Python Essential Reference

The New Riders Professional Library

R. Virella y

Python Essential Reference

David M. Beazley

New
Riders

201 West 103rd Street, Indianapolis, IN 46290

Python Essential Reference

Copyright © 2000 by New Riders Publishing

International Standard Book Number: 0-7357-0901-7

Library of Congress Catalog Card Number: 99-65209

Printed in the United States of America

First Printing: October, 1999

03 02 01 00   7 6 5 4 3

Interpretation of the printing code: The rightmost double-digit number is the year of the book's printing; the rightmost single-digit number is the number of the book's printing. For example, the printing code 99-1 shows that the first printing of the book occurred in 1999.

Trademarks

Warning and Disclaimer

Publisher
David Dwyer

Executive Editor
Laurie Petrycki

Acquisitions Editor
Katie Purdum

Managing Editor
Sarah Kearns

Product Marketing Manager
Stephanie Layton

Editor
Robin Drake

Technical Reviewers
David Ascher
Paul Dubois

Book Designer
Louisa Klucznik

Cover Production
Aren Howell

Indexer
Craig Small

Proofreader
John Rahm

Compositor
Wil Cruz

*This book is dedicated to Peter Lomdahl for being
a great boss, mentor, and friend.*

About the Author

David M. Beazley is the developer of SWIG, a popular software package for integrating C and C++ software with interpreted languages including Python, Perl, and Tcl. Beazley spent seven years working in the Theoretical Physics Division at Los Alamos National Laboratory and has been at the forefront of integrating Python with high-performance simulation software running on parallel computers. He is currently an assistant professor in the Department of Computer Science at the University of Chicago, where he enjoys tormenting students with insane systems-programming projects. He can be reached at `beazley@cs.uchicago.edu`.

About the Technical Reviewers

David Ascher, Ph.D., is a vision researcher, Python consultant, trainer, and book author. He has been actively involved in Python development since 1994, and his special interests are object-oriented programming, scientific computation, and user interfaces.

Paul F. Dubois graduated from the University of California at Berkeley with a degree in mathematics. He obtained a Ph.D. in mathematics from the University of California at Davis in 1970. After six years of teaching and research, in 1976 he joined Lawrence Livermore National Laboratory. He has held a variety of positions at LLNL as a technical leader in numerical mathematics and computer science. In 1999 he joined the Program for Climate Model Diagnosis and Intercomparison in the Atmospheric Sciences Division, where he is putting Python to work creating analysis tools for climate modelers.

Paul's work includes pioneering work on computational steering and the use of object technology for scientific programming. He is the editor of the Scientific Programming Department for the journal *IEEE Computers in Science and Engineering*.

Contents

Foreword

As Python's creator, I'm really happy that this book has appeared. It marks a point in time when Python is becoming a mainstream language, with a rapidly growing community of users. If you consider yourself an (established or aspiring) member of this community, you need neither evangelizing nor proselytizing, and you already know Python well enough to have chosen it as an essential element of your personal toolbox.

This book aims to be your guide on the rest of your journey through the Python world. It documents every detail of the language's syntax and semantics, provides reference documentation and examples for most standard library modules, and even contains a quick reference for writing extension modules. All this information is thoroughly indexed and cross-referenced, and where necessary contains pointers to additional online documentation for obscure details.

You might think that all this information is already available for free on the Python Web site (www.python.org). Sure, it's all there—in fact, I'm certain that the author, my good friend David Beazley, consulted the Web site many times. He would have been a fool not to!

However, with all due respect for the authors of Python's online documentation (myself included!), this book has a huge advantage over the Web site: You can easily take it with you on a trip into the desert. Seriously, David has reorganized and rewritten all the information for maximum clarity, pulled things together from different sources, removed redundancies, clarified ambiguities, added better examples, and so on. He also had a benefit that few readers of the Web site have: direct access to my brain! This summer, David spent a few weeks visiting CNRI, the research lab in Reston that Python calls home. During this time we had many interesting and fruitful discussions about Python, this book, the meaning of life, southwestern cooking, the joys and pains of teaching computer science to non-computer scientists, and the Spanish Inquisition. (Remember? *Nobody* expects the Spanish Inquisition!)

I hope that you will enjoy using this book, and that it will serve you well. I also hope that you will continue to enjoy using Python, and that *it* will serve you well. Python is a great programming language, and I would like to use this opportunity to thank the entire Python community for making Python what it is today. Without the thousands of believers, users, contributors, entrepreneurs, and developers who make up the Python community, my own energy directed toward Python would have dried up long ago. I see this as the essence of open source projects: The energy and creativity of many people with diverse goals together can work miracles!

—Guido van Rossum
Baltimore, MD
9/13/1999

Acknowledgments

This book would not be possible without the input and support of many people. First, I would like to thank technical reviewers David Ascher and Paul Dubois for their valuable comments and continued advice. I would also like to thank Guido van Rossum, Jeremy Hylton, Fred Drake, Roger Masse, Barry Warsaw, and the rest of the Python developers at the Corporation for National Initiatives for their feedback during my visit. A special thanks is also in order for Allen and Joan Sears for providing me with a place to crash for a few weeks.

I would also like to thank Katie Purdum, Louisa Klucznik, and the rest of the New Riders staff for making this book possible. A special thanks is also in order for Robin Drake for her amazing editing skills and work on this project. I'd also like to thank Ivan Van Laningham for his great colophon.

There are many other people that I need to thank as well. I'd like to acknowledge Peter Lomdahl, Tim Germann, Niels Jensen, Brad Holian, Zhujia Zhou, and the rest of the SPaSM team at Los Alamos National Laboratory for their continued support over the years and their willingness to take a chance with a risky idea—fight the power. I'd also like to acknowledge all of my friends back at the University of Utah for putting up with my crazy rantings and providing a place to store my skis. In addition, a special thanks is in order for the faculty of Fort Lewis College for giving me the confidence to accomplish anything. Finally, I would especially like to thank my parents for their continued love, understanding, and support of all of my endeavors—I would not be where I am today without you.

Oh, and last but not least I would like to thank Commonwealth Edison for the relentless power supplied to my air conditioner during the Chicago heat wave of '99.

Tell Us What You Think!

As the reader of this book, *you* are our most important critic and commentator. We value your opinion and want to know what we're doing right, what we could do better, what areas you'd like to see us publish in, and any other words of wisdom you're willing to pass our way.

As the Executive Editor for the Open Source team at New Riders Publishing, I welcome your comments. You can fax, email, or write me directly to let me know what you did or didn't like about this book—as well as what we can do to make our books stronger.

Please note that I cannot help you with technical problems related to the topic of this book, and that due to the high volume of mail I receive, I might not be able to reply to every message.

When you write, please be sure to include this book's title and author, as well as your name and phone or fax number. I will carefully review your comments and share them with the author and editors who worked on the book.

Fax: 317-581-4663

Email: newriders@mcp.com

Mail: Laurie Petrycki
           Executive Editor
           Open Source
           New Riders Publishing
           201 West 103rd Street
           Indianapolis, IN 46290 USA

Introduction

This book is intended to be a concise reference to the Python programming language. Although an experienced programmer will probably be able to learn Python from this book, it's not intended to be an extended tutorial or a treatise on software design. Rather, the goal is to present the core Python language, the contents of the Python library, and the Python extension API in a manner that's accurate and succinct. This book assumes that the reader has prior programming experience with Python or other languages such as C or Java. In addition, a general familiarity with systems programming topics (for example, basic operating system calls, process management, and network programming) may be useful in understanding certain parts of the library reference.

Python is freely available for download at http://www.python.org. Versions are available for Unix, Windows, Macintosh, and Java. In addition, this site includes links to documentation, how-to guides, and a wide assortment of extension modules.

The contents of this book are based on Python 1.5.2. However, readers should be aware that Python is a constantly evolving language. Most of the topics described herein are likely to be applicable to future versions of Python 1.x. In addition, most topics are applicable to earlier releases. To a lesser extent, the topics in this book also apply to JPython, an implementation of Python entirely in Java. However, as of this writing, JPython is still in beta release and undergoing active development—making it a difficult target for up-to-date reference material.

Finally, it should be noted that Python is distributed with well over 500 pages of reference documentation. The contents of this book are largely based on this documentation, but with a number of enhancements, additions, and omissions. First, this reference presents most of the same material in a more compact form with different examples and alternative descriptions of many topics. Second, a number of topics in the library reference have been expanded to include additional outside reference material. This is especially true for low-level system and networking modules in which effective use of a module normally relies on a myriad of options listed in Unix manual pages and outside reference material. In addition, in order to produce a more concise reference, a number of deprecated and relatively obscure library modules have been omitted. Finally, this reference doesn't attempt to cover large frameworks such as Tkinter or the COM extension, as these topics are beyond the scope of this book and are described in books of their own.

In writing this book, it has been my goal to produce a reference containing virtually everything I have needed to use Python and its large collection of modules. To do this, I have incorporated and condensed a considerable amount of information from manual pages, online documentation, and several thousand pages of systems programming books. Although this is by no means a gentle introduction to the Python language, I hope that you find the contents of this book to be a useful addition to your programming reference library for many years to come. I welcome your comments.

—David Beazley
Chicago, IL
9/9/1999

Conventions and Typographical Features

Convention	Usage
monospace text	Datatypes, classes, modules, constants, and so on—basically, anything that constitutes part of the Python language or any command you could present to the computer. The monospaced font is also used for Internet addresses such as www.python.org.
italic monospace	Variables such as *x* in abs(*x*).
[ ]	Brackets are used in syntax lines to indicate optional elements, such as *object* in dir([*object*]). In the syntax [*arg* = *value*], *value* indicates the default value of *arg*. Brackets are also used to denote Python lists; in all coding examples, this is the interpretation.
➡	Code-continuation characters are inserted into code when a line shouldn't be broken, but we simply ran out of room on the page.

1
A Tutorial
Introduction

This chapter provides a quick introduction to Python. The goal is to illustrate Python's essential features without getting too bogged down in special rules or details. To do this, the chapter briefly covers basic concepts such as variables, expressions, control flow, functions, and input/output. This chapter is not intended to provide comprehensive coverage, nor does it cover many of Python's more advanced features. However, experienced programmers should be able to extrapolate from the material in this chapter to create more advanced programs. Beginners are encouraged to try a few examples to get a feel for the language.

Running Python

Python programs are executed by an interpreter. On Unix machines, the interpreter is started by typing python. On Windows and the Macintosh, the interpreter is launched as an application (either from the Start menu or by double-clicking on the interpreter's icon). When the interpreter starts, a prompt appears at which you can start typing programs into a simple read-evaluation loop. For example, in the following output, the interpreter displays its copyright message and presents the user with the >>> prompt, at which the user types the familiar "Hello World" command:

```
Python 1.5.2 (#0, Jun 1 1999, 20:22:04)
Copyright 1991-1995 Stichting Mathematisch Centrum, Amsterdam
>>> print "Hello World"
Hello World
>>>
```

Programs can also be placed in a file such as the following:

```
# helloworld.py
print "Hello World"
```

Python source files have a .py suffix. The # character in the preceding example denotes a comment that extends to the end of the line.

To execute the helloworld.py file, you provide the filename to the interpreter as follows:

```
% python helloworld.py
Hello World
%
```

On Windows, Python programs can be started by double-clicking on a .py file. This launches the interpreter and runs the program in a console window. In this case, the console window disappears immediately after the program completes its execution (often before you can read its output). To prevent this, you may want to use an integrated development environment such as Idle or Pythonwin. An alternative approach is to launch the program using a .bat file containing a statement such as python -i helloworld.py that instructs the interpreter to enter interactive mode after program execution.

On the Macintosh, programs can be executed from the included integrated development environment. In addition, the BuildApplet utility (included in the distribution) turns a Python program into a document that automatically launches the interpreter when opened.

Within the interpreter, the execfile() function runs a program, as in the following example:

```
>>> execfile("helloworld.py")
Hello World
```

On Unix, you can also invoke Python using #! in a shell script:

```
#!/usr/local/bin/python
print "Hello World"
```

The interpreter runs until it reaches the end of the input file. If running interactively, you can exit by typing the EOF (end of file) character or selecting Exit from a pull-down menu (if available). On Unix, EOF is Ctrl+D; on Windows, Ctrl+Z. A program can also exit by calling the sys.exit() function or raising the SystemExit exception (which is equivalent). For example:

```
>>> import sys
>>> sys.exit()
```

or

```
>>> raise SystemExit
```

Variables and Arithmetic Expressions

The program in Listing 1.1 shows the use of variables and expressions by performing a simple compound-interest calculation:

Listing 1.1. Simple Compound–Interest Calculation.

```
principal = 1000       # Initial amount
rate = 0.05            # Interest rate
numyears = 5           # Number of years
year = 1
while year <= numyears:
        principal = principal*(1+rate)
        print year, principal
        year = year + 1
```

The output of this program is the following table:

```
1 1050.0
2 1102.5
3 1157.625
4 1215.50625
5 1276.2815625
```

Python is a dynamically typed language in which names can represent values of different types during the execution of the program. In fact, the names used in a program are really just labels for various quantities and objects. The assignment operator simply creates an association between that name and a value. This is different from C, for example, in which a name represents a fixed size and location in memory into which results are placed. The dynamic behavior of Python can be seen in Listing 1.1 with the `principal` variable. Initially, it's assigned to an integer value. However, later in the program it's reassigned as follows:

```
principal = principal*(1+rate)
```

This statement evaluates the expression and reassociates the name `principal` with the result. When this occurs, the original binding of `principal` to the integer 1000 is lost (at which point, the integer may be marked for garbage collection). Furthermore, the result of assignment may change the *type* of a variable. In this case, the type of `principal` changes from an integer to a floating-point number, because `rate` is a floating-point number.

A newline terminates each individual statement. You also can use a semicolon to separate statements, as shown here:

```
principal = 1000; rate = 0.05; numyears = 5;
```

The `while` statement tests the conditional expression that immediately follows. If the tested statement is true, the body of the `while` statement executes. The condition is then retested and the body executed again until the condition becomes false. Because the body of the loop is denoted by indentation, the three statements following the `while` in Listing 1.1 execute on each iteration. Python doesn't specify the amount of required indentation, as long as it's consistent within a block.

One problem with the program in Listing 1.1 is that the output isn't very pretty. To make it better, you could right-align the columns and limit the precision of `principal` to two digits by modifying the `print` to use a *format string*, like this:

```
print "%3d %0.2f" % (year, principal)
```

Now the output of the program looks like this:

```
1    1050.00
2    1102.50
3    1157.63
4    1215.51
5    1276.28
```

Format strings contain ordinary text and special formatting-character sequences such as `"%d"`, `"%s"`, or `"%f"`. These sequences specify the formatting of a particular type of data such as an integer, string, or floating-point number, respectively. The special-character sequences can also contain modifiers that specify a width and precision. For example, `"%3d"` formats an integer right-aligned in a column of width 3 and `"%0.2f"` formats a floating-point number so that only two digits appear after the decimal point. The behavior of format strings is almost identical to the C `printf()` function and is described in detail in Chapter 4, "Operators and Expressions."

Conditionals

The if and else statements can perform simple tests. For example:

```
# Compute the maximum (z) of a and b
if a < b:
        z = b
else:
        z = a
```

The bodies of the if and else clauses are denoted by indentation. The else clause is optional.

To create an empty clause, use the pass statement as follows:

```
if a < b:
        pass      # Do nothing
else:
        z = a
```

You can form Boolean expressions by using the or, and, and not keywords:

```
if b >= a and b <= c:
        print "b is between a and c"
if not (b < a or b > c):
        print "b is still between a and c"
```

To handle multiple-test cases, use the elif statement, like this:

```
if a == '+':
        op = PLUS
elif a == '-':
        op = MINUS
elif a == '*':
        op = MULTIPLY
else:
        raise RuntimeError, "Unknown operator"
```

File Input and Output

The following program opens a file and reads its contents line by line:

```
f = open("foo.txt")        # Returns a file object
line = f.readline()        # Invokes readline() method on file
while line:
        print line,        # trailing ',' omits newline character
        line = f.readline()
f.close()
```

The open() function returns a new file object. By invoking methods on this object, you can perform various file operations. The readline() method reads a single line of input, including the terminating newline. The empty string is returned at the end of the file. Similarly, you can use the write() method to make the compound-interest program write the results to a file:

```
f = open("out","w")        # Open file for writing
while year <= numyears:
        principal = principal*(1+rate)
        f.write("%3d    %0.2f\n" % (year,principal))  # File output
        year = year + 1
f.close()
```

Strings

To create *string literals*, enclose them in single, double, or triple quotes as follows:

```
a = "Hello World"
b = 'Python is groovy'
c = """What is footnote 5?"""
```

The same type of quote used to start a string must be used to terminate it. Triple-quoted strings capture all the text that appears prior to the terminating triple quote, as opposed to single- and double-quoted strings, which must be specified on one logical line. Triple-quoted strings are useful when the contents of a string literal span multiple lines of text such as the following:

```
print '''Content-type: text/html

<h1> Hello World </h1>
Click <a href="http://www.python.org">here</a>.
'''
```

Strings are sequences of characters indexed by integers starting at zero. To extract a single character, use the indexing operator $s[i]$ like this:

```
a = "Hello World"
b = a[4]                 # b = 'o'
```

To extract a *substring*, use the *slicing operator* $s[i:j]$. This extracts all elements from s whose index k is in the range $i \leq k < j$. If either index is omitted, the beginning or end of the string is assumed, respectively:

```
c = a[0:5]               # c = "Hello"
d = a[6:]                # d = "World"
e = a[3:8]               # e = "lo Wo"
```

Strings are concatenated with the plus (+) operator:

```
g = a + " This is a test"
```

Other datatypes can be converted into a string using either the `str()` or `repr()` function or backquotes (`), which are a shortcut notation for `repr()`. For example:

```
s = "The value of x is " + str(x)
s = "The value of y is " + repr(y)
s = "The value of y is " + `y`
```

In many cases, `str()` and `repr()` return identical results. However, there are subtle differences in semantics that are described in later chapters.

Lists and Tuples

Just as strings are sequences of characters, lists and tuples are sequences of arbitrary objects. You create a list as follows:

```
names = [ "Dave", "Mark", "Ann", "Phil" ]
```

Lists are indexed by integers starting with zero. Use the indexing operator to access and modify individual members of the list:

```
a = names[2]             # Returns the third element of the list "Ann"
names[0] = "Jeff"        # Changes the first element to "Jeff"
```

To append new members to a list, use the append() method:

```
names.append("Kate")
```

You can extract or reassign a portion of a list by using the slicing operator:

```
b = names[0:2]                          # Returns [ "Jeff", "Mark" ]
c = names[2:]                           # Returns [ "Ann", "Phil", "Kate" ]
names[1] = 'Jeff'                       # Replace the 2nd item in names with 'Jeff'
names[0:2] = [ 'Dave', 'Mark', 'Jeff' ] # Replace the first two elements of
                                        # the list with the sublist on the right.
```

Use the plus (+) operator to concatenate lists:

```
a = [1,2,3] + [4,5]     # Result is [1,2,3,4,5]
```

Lists can contain any kind of Python object, including other lists, as in the following example:

```
a = [1,"Dave",3.14, ["Mark", 7, 9, [100,101]], 10]
```

Nested lists are accessed as follows:

```
a[1]            # Returns "Dave"
a[3][2]         # Returns 9
a[3][3][1]      # Returns 101
```

The program in Listing 1.2 illustrates a few more advanced features of lists by reading a list of numbers from a file and outputting the minimum and maximum values.

Listing 1.2. Advanced List Features.

```
import string             # Load the string module
import sys                # Load the sys module
f = open(sys.argv[1])     # Filename on the command line
svalues = f.readlines()   # Read all lines into a list
f.close()

# Convert all of the values from strings to floats
fvalues = map(string.atof, svalues)

# Print min and max values
print "The minimum value is ", min(fvalues)
print "The maximum value is ", max(fvalues)
```

The first two lines of this program use the import statement to load the string module and sys module from the Python library.

The readlines() method reads all the input lines into a list of strings.

The map() function applies a function to all the elements in the list, returning a new list. In this case, the string.atof() function is applied to all the lines in svalues to create a list of floating-point numbers. Afterwards, the built-in min() and max() functions are used to compute the minimum and maximum values.

Closely related to lists is the tuple datatype. You create tuples by enclosing a group of values in parentheses or with a comma-separated list, like this:

```
a = (1,4,5,-9,10)
b = (7,)                                 # Singleton (note extra ,)
person = (first_name, last_name, phone)
person = first_name, last_name, phone    # Same as previous line
```

Tuples support most of the same operations as lists, such as indexing, slicing, and concatenation. The only difference is that you can't modify the contents of a tuple after creation (that is, you can't modify individual elements, or append new elements to a tuple).

Loops

The simple loop shown earlier used the `while` statement. The other looping construct is the `for` statement, which iterates over the members of a sequence, such as a string, list, or tuple. Here's an example:

```
for i in range(1,10):
        print "2 to the %d power is %d" % (i, 2**i)
```

The `range(i,j)` function constructs a list of integers with values from i to j-1. If the starting value is omitted, it's taken to be zero. An optional stride can also be given as a third argument. For example:

```
a = range(5)         # a = [0,1,2,3,4]
b = range(1,8)       # b = [1,2,3,4,5,6,7]
c = range(0,14,3)    # c = [0,3,6,9,12]
d = range(8,1,-1)    # d = [8,7,6,5,4,3,2]
```

The `for` statement can iterate over any sequence type and isn't limited to sequences of integers:

```
a = "Hello World"
# Print out the characters in a
for c in a:
        print c

b = ["Dave","Mark","Ann","Phil"]
# Print out the members of a list
for name in b:
        print name
```

`range()` works by constructing a list and populating it with values according to the starting, ending, and stride values. For large ranges, this process is expensive in terms of both memory and runtime performance. To avoid this, you can use the `xrange()` function, as shown here:

```
for i in xrange(1,10):
        print "2 to the %d power is %d" % (i, 2**i)

a = xrange(100000000)        # a = [0,1,2, ..., 99999999]
b = xrange(0,100000000,5)    # a = [0,5,10, ...,99999995]
```

Rather than creating a sequence populated with values, the sequence returned by `xrange()` computes its values from the starting, ending, and stride values whenever it's accessed.

Dictionaries

A *dictionary* is an associative array or hash table that contains objects indexed by keys. Create a dictionary by enclosing the values in curly braces ({ }) like this:

```
a = {
        "username" : "beazley",
        "home" : "/home/beazley",
        "uid" : 500
    }
```

To access members of a dictionary, use the key-indexing operator as follows:

```
u = a["username"]
d = a["home"]
```

Inserting or modifying objects works like this:

```
a["username"] = "pxl"
a["home"] = "/home/pxl"
a["shell"] = "/usr/bin/tcsh"
```

Although strings are the most common type of key, you can use many other Python objects, including numbers and tuples. Some objects, including lists and dictionaries, cannot be used as keys, because their contents are allowed to change.

Dictionary membership is tested with the has_key() method, as in the following example:

```
if a.has_key("username"):
        username = a["username"]
else:
        username = "unknown user"
```

This particular sequence of steps can also be performed more compactly as follows:

```
username = a.get("username", "unknown user")
```

To obtain a list of dictionary keys, use the keys() method:

```
k = a.keys()            # k = ["username","home","uid","shell"]
```

Use the del statement to remove an element of a dictionary:

```
del a["username"]
```

Functions

You use the def statement to create a function, as shown in the following example:

```
def remainder(a,b):
        q = a/b
        r = a - q*b
        return r
```

To invoke a function, simply use the name of the function followed by its arguments enclosed in parentheses, such as result = remainder(37,15). You can use a tuple to return multiple values from a function, as shown here:

```
def divide(a,b):
        q = a/b         # If a and b are integers, q is an integer.
        r = a - q*b
        return (q,r)
```

When returning multiple values in a tuple, it's often useful to invoke the function as follows:

```
quotient, remainder = divide(1456,33)
```

To assign a default value to a parameter, use assignment:

```
def connect(hostname,port,timeout=300):
# Function body
```

When default values are given in a function definition, they can be omitted from subsequent function calls. For example:

```
connect('www.python.org', 80)
```

You also can invoke functions by using keyword arguments and supplying the arguments in arbitrary order. For example:

```
connect(port=80,hostname="www.python.org")
```

When variables are created or assigned inside a function, their scope is local. To modify the value of a global variable from inside a function, use the global statement as follows:

```
a = 4.5
...
def foo():
      global a
      a = 8.8            # Changes the global variable a
```

Classes

The class statement is used to define new types of objects and for object-oriented programming. For example, the following class defines a simple stack:

```
class Stack:
      def __init__(self):          # Initialize the stack
            self.stack = [ ]
      def push(self,object):
            self.stack.append(object)
      def pop(self, object):
            return self.stack.pop()
      def length(self):
            return len(self.stack)
```

In the class definition, methods are defined using the def statement. The first argument in each method always refers to the object. By convention, self is the name used for this argument (much like this refers to an object in C++). All operations involving the attributes of an object must explicitly refer to the self variable. Methods with leading and trailing double underscores are special methods. For example, __init__ is used to initialize an object after it's created.

To use a class, write code such as the following:

```
s = Stack()            # Create a stack
s.push("Dave")         # Push some things onto it
s.push(42)
s.push([3,4,5])
x = s.pop()            # x gets [3,4,5]
y = s.pop()            # y gets 42
del s                  # Destroy s
```

Exceptions

If an error occurs in your program, an exception is raised and an error message such as the following appears:

```
Traceback (innermost last):
 File "<interactive input>", line 42, in foo.py
NameError: a
```

The error message indicates the type of error that occurred, along with its location. Normally, errors cause a program to abort. However, you can catch and handle exceptions using the try and except statements, like this:

```
try:
    f = open("file.txt","r")
except IOError, e:
    print e
```

If an IOError occurs, details concerning the cause of the error are placed in e and control passes to the code in the except block. If some other kind of exception is raised, it's passed to the enclosing code block (if any). If no errors occur, the code in the except block is ignored.

The raise statement is used to signal an exception. When raising an exception, you can use one of the built-in exceptions, like this:

```
raise RuntimeError, "Unrecoverable error"
```

Or you can create your own exceptions, as described in the section "Defining New Exceptions" in Chapter 5, "Control Flow."

Modules

As your programs grow in size, you'll probably want to break them up into multiple files for easier maintenance. To do this, Python allows you to put definitions in a file and use them as a *module* that can be imported into other programs and scripts. To create a module, put the relevant statements and definitions into a file that has the same name as the module. (*Note:* The file must have a .py suffix.) For example:

```
# file :  div.py
def divide(a,b):
    q = a/b         # If a and b are integers, q is an integer
    r = a - q*b
    return (q,r)
```

To use your module in other programs, you can use the import statement:

```
import div
a, b = div.divide(2305, 29)
```

import creates a new namespace that contains all the objects defined in the module. To access this namespace, simply use the name of the module as a prefix, as in div.divide() in the preceding example.

To import specific definitions into the current namespace, use the from statement:

```
from div import divide
a,b = divide(2305,29)       # No longer need the div prefix
```

To load all of a module's contents into the current namespace, you can also use the following:

```
from div import *
```

The dir() function lists the contents of a module and is a useful tool for interactive experimentation:

```
>>> import string
>>> dir(string)
['__builtins__', '__doc__', '__file__', '__name__', '_idmap',
 '_idmapL', '_lower', '_swapcase', '_upper', 'atof', 'atof_error',
 'atoi', 'atoi_error', 'atol', 'atol_error', 'capitalize',
 'capwords', 'center', 'count', 'digits', 'expandtabs', 'find',
...
>>>
```

2

Lexical Conventions and Syntax

This chapter describes the syntactic and lexical conventions of a Python program. Topics include line structure, grouping of statements, reserved words, literals, operators, and tokens.

Line Structure and Indentation

Each statement in a program is terminated with a newline. Long statements can span multiple lines by using the line-continuation character (\), as shown in the following example:

```
a = math.cos(3*(x-n)) + \
    math.sin(3*(y-n))
```

You don't need the line-continuation character when the definition of a triple-quoted string, list, tuple, or dictionary spans multiple lines. More generally, any part of a program enclosed in parentheses (...), brackets [...], braces {...}, or triple quotes can span multiple lines without use of the line-continuation character.

Indentation is used to denote different blocks of code, such as the bodies of functions, conditionals, loops, and classes. The amount of indentation used for the first statement of a block is arbitrary, but the indentation of the entire block must be consistent. For example:

```
if a:
    statement1     # Consistent indentation
    statement2
else:
    statement3
      statement4    # Inconsistent indentation (error)
```

If the body of a function, conditional, loop, or class is short and contains only a few statements, they can be placed on the same line, like this:

```
if a:   statement1
else:   statement2
```

When tabs are used for indentation, they're converted into the number of spaces required to move to the next column that's a multiple of 8 (for example, a tab appearing in column 11 inserts enough spaces to move to column 16). The interpreter ignores blank lines except when running in interactive mode.

To place more than one statement on a line, separate the statements with a semi-colon (;). A line containing a single statement can also be terminated by a semicolon, although this is unnecessary.

The # character denotes a comment that extends to the end of the line. A # appearing inside a quoted string doesn't start a comment, however.

Identifiers and Reserved Words

An *identifier* is a name used to identify variables, functions, classes, modules, and other objects. Identifiers can include letters, numbers, and the underscore character (_), but must always start with a non-numeric character. Letters are currently confined to the characters A–Z and a–z in the ISO–Latin character set. Because identifiers are case sensitive, FOO is different from foo. Special symbols such as $, %, and @ are not allowed in identifiers. In addition, words such as if, else, and for are reserved and cannot be used as identifier names. The following list shows all the reserved words:

and	elif	global	or
assert	else	if	pass
break	except	import	print
class	exec	in	raise
continue	finally	is	return
def	for	lambda	try
del	from	not	while

Identifiers starting or ending with underscores often have special meanings. For example, identifiers starting with a single underscore such as _foo are not imported by the from module import * statement. Identifiers with leading and trailing double underscores such as __init__ are reserved for special methods, and identifiers with leading double underscores such as __bar are used to implement private class members. Avoid using similar identifiers for any other purpose.

Literals

There are four built-in numeric types:

- integers
- long integers
- floating-point numbers
- complex numbers

A number such as 1234 is interpreted as a decimal integer. To specify octal and hexadecimal integers, precede the value with 0 or 0x, respectively—0644 or 0x100fea8. Write a long integer using a trailing l (ell) or L character, as in 1234567890L. Unlike integers, which are limited by machine precision, long integers can be of any length (up to the maximum memory of the machine). Numbers such as 123.34 and 1.2334e+02 are interpreted as floating-point numbers. An integer or floating-point number with a trailing j or J, such as 12.34J, is an imaginary number. You can create complex numbers with real and imaginary parts by adding a real number and an imaginary number, as in 1.2 + 12.34J.

String literals are enclosed using single ('), double ("), or triple (''' or """) quotes. You must use the same type of quote to start and terminate a string. Adjacent strings (separated by white space or a newline) such as "hello" 'world' are concatenated to form a single string: "helloworld". The backslash (\) character is used to escape special characters such as newlines, the backslash itself, quotes, and nonprinting characters. Table 2.1 shows the accepted escape codes. Unrecognized escape sequences are left in the string unmodified and include the leading backslash.

Triple-quoted strings can span multiple lines and include unescaped newlines and quotes.

Table 2.1   Character Escape Codes

Character	Description
\	Newline continuation
\\	Backslash
\'	Single quote
\"	Double quote
\a	Bell
\b	Backspace
\e	Escape
\0	Null
\n	Line feed
\v	Vertical tab
\t	Horizontal tab
\r	Carriage return
\f	Form feed
\0XX	Octal value
\xXX	Hexadecimal value

Optionally, you can precede a string with an r or R such as in r"\n\"". These strings are known as *raw strings* because all of their backslash characters are left intact (that is, the string literally contains the enclosed text, including the backslashes). Raw strings cannot end in a single backslash, such as r"\".

Values enclosed in square brackets [...], parentheses (...), and braces { ... } denote lists, tuples, and dictionaries, respectively, as in the following example:

```
a = [ 1, 3.4, 'hello' ]      # A list
b = ( 10, 20, 30 )           # A tuple
c = { 'a': 3, 'b':42 }       # A dictionary
```

Operators, Delimiters, and Special Symbols

The following operator tokens are recognized:

```
+     -     *     **     /     %     <<     >>     &
|     ^     ~     <     >     <=     >=     ==     !=     <>
```

The following tokens serve as delimiters for expressions, lists, dictionaries, and various parts of a statement:

```
(     )     [     ]     {     }
,     :     .     `     =     ;
```

For example, the equal (=) character serves as a delimiter between the name and value of an assignment, while the comma (,) character is used to delimit arguments to a function. The period (.) is also used in floating-point numbers and in the ellipsis (. . .) used in extended slicing operations.

Finally, the following special symbols are also used:

```
'     "     #     \
```

The characters @, $, and ? cannot appear in a program except inside a quoted string literal.

Documentation Strings

If the first statement of a module, class, or function definition is a string, that string becomes a *documentation string* for the associated object, as in the following example:

```
def fact(n):
    "This function computes a factorial"
    if (n <= 1): return 1
    else: return n*fact(n-1)
```

Code-browsing and documentation-generation tools sometimes use documentation strings. The strings are accessible in the __doc__ attribute of an object, as shown here:

```
>>> print fact.__doc__
This function computes a factorial
>>>
```

The indentation of the documentation string must be consistent with all the other statements in a definition.

3

Types and Objects

All the data stored in a Python program is built around the concept of an object. Objects include fundamental datatypes such as numbers, strings, lists, and dictionaries. It's also possible to create user-defined objects in the form of classes or extension types. This chapter describes the Python object model and provides an overview of the built-in datatypes. Chapter 4, "Operators and Expressions," further describes operators and expressions.

Terminology

Every piece of data stored in a program is an *object*. Each object has an identity, a type, and a value.

For example, when you write a = 42, an integer object is created with the value of 42. You can view the *identity* of an object as a pointer to its location in memory. a is a name that refers to this specific location.

The *type* of an object (which is itself a special kind of object) describes the internal representation of the object as well as the methods and operations that it supports. When an object of a particular type is created, that object is sometimes called an *instance* of that type (although an instance of a type should not be confused with an instance of a user-defined class). After an object is created, its identity and type cannot be changed. If an object's value can be modified, the object is said to be *mutable*. If the value cannot be modified, the object is said to be *immutable*. An object that contains references to other objects is said to be a *container* or *collection*.

In addition to holding a value, many objects define a number of data attributes and methods. An *attribute* is a property or value associated with an object. A *method* is a function that performs some sort of operation on an object when the method is invoked. Attributes and methods are accessed using the dot (.) operator, as shown in the following example:

```
a = 3 + 4j      # Create a complex number
r = a.real      # Get the real part (an attribute)

b = [1, 2, 3]   # Create a list
b.append(7)     # Add a new element using the append method
```

Object Identity and Type

The built-in function id() returns the identity of an object as an integer. This integer usually corresponds to the object's location in memory, although this is specific to the implementation. The is operator compares the identity of two objects. The built-in function type() returns the type of an object. For example:

```
# Compare two objects
def compare(a,b):
    print 'The identity of a is ', id(a)
    print 'The identity of b is ', id(b)
    if a is b:
        print 'a and b are the same object'
    if a == b:
        print 'a and b have the same value'
    if type(a) == type(b):
        print 'a and b have the same type'
```

The type of an object is itself an object. The standard module types contains the type objects for all the built-in types and can be used to perform type-checking. For example:

```
import types
if isinstance(s, types.ListType):
    print 'Is a list'
else:
    print 'Is not a list'
```

The isinstance() function tests an object to see if it's an instance of a specific type. (This function is also used in conjunction with user-defined classes, as described in Chapter 7, "Classes and Object-Oriented Programming.")

Reference Counting

All objects are reference counted. An object's reference count is increased whenever it's assigned to a new name or placed in a container such as a list, tuple, or dictionary, as shown here:

```
a = 3.4     # Creates an object '3.4'
b = a       # Increases reference count on '3.4'
c = []
c.append(b) # Increases reference count on '3.4'
```

This example creates a single object containing the value 3.4. a is merely a name that refers to the newly created object. When b is assigned to a, b becomes a new name for the same object, and the object's reference count increases. Likewise, when you place b into a list, the object's reference count increases again. Throughout the example, only one object contains 3.4. All other operations are simply creating new references to the object.

An object's reference count is decreased by the del statement or whenever a local reference goes out of scope (or is reassigned). For example:

```
del a     # Decrease reference count of 3.4
b = 7.8   # Decrease reference count of 3.4
c[0]=2.0  # Decrease reference count of 3.4
```

When an object's reference count reaches zero, it is garbage collected. However, in some cases a circular dependency may exist between a collection of objects that are no longer in use. For example:

```
a = { }
b = { }
a['b'] = b              # a contains reference to b
b['a'] = a              # b contains reference to a
del a
del b
```

In this example, the del statements decrease the reference count of a and b and destroy the names used to refer to the underlying objects. However, because each object contains a reference to the other, the reference count doesn't drop to zero and the objects are not garbage collected. As a result, the objects remain allocated even though there's no longer any way for the interpreter to access them (that is, the names used to refer to the objects are gone).

References and Copies

When a program makes an assignment such as a = b, a new reference to b is created. For simple objects such as numbers and strings, this assignment effectively creates a copy of b. However, the behavior is quite different for mutable objects such as lists and dictionaries. For example:

```
b = [1,2,3,4]
a = b                   # a is a reference to b
a[2] = -100             # Change an element in 'a'
print b                 # Produces '[1, 2, -100, 4]'
```

Because a and b refer to the same object in this example, a change made to one of the variables is reflected in the other. To avoid this, you have to create a copy of an object rather than a new reference.

There are two types of copy operations that are applied to container objects such as lists and dictionaries: a shallow copy and a deep copy. A *shallow copy* creates a new object, but populates it with references to the items contained in the original object. For example:

```
b = [ 1, 2, [3,4] ]
a = b[:]                # Create a shallow copy of b
a.append(100)           # Append element to a
print b                 # Produces '[1,2, [3,4]]'. b unchanged.
a[2][0] = -100          # Modify an element of a.
print b                 # Produces '[1,2, [-100,4]]'.
```

In this case, a and b are separate list objects, but the elements they contain are shared. Thus, a modification to one of the elements of a also modifies an element of b as shown.

A *deep copy* creates a new object and recursively copies all of the objects it contains. There is no built-in function to create deep copies of objects. However, the copy.deepcopy() function in the standard library can be used, as shown in the following example:

```
import copy
b = [1, 2, [3, 4] ]
a = copy.deepcopy(b)
```

Built-in Types

Approximately two dozen types are built into the Python interpreter and grouped into a few major categories, as shown in Table 3.1. Some categories include familiar objects such as numbers and sequences. Others are used during program execution and are of little practical use to most programmers. The next few sections describe the most commonly used built-in types.

Table 3.1   Built-in Python Types

Type Category	Type Name	Description
None	NoneType	The null object.
Numbers	IntType	Integer.
	LongType	Arbitrary precision integer.
	FloatType	Floating point.
	ComplexType	Complex number.
Sequences	StringType	Character strings.
	ListType	List.
	TupleType	Tuple.
	XRangeType	Returned by $xrange(i,j,k)$.
Mapping	DictType	Dictionary.
Callable	BuiltinFunctionType	Built-in functions.
	BuiltinMethodType	Built-in methods.
	ClassType	Class object.
	FunctionType	User-defined function.
	InstanceType	Class object instance.
	MethodType	Bound class method.
	UnboundMethodType	Unbound class method.
Modules	ModuleType	Module.
Classes	ClassType	Class definition.
Class Instance	InstanceType	Class instance.
Files	FileType	File.
Internal	CodeType	Byte-compiled code.
	FrameType	Execution frame.
	TracebackType	Stacks traceback of an exception.
	SliceType	Generated by extended slices.
	EllipsisType	Used in extended slices.

Note: ClassType and InstanceType appear twice in Table 3.1 because classes and instances are both callable under special circumstances.

The *None* Type

The None type denotes a null object. Python provides exactly one null object, which is written as None in a program. This object is returned by functions that don't explicitly return a value. (You also can pass it to functions and methods to indicate an empty list of arguments.) None has no attributes and evaluates to false in expressions.

Numeric Types

Python uses four numeric types: integers, long integers, floating-point numbers, and complex numbers. All numeric objects are signed and immutable.

Integers represent whole numbers in the range of -2147483648 to 2147483647 (the range may be larger on some machines). Internally, integers are stored as 2's complement binary values, in 32 or more bits. If the result of an operation exceeds the allowed range of values, an OverflowError exception is raised. Long integers represent whole numbers of unlimited range (limited only by available memory).

Floating-point numbers are represented using the native double-precision (64-bit) representation of floating-point numbers on the machine. Normally this is IEEE 754, which provides approximately 17 digits of precision and an exponent in the range of -308 to 308. Python doesn't support 32-bit single-precision floating-point numbers.

Complex numbers are represented as a pair of floating-point numbers. The real and imaginary parts of a complex number z are available in z.real and z.imag.

Sequence Types

Sequences represent ordered sets of objects indexed by natural numbers, and include strings, lists, and tuples. Strings are sequences of characters; lists and tuples are sequences of arbitrary Python objects. Strings and tuples are immutable; lists allow insertion, deletion, and substitution of elements.

Table 3.2 shows the operators and methods that you can apply to all sequence types. Element i of a sequence s is selected using the indexing operator s[i], and a subsequence is selected using the slicing operator s[i:j] (these operations are described in Chapter 4). The length of any sequence is returned using the built-in len(s) function. You can find the minimum and maximum values of a sequence by using the built-in min(s) and max(s) functions.

Table 3.2   Sequence Operations and Methods

Item	Description
s[i]	Returns element i of a sequence.
s[i:j]	Returns a slice.
len(s)	Number of elements in s.
min(s)	Minimum value in s.
max(s)	Maximum value in s.

Additionally, lists support the methods shown in Table 3.3. The built-in function `list(s)` converts any sequence type to a list. If s is already a list, this function constructs a new list that's a shallow copy of s. The `s.index(x)` method searches the list for the first occurrence of x. If no such element is found, a `ValueError` exception is raised. Similarly, the `s.remove(x)` method removes the first occurrence of x from the list. The `s.extend(t)` method extends the list s by appending the elements in list t. The `s.sort()` method sorts the elements of a list and optionally accepts a comparison function. This function should take two arguments and return negative, zero, or positive, depending on whether the first argument is smaller, equal to, or larger than the second argument. The `s.reverse()` method reverses the order of the items in the list. Both the `sort()` and `reverse()` methods operate on the list elements in place and return `None`.

Table 3.3   List Methods

Method	Description
`list(s)`	Converts sequence s to a list.
`s.append(x)`	Appends a new element x to the end of s.
`s.extend(l)`	Appends a new list l to the end of s.
`s.count(x)`	Counts occurrences of x in s.
`s.index(x)`	Returns the smallest i where s[i] == x.
`s.insert(i,x)`	Inserts x at index i.
`s.pop([i])`	Returns the element i and removes it from the list. If i is omitted, the last element is returned.
`s.remove(x)`	Searches for x and removes it from s.
`s.reverse()`	Reverses items of s in place.
`s.sort([cmpfunc])`	Sorts items of s in place. cmpfunc is a comparison function.

The built-in function `range(i,j [,stride])` constructs a list of integers and populates it with the values k such that $i \le k < j$. You can also specify an optional stride. The built-in `xrange()` function performs a similar operation, but returns an immutable sequence of type `XRangeType`. Rather than storing all the values in a list, this sequence calculates its values whenever it's accessed. Consequently, it's much more memory efficient when working with large sequences of integers. The `XRangeType` provides a single method, `s.tolist()`, that converts its values to a list.

Mapping Types

A *mapping object* represents an arbitrary collection of objects that are indexed by another collection of nearly arbitrary key values. Unlike a sequence, a mapping object is unordered and can be indexed by numbers, strings, and other objects. Mappings are mutable.

Dictionaries are the only built-in mapping type and are Python's version of a hash table or associative array. You can use any immutable object as a dictionary key value (strings, numbers, tuples, and so on). Lists, dictionaries, or tuples containing mutable objects cannot be used as keys (the dictionary type requires key values to remain constant).

To select an item in a mapping object, use the key index operator $m[k]$ where k is a key value. If the key is not found, a KeyError exception is raised. The len(m) function returns the number of items contained in a mapping object. Table 3.4 lists methods and operations.

Table 3.4   Methods and Operations for Mapping Types

Item	Description
len(*m*)	Returns the number of items in *m*.
m[*k*]	Returns the item of *m* with key *k*.
m[*k*]=*x*	Sets *m*[*k*] to *x*.
del *m*[*k*]	Removes *m*[*k*] from *m*.
m.clear()	Removes all items from *m*.
m.copy()	Makes a copy of *m*.
m.has_key(*k*)	Returns 1 if *m* has key *k*, 0 otherwise.
m.items()	Returns a list of (key,value) pairs.
m.keys()	Returns a list of key values.
m.update(*b*)	Adds all objects from *b* to *m*.
m.values()	Returns a list of all values in *m*.
m.get(*k* [,*f*])	Returns *m*[*k*] if found; otherwise, returns *f*.

The m.clear() method removes all items. The m.copy() method makes a shallow copy of the items contained in a mapping object and places them in a new mapping object. The m.items() method returns a list containing (key,value) pairs. The m.keys() method returns a list with all the key values and the m.values() method returns a list with all the objects. The m.update(b) method updates the current mapping object by inserting all the (key,value) pairs found in the mapping object b. The m.get(k [,f]) method retrieves an object, but allows for an optional default value f that's returned if no such object exists.

Callable Types

Callable types represent objects that support the function call operation. There are several flavors of objects with this property, including user-defined functions, built-in functions, and methods associated with classes.

User-defined functions are callable objects created at the module level by using the def statement or lambda operator (functions defined within class definitions are called *methods* and are described shortly). Functions are first-class objects that behave just like any other Python object. As a result, you can assign them to variables or place them in lists, tuples, and dictionaries, as shown in the following example:

```
def foo(x,y):
    print '%s + %s is %s' % (str(x), str(y), str(x+y))

# Assign to a new variable
bar = foo
bar(3,4)            # Invokes 'foo' defined above
```

continues >>

>>continued
```
# Place in a container
d = { }
d['callback'] = foo
d['callback'](3,4)  # Invokes 'foo'
```

A user-defined function *f* has the following attributes:

Attribute(s)	Description
f.__doc__ or f.func_doc	Documentation string.
f.__name__ or f.func_name	Function name.
f.func_code	Byte-compiled code.
f.func_defaults	Tuple containing the default arguments.
f.func_globals	Dictionary defining the global namespace.

Methods are functions that operate only on instances of an object. Typically, methods are defined inside a class definition, as shown here:

```
# A queue of objects ranked by priorities
class PriorityQueue:
    def __init__(self):
        self.items = [ ]            # List of (priority, item)
    def insert(self,priority,item):
        for i in range(len(self.items)):
            if self.items[i][0] > priority:
                self.items.insert(i,(priority,item))
                break
        else:
            self.items.append((priority,item))
    def remove(self):
        try:
            return self.items.pop(0)[1]
        except IndexError:
            raise RuntimeError, 'Queue is empty'
```

An *unbound method object* is a method that hasn't yet been associated with a specific instance of an object. The methods contained within a class definition are unbound until they're attached to a specific object. For example:

```
m = PriorityQueue.insert     # Unbound method
```

To invoke an unbound method, supply an instance of an object as the first argument:

```
pq = PriorityQueue()
m = PriorityQueue.insert
m(pq,5,"Python")                      # Invokes pq.insert(5,"Python")
```

A *bound method object* is a function that has been bound to a specific object instance. For example:

```
pq = PriorityQueue()     # Create a PriorityQueue instance
n = pq.insert            # n is a method bound to pq
```

A bound method implicitly contains a reference to the associated instance, so it can be invoked as follows:

```
n(5,"Python")                       # Invokes pq.insert(5,"Python")
```

Bound and unbound methods are no more than a thin wrapper around an ordinary function object. The following attributes are defined for method objects:

Attribute	Description
`m.__doc__`	Documentation string.
`m.__name__`	Method name.
`m.im_class`	Class in which this method was defined.
`m.im_func`	Function object implementing the method.
`m.im_self`	Instance associated with method (`None` if unbound).

So far, this discussion has focused on functions and methods, but class objects (described shortly) are also callable. When a class is called, a new class instance is created. In addition, if the class defines an `__init__()` method, it's called to initialize the newly created instance. The creation of a `PriorityQueue` in the earlier example illustrates this behavior.

A class instance is also callable if its class defines a special method `__call__()`. If this method is defined for a class instance x, then $x(args)$ invokes the method $x.\_\_call\_\_(args)$.

The final types of callable objects are *built-in functions* and *methods*. Built-in functions/methods correspond to code written in extension modules and are usually written in C or C++. The following attributes are available for built-in methods:

Attribute	Description
`b.__doc__`	Documentation string.
`b.__name__`	Function/method name.
`b.__self__`	Instance associated with method.

For built-in functions such as `len()`, the `__self__` is set to `None`, indicating that the function isn't bound to any specific object. For built-in methods such as `x.append()` where x is a list object, `__self__` is set to x.

Modules

The *module* type is a container that holds objects loaded with the `import` statement. When the statement `import foo` appears in a program, for example, the name `foo` is assigned to the corresponding module object. Modules define a namespace that's implemented using a dictionary accessible in the attribute `__dict__`. Whenever an attribute of a module is referenced (using the dot operator), it's translated into a dictionary lookup. For example, $m.x$ is equivalent to `m.__dict__["x"]`. Likewise, assignment to an attribute such as $m.x = y$ is equivalent to `m.__dict__["x"] = y`. The following attributes are available:

Attribute	Description
`m.__dict__`	Dictionary associated with the module.
`m.__doc__`	Module documentation string.
`m.__name__`	Name of the module.
`m.__file__`	File from which the module was loaded.
`m.__path__`	Fully qualified package name, defined when the module object refers to a package.

Classes

Classes are created using the `class` statement, as described in Chapter 7. Like modules, classes are implemented using a dictionary that contains all the objects defined within the class, and defines a namespace. References to class attributes such as `c.x` are translated into a dictionary lookup `c.__dict__["x"]`. If an attribute isn't found in this dictionary, the search continues in the list of base classes. This search is depth first, left to right, in the order that base classes were specified in the class definition. Attribute assignment such as `c.y = 5` always updates the `__dict__` attribute of `c`, not the dictionaries of any base class.

The following attributes are defined by class objects:

Attribute	Description
`c.__dict__`	Dictionary associated with class.
`c.__doc__`	Class documentation string.
`c.__name__`	Name of the class.
`c.__module__`	Module name in which the class was defined.
`c.__bases__`	Tuple containing base classes.

Class Instances

A *class instance* is an object created by calling a class object. Each instance has its own local namespace that's implemented as a dictionary. This dictionary and the associated class object are available in the following attributes:

Attribute	Description
`x.__dict__`	Dictionary associated with an instance.
`x.__class__`	Class to which an instance belongs.

When the attribute of an object is referenced, such as in `x.a`, the interpreter first searches in the local dictionary for `x.__dict__["a"]`. If it doesn't find the name locally, the search continues by performing a lookup on the class defined in the `__class__` attribute. If no match is found, the search continues with base classes as described earlier. If still no match is found and the object's class defines a `__getattr__()` method, it's used to perform the lookup. The assignment of attributes such as `x.a = 4` always updates `x.__dict__`, not the dictionaries of classes or base classes.

Files

The file object represents an open file and is returned by the built-in `open()` function (as well as a number of functions in the standard library). For more details about this type, see Chapter 9, "Input and Output."

Internal Types

A number of objects used by the interpreter are exposed to the user. These include traceback objects, code objects, frame objects, slice objects, and the Ellipsis object.

Code Objects

Code objects represent raw byte-compiled executable code or bytecode and are typically returned by the built-in `compile()` function. Code objects are similar to functions except that they don't contain any context related to the namespace in which the code was defined, nor do code objects store information about default argument values. A code object `c` has the following read-only attributes:

Attribute	Description
c.co_name	Function name.
c.co_argcount	Number of positional arguments (including default values).
c.co_nlocals	Number of local variables used by the function.
c.co_varnames	Tuple containing names of local variables.
c.co_code	String representing raw bytecode.
c.co_consts	Tuple containing the literals used by the bytecode.
c.co_names	Tuple containing names used by the bytecode.
c.co_filename	Filename of the file in which the code was compiled.
c.co_firstlineno	First line number of the function.
c.co_lnotab	String encoding bytecode offsets to line numbers.
c.co_stacksize	Required stack size (including local variables).
c.co_flags	Integer containing interpreter flags. Bit 2 is set if the function uses a variable number of positional arguments using `"*args"`. Bit 3 is set if the function allows arbitrary keyword arguments using `"**kwargs"`. All other bits are reserved.

Frame Objects

Frame objects are used to represent execution frames and most frequently occur in traceback objects (described next). A frame object `f` has the following read-only attributes:

Attribute	Description
f.f_back	Previous stack frame (toward the caller).
f.f_code	Code object being executed.
f.f_locals	Dictionary used for local variables.
f.f_globals	Dictionary used for global variables.
f.f_builtins	Dictionary used for built-in names.
f.f_restricted	Set to 1 if executing in restricted execution mode.
f.f_lineno	Line number.
f.f_lasti	Current instruction. This is an index into the bytecode string of f_code.

The following attributes can be modified (and are used by debuggers and other tools):

Attribute	Description
f.f_trace	Function called at the start of each source code line.
f.f_exc_type	Most recent exception type.
f.f_exc_value	Most recent exception value.
f.f_exc_traceback	Most recent exception traceback.

Traceback Objects

Traceback objects are created when an exception occurs and contains stack trace information. When an exception handler is entered, the stack trace can be retrieved using the sys.exc_info() function. The following read-only attributes are available in traceback objects:

Attribute	Description
t.tb_next	Next level in the stack trace (toward the execution frame where the exception occurred).
t.tb_frame	Execution frame object of the current level.
t.tb_line	Line number where the exception occurred.
t.tb_lasti	Instruction being executed in the current level.

Slice Objects

Slice objects are used to represent slices given in extended slice syntax, such as a[i:j:stride], a[i:j, n:m], or a[..., i:j]. Slice objects are also created using the built-in slice([i,] j [,stride]) function. The following read-only attributes are available:

Attribute	Description
s.start	Lower bound of the slice; none if omitted.
s.stop	Upper bound of the slice; none if omitted.
s.step	Stride of the slice; none if omitted.

Ellipsis Object

The *Ellipsis object* is used to indicate the presence of an ellipsis (...) in a slice. There is a single object of this type, accessed through the built-in name Ellipsis. It has no attributes and evaluates as true.

Special Methods

All the built-in datatypes consist of some data and a collection of special object methods. The names of special methods are always preceded and followed by double underscores (__). These methods are automatically triggered by the interpreter as a program executes. For example, the operation x + y is mapped to an internal method x.__add__(y), and an indexing operation x[k] is mapped to x.__getitem__(k). The behavior of each datatype depends entirely on the set of special methods that it implements.

Although it's not possible to alter the behavior of built-in types (or to even invoke any of their special methods directly by name, as just suggested), it's possible to use class definitions to define new objects that behave like the built-in types. To do this, supply implementations of the special methods described in this section.

Object Creation, Destruction, and Representation

The methods in Table 3.5 initialize, destroy, and represent objects. The __init__() method initializes the attributes of an object and is called immediately after an object has been newly created. The __del__() method is invoked when an object is about to be destroyed and is called a *destructor*. This method is invoked only when an object is no longer in use. It's important to note that the statement del x only decrements an object's reference count and doesn't necessarily result in a call to this function.

Table 3.5   Special Methods for Object Creation, Destruction, and Representation

Method	Description
__init__(self [,args])	Called to initialize a new instance.
__del__(self)	Called to destroy an instance.
__repr__(self)	Creates a full string representation of an object.
__str__(self)	Creates an informal string representation.
__cmp__(self,other)	Compares two objects and returns negative, zero, or positive.
__hash__(self)	Computes a 32-bit hash index.
__nonzero__(self)	Returns 0 or 1 for truth-value testing.

The __repr__() and __str__() methods create string representations of an object. The __repr__() method normally returns an expression string that can be evaluated to re-create the object. This method is invoked by the built-in repr() function and by the backquotes operator. For example:

```
a = [2,3,4,5]      # Create a list
s = repr(a)        # s = '[2, 3, 4, 5]'
                   # Note : could have also used s = `a`
b = eval(s)        # Turns s back into a list
```

If a string expression cannot be created, the convention is for __repr__() to return a string of the form <...*message*...>, as shown here:

```
f = open("foo")
a = repr(f)        # a = "<open file 'foo', mode 'r' at dc030>"
```

The __str__() method is called by the built-in str() function and by the print statement. It differs from __repr__() in that the string it returns can be more concise and informative to the user. If this method is undefined, the __repr__() method is invoked.

The __cmp__(*self*,*other*) method is used by all the comparison operators. It returns a
negative number if *self* < *other*, zero if *self* == *other*, and positive if *self* > *other*.
If this method is undefined for an object, the object will be compared by object
identity. The __nonzero__() method is used for truth-value testing and should return 0
or 1. If undefined, the __len__() method is invoked to determine truth. Finally, the
__hash__() method computes an integer hash key used in dictionary operations
(the hash value can also be returned using the built-in function hash()). The value
returned should be identical for two objects that compare as equal. Furthermore,
mutable objects should not define this method; any changes to an object will alter
the hash value and make it impossible to locate an object on subsequent dictionary
lookups. An object should not define a __hash__() method without also defining
__cmp__().

Attribute Access

The methods in Table 3.6 read, write, and delete the attributes of an object using the
dot (.) operator and the del operator, respectively.

Table 3.6   Special Methods for Attribute Access

Method	Description
__getattr__(*self*, *name*)	Returns the attribute *self.name*.
__setattr__(*self*, *name*, *value*)	Sets the attribute *self.name* = *value*.
__delattr__(*self*, *name*)	Deletes the attribute *self.name*.

For example:

```
a = x.s       # Invokes __getattr__(x,"s")
x.s = b       # Invokes __setattr__(x,"s", b)
del x.s       # Invokes __delattr__(x,"s")
```

For class instances, the __getattr__() method is invoked only if the search for the
attribute in the object's local dictionary or corresponding class definition fails. This
method should return the attribute value or raise an AttributeError exception on
failure.

Sequence and Mapping Methods

The methods in Table 3.7 are used by objects that want to emulate sequence and
mapping objects.

Table 3.7   Methods for Sequences and Mappings

Method	Description
__len__(*self*)	Returns the length of *self*.
__getitem__(*self*, *key*)	Returns *self*[*key*].
__setitem__(*self*, *key*, *value*)	Sets *self*[*key*] = *value*.
__delitem__(*self*, *key*)	Deletes *self*[*key*].
__getslice__(*self*,*i*,*j*)	Returns *self*[*i*:*j*].
__setslice__(*self*,*i*,*j*,*s*)	Sets *self*[*i*:*j*] = *s*.
__delslice__(*self*,*i*,*j*)	Deletes *self*[*i*:*j*].

For example:

```
a = [1,2,3,4,5,6]
len(a)                    # __len__(a)
x = a[2]                  # __getitem__(a,2)
a[1] = 7                  # __setitem__(a,1,7)
del a[2]                  # __delitem__(a,2)
x = a[1:5]                # __getslice__(a,1,5)
a[1:3] = [10,11,12]       # __setslice__(a,1,3,[10,11,12])
del a[1:4]                # __delslice__(a,1,4)
```

The __len__ method is called by the built-in len() function to return a non-negative length. This function also determines truth values unless the __nonzero__() method has also been defined.

For manipulating individual items, the __getitem__() method can return an item by key value. The key can be any Python object, but is typically an integer for sequences. The __setitem__() method assigns a value to an element. The __delitem__() method is invoked whenever the del operation is applied to a single element.

The slicing methods support the slicing operator s[i:j]. The __getslice__() method returns a slice, which must be of the same type as the original object. The indices i and j must be integers, but their interpretation is up to the method. Missing values for i and j are replaced with 0 and sys.maxint, respectively. The __setslice__() method assigns values to a slice. Similarly, __delslice__() deletes all the elements in a slice.

In addition to implementing the methods just described, sequences and mappings implement a number of mathematical methods, including __add__(), __radd__(), __mul__(), and __rmul__() to support concatenation and sequence replication. These methods are described shortly.

Finally, Python supports an extended slicing operation that's useful for working with multidimensional data structures such as matrices and arrays. Syntactically, you specify an extended slice as follows:

```
a = m[0:100:10]          # Strided slice (stride=10)
b = m[1:10, 3:20]        # Multidimensional slice
c = m[0:100:10, 50:75:5] # Multiple dimensions with strides
m[0:5, 5:10] = n         # extended slice assignment
del m[:10, 15:]          # extended slice deletion
```

The general format for each dimension of an extended slice is i:j[:stride], where stride is optional. As with ordinary slices, you can omit the starting or ending values for each part of a slice. In addition, a special object known as the *Ellipsis* and written as ... is available to denote any number of trailing or leading dimensions in an extended slice:

```
a = m[..., 10:20]     # extended slice access with ellipsis
m[10:20, ...] = n
```

When using extended slices, the __getitem__(), __setitem__(), and __delitem__() methods implement access, modification, and deletion. However, instead of an integer, the value passed to these methods is a tuple containing one or more slice objects and at most one instance of the Ellipsis type. For example,

```
a = m[0:10, 0:100:5, ...]
```

invokes __getitem__() as follows:

```
a = __getitem__(m, (slice(0,10,None), slice(0,100,5), Ellipsis))
```

At this time, none of the built-in datatypes support extended slices, so using them is likely to result in an error. However, special-purpose extensions, especially those with a scientific flavor, may provide new types and objects that support the extended slicing operation.

Mathematical Operations

Table 3.8 lists special methods that objects must implement to emulate numbers. Mathematical operations are always evaluated from left to right; when an expression such as x + y appears, the interpreter tries to invoke the method x.__add__(y). The special methods beginning with r support operations with reversed operands. These are invoked only if the left operand doesn't implement the specified operation. For example, if x in x + y doesn't support the __add__() method, the interpreter tries to invoke the method y.__radd__(x).

Table 3.8   Methods for Mathematical Operations

Method	Result
__add__(self,other)	self + other
__sub__(self,other)	self - other
__mul__(self,other)	self * other
__div__(self,other)	self / other
__mod__(self,other)	self % other
__divmod__(self,other)	divmod(self,other)
__pow__(self,other [,modulo])	self ** other,pow(self, other, modulo)
__lshift__(self,other)	self << other
__rshift__(self,other)	self >> other
__and__(self,other)	self & other
__or__(self,other)	self ¦ other
__xor__(self,other)	self ^ other
__radd__(self,other)	other + self
__rsub__(self,other)	other - self
__rmul__(self,other)	other * self
__rdiv__(self,other)	other / self
__rmod__(self,other)	other % self
__rdivmod__(self,other)	divmod(other,self)
__rpow__(self,other)	other ** self
__rlshift__(self,other)	other << self
__rrshift__(self,other)	other >> self
__rand__(self,other)	other & self
__ror__(self,other)	other ¦ self
__rxor__(self,other)	other ^ self
__neg__(self)	-self
__pos__(self)	+self

Method	Result
__abs__(*self*)	abs(*self*)
__invert__(*self*)	~*self*
__int__(*self*)	int(*self*)
__long__(*self*)	long(*self*)
__float__(*self*)	float(*self*)
__complex__(*self*)	complex(*self*)
__oct__(*self*)	oct(*self*)
__hex__(*self*)	hex(*self*)
__coerce__(*self*,*other*)	Type coercion

The conversion methods __int__(), __long__(), __float__(), and __complex__() convert an object into one of the four built-in numerical types. The __oct__() and __hex__() methods return strings representing the octal and hexadecimal values of an object, respectively.

The __coerce__(*x*,*y*) method is used in conjunction with mixed-mode arithmetic. This method returns either a 2-tuple containing the values of *x* and *y* converted to a common numerical type, or None if no such conversion is possible. To evaluate an operation *x* op *y* where op is an operation such as +, the following rules are applied, in order:

1. If *x* has a __coerce__() method, replace *x* and *y* with the values returned by *x*.__coerce__(*y*). If None is returned, skip to step 3.

2. If *x* has a method __op__(), return *x*.__op__(*y*). Otherwise, restore *x* and *y* to their original values and continue.

3. If *y* has a __coerce__() method, replace *x* and *y* with the values returned by *y*.__coerce__(*x*). If None is returned, raise an exception.

4. If *y* has a method __rop__(), return *y*.__rop__(*x*). Otherwise, raise an exception.

The interpreter supports only a limited number of mixed-type operations involving the built-in types, in particular the following:

- If *x* is a string, *x* % *y* invokes the string-formatting operation, regardless of the type of *y*.

- If *x* is a sequence, *x* + *y* invokes sequence concatenation.

- If either *x* or *y* is a sequence and the other operand is an integer, *x* * *y* invokes sequence repetition.

Callable Objects

Finally, an object can emulate a function by providing the __call__(*self* [,*args*]) method. If an object *x* provides this method, it can be invoked like a function. That is, *x*(*arg1*, *arg2*, ...) invokes *x*.__call__(*self*, *arg1*, *arg2*, ...).

Performance and Memory Considerations

All Python objects minimally include an integer reference count, a descriptor defining the type, and the representation of the actual data. Table 3.9 shows the approximate memory requirements of various built-in objects based on the C implementation running on a 32-bit machine. The precise values may vary slightly according to the implementation of the interpreter and machine architecture (for instance, the memory requirements may double on a 64-bit machine). Although you may never need to think about memory utilization, Python is used in a variety of high-performance and memory-critical applications ranging from supercomputing to mobile computing. The memory footprint of the built-in types is presented here to help programmers make informed design decisions in memory-critical settings.

Table 3.9   Memory Size of Built-in Datatypes

Type	Size
Integer	12 bytes
Long Integer	12 bytes + ($n$bits/16 + 1)*2 bytes
Floats	16 bytes
Complex	24 bytes
List	16 bytes + 4 bytes for each item
Tuple	16 bytes + 4 bytes for each item
String	20 bytes + 1 byte per character
Dictionary	24 bytes + $12*2^n$ bytes, $n = \log_2(n\text{items})+1$
Class Instance	16 bytes plus a dictionary object
Xrange object	24 bytes

Because strings are used so frequently, the interpreter uses a number of optimizations. First, a string s can be *interned* using the built-in function intern(s). This function looks in an internal hash table to see whether the string value already exists. If so, a reference to that string—instead of a copy of the string data—is stored in the string object. If not, the data in s is added to the hash table. Interned strings live until the interpreter exits; if you're concerned about memory, you shouldn't intern infrequently used strings. Also, to increase the performance of dictionary lookups, strings cache their last computed hash-table value.

Dictionaries are implemented using a hash table with open indexing. The number of entries allocated to a dictionary is equal to twice the smallest power of 2 that's greater than the number of objects stored in the dictionary. When a dictionary expands, its size doubles. On average, about a half of the entries allocated to a dictionary are unused.

The execution of a Python program is primarily a sequence of function calls involving the special methods described in the earlier section "Special Methods." Next to choosing the most efficient algorithm, performance improvements can be made by understanding Python's object model and trying to minimize the number of special method calls that occur during execution. This is especially true for name lookups on modules and classes. For example, consider the following code:

```
import math
d= 0.0
for i in xrange(1000000):
    d = d + math.sqrt(i)
```

In this case, each iteration of the loop involves two name lookups. First, the math module is located in the global namespace; then it's searched for a function object named sqrt. Now consider the following modification:

```
from math import sqrt
d = 0.0
for i in xrange(1000000):
    d = d + sqrt(i)
```

In this case, one name lookup is eliminated from the inner loop. In fact, when running on a 200 MHz Pentium, this simple change makes the code run more than twice as fast as before.

Unnecessary method calls can also be eliminated by making careful use of temporary values and avoiding unnecessary lookups on sequences and dictionaries. For example, consider the following two classes:

```
class Point:
    def __init__(self,x,y,z):
        self.x = x
        self.y = y
        self.z = z

class Poly:
    def __init__(self):
        self.pts = [ ]
    def addpoint(self,pt):
        self.pts.append(pt)
    def perimeter(self):
        d = 0.0
        self.pts.append(self.pts[0])         # Temporarily close the polygon
        for i in xrange(len(self.pts)-1):
            d2 = (self.pts[i+1].x - self.pts[i].x)**2 + \
                 (self.pts[i+1].y - self.pts[i].y)**2 + \
                 (self.pts[i+1].z - self.pts[i].z)**2
            d = d + math.sqrt(d2)
        self.pts.pop()                       # Restore original list of points
        return d
```

In the `perimeter()` method, each occurrence of `self.pts[i]` involves two special-method lookups—one involving a dictionary and another involving a sequence. You can reduce the number of lookups by rewriting the method as follows:

```
class Poly:
    ...
    def perimeter(self):
        d = 0.0
        pts = self.pts
        pts.append(pts[0])
        for i in xrange(len(pts)-1):
            p1 = pts[i+1]
            p2 = pts[i]
            d2 = (p1.x - p2.x)**2 + \
                 (p1.y - p2.y)**2 + \
                 (p1.z - p2.z)**2
            d = d + math.sqrt(d2)
        pts.pop()
        return d
```

Although the performance gains made by such modifications are often modest (15–20%), an understanding of the underlying object model and the manner in which special methods are invoked can result in faster programs. Of course, if performance is extremely critical, you often can export functionality to a Python extension module written in C or C++.

4

Operators and Expressions

This chapter describes Python's built-in operators as well as precedence rules used in the evaluation of expressions.

Operations on Numbers

The following operations can be applied to all numeric types:

Operation	Description
x + y	Addition.
x - y	Subtraction.
x * y	Multiplication.
x / y	Division.
x ** y	Power (x^y).
x % y	Modulo (x mod y).
-x	Unary minus.
+x	Unary plus.

For integers, division truncates the result to an integer. Thus, 7/4 is 1, not 1.75. The modulo operator returns the remainder of the division x / y. For example, 7 % 4 is 3. For floating-point numbers, the modulo operator returns the floating-point remainder of x / y, which is x - int(x / y) * y. For complex numbers, the modulo operator returns x - int((x / y).real) * y.

The following shifting and bitwise logical operators can only be applied to integers and long integers:

Operation	Description
x << y	Left shift.
x >> y	Right shift.
x & y	Bitwise and.
x ¦ y	Bitwise or.
x ^ y	Bitwise xor (exclusive or).
~x	Bitwise negation.

The bitwise operators assume that integers are represented in a 2's complement binary representation. For long integers, the bitwise operators operate as if the sign bit is infinitely extended to the left.

In addition, you can apply the following built-in functions to all the numerical types:

Function	Description
abs(x)	Absolute value.
divmod(x,y)	Returns (int(x / y), x % y).
pow(x,y [,modulo])	Returns (x ** y) % modulo.
round(x,[n])	Rounds to the nearest integer (floating-point numbers only).

The abs() function returns the absolute value of a number. The divmod() function returns the quotient and remainder of a division operation. The pow() function can be used in place of the ** operator, but also supports the ternary power–modulo function (often used in cryptographic algorithms). The round() function rounds a floating-point number x to the nearest multiple of 10 to the power n. If n is omitted, it is set to 0. If x is equally close to two multiples, rounding is performed away from zero (for example, 0.5 is rounded to 1 and -0.5 is rounded to -1).

The following comparison operators have the standard mathematical interpretation and return an integer value of 1 for true, 0 for false:

Operation	Description
x < y	Less than.
x > y	Greater than.
x == y	Equal to.
x != y	Not equal to (same as <>).
x >= y	Greater than or equal to.
x <= y	Less than or equal to.

Comparisons can be chained together, such as in w < x < y < z. Such expressions are evaluated as w < x and x < y and y < z. Expressions such as x < y > z are legal, but are likely to confuse anyone else reading the code (it's important to note that no comparison is made between x and z in such an expression).

Comparisons involving complex numbers first compare the real components and then the imaginary components. Thus, 3 + 2j is less than 4 + 10000j and 2 + 1j is less than 2 + 4j.

Operations involving numbers are valid only if the operands are of the same type. If the types differ, a coercion operation is performed to convert one of the types to the other:

1. If either operand is a complex number, the other operand is converted to a complex number.

2. If either operand is a floating-point number, the other is converted to a float.

3. If either operand is a long integer, the other is converted to a long integer.

4. Otherwise, both numbers must be integers and no conversion is performed.

Operations on Sequences

The following operators can be applied to sequence types, including strings, lists, and tuples:

Operation	Description
s + r	Concatenation.
s * n, n * s	Makes n copies of s, where n is an integer.
s % d	String formatting (strings only).
s[i]	Indexing.
s[i:j]	Slicing.
x in s, x not in s	Membership.
for x in s:	Iteration.
len(s)	Length.
min(s)	Minimum item.
max(s)	Maximum item.

The + operator concatenates two sequences. The s * n operator makes n copies of a sequence. However, these are shallow copies that replicate elements by reference only. For example, consider the following code:

```
a = [3,4,5]     # A list
b = (a,)        # A tuple (containing a)
c = 4*b         # Make four copies of b

# Now modify a
a[0] = -7

# Look at c
print c
```

The output of this program is the following:

```
([-7, 4, 5], [-7, 4, 5], [-7, 4, 5], [-7, 4, 5])
```

In this case, a reference to the list a was placed in the tuple b. When b was replicated, four additional references to a were created. Finally, when a was modified, this change was propagated to all of the other "copies" of a. This behavior of sequence multiplication is often unexpected and not the intent of the programmer. One way to work around the problem is to manually construct the replicated sequence by duplicating the contents of a. For example:

```
a = [ 3, 4, 5 ]
b = (a, )
c = []
for i in range(4):
    for item in b:
        c.append(item[:])    # [:] makes a copy of a list
c = tuple(c)
```

The copy module in the standard library can also be used to make copies of objects.

The indexing operator s[n] returns the nth object from a sequence where s[0] is the first object. Negative indices can be used to fetch characters from the end of a sequence. For example, s[-1] returns the last item. Otherwise, attempts to access elements that are out of range result in an IndexError exception.

The slicing operator s[i:j] extracts a subsequence from s consisting of the elements with index k where i ≤ k < j. If the starting or ending index is omitted, the beginning or end of the sequence is assumed, respectively. Negative indices are allowed and assumed to be relative to the end of the sequence. If i or j is out of range, they're assumed to refer to the beginning or end of a sequence, depending on whether their value refers to an element before the first item or after the last item, respectively.

The x in s operator tests to see whether the object x is in the sequence s and returns 1 if true, 0 if false. Similarly, the x not in s operator tests whether x is not in the sequence s. The for x in s operator iterates over all the elements of a sequence and is described further in Chapter 5, "Control Flow." len(s) returns the number of elements in a sequence. min(s) and max(s) return the minimum and maximum values of a sequence, although the result may only make sense if the elements can be ordered with respect to the <= and >= operators (for example, it would make little sense to find the maximum value of a list of file objects).

Strings and tuples are immutable and cannot be modified after creation. Lists can be modified with the following operators:

Operation	Description
s[i] = x	Index assignment.
s[i:j] = r	Slice assignment.
del s[i]	Delete an element.
del s[i:j]	Delete a slice.

The s[i] = x operator changes element i of a list to refer to object x, increasing the reference count of x. Negative indices are relative to the end of the list and attempts to assign a value to an out-of-range index result in an IndexError exception. The slicing assignment operator s[i:j] = r replaces elements k where i ≤ k < j with elements from sequence r. Indices may have the same values as for slicing and are adjusted to the beginning or end of the list if they're out of range. If necessary, the sequence s is expanded or reduced to accommodate all the elements in r. For example:

```
a = [1,2,3,4,5]
a[1] = 6              # a = [1,6,3,4,5]
a[2:4] = [10,11]      # a = [1,6,10,11,5]
a[3:4] = [-1,-2,-3]   # a = [1,6,10,-1,-2,-3,5]
a[2:] = [0]           # a = [1,6,0]
```

The del s[i] operator removes element i from a list and decrements its reference count. del s[i:j] removes all the elements in a slice.

Sequences are compared using the operators <, >, <=, >=, ==, and !=. When comparing two sequences, the first elements of each sequence are compared. If they differ, this determines the result. If they're the same, the comparison moves to the second element of each sequence. This process continues until two different elements are found or no more elements exist in either of the sequences. If a is a subsequence of b, then a < b. Strings are compared using lexicographical ordering. Each character is assigned a unique index determined by the machine's character set (such as ASCII or Unicode). A character is less than another character if its index is less.

The modulo operator (s % d) produces a formatted string, given a format string s and a collection of objects in a tuple or mapping object (dictionary). The behavior of this operator is similar to the C printf() function. The format string contains two types of objects: ordinary characters (which are left unmodified) and conversion specifiers— each of which is replaced with a formatted string representing an element of the associated tuple or mapping. If *d* is a tuple, the number of conversion specifiers must exactly match the number of objects in *d*. If *d* is a mapping, each conversion specifier must be associated with a valid key name in the mapping (using parentheses, as described shortly). Each conversion specifier starts with the % character and ends with one of the conversion characters shown in Table 4.1.

Table 4.1   String Formatting Conversions

Character	Output Format
d,i	Decimal integer.
u	Unsigned integer.
o	Octal integer.
x	Hexadecimal integer.
X	Hexadecimal integer (uppercase letters).
f	Floating point as [-]m.dddddd.
e	Floating point as [-]m.dddddde±xx.
E	Floating point as [-]m.ddddddE±xx.
g,G	Use %e or %E for exponents less than −4 or greater than the precision; otherwise use %f.
s	String or any object.
c	Single character.
%	Literal %.

Between the % and the conversion character, the following modifiers may appear, in order:

1. A key name in parentheses, which selects a specific item out of the mapping object. If no such element exists, a KeyError exception is raised.

2. One or more of the following:

    ■ A - sign, indicating left alignment.

    ■ A + sign, indicating that the numeric sign should be included (even if positive).

    ■ A 0, indicating a zero fill.

3. A number specifying the minimum field width. The converted value will be printed in a field at least this wide and padded on the left (or right if the - flag is given) to make up the field width.

4. A period separating the field width from a precision.

5. A number specifying the maximum number of characters to be printed from a string, the number of digits following the decimal point in a floating-point number, or the minimum number of digits for an integer.

In addition, the asterisk (*) character may used in place of a number in any width field. If present, the width will be read from the next item in the tuple.

The following code illustrates a few examples:

```
a = 42
b = 13.142783
c = "hello"
d = {'x':13, 'y':1.54321, 'z':'world'}

print 'a is %d' % a              # "a is 42"
print '%10d %f' % (a,b)          # "        42 13.142783"
print '%+010d %E' % (a,b)        # "+000000042 1.314278E+01"
print '%(x)-10d %(y)0.3g' % d    # "13         1.54"
print '%0.4s %s' % (c, d['z'])   # "hell world"
print '%*.*f' % (5,3,b)          # "13.143"
```

Operations on Dictionaries

Dictionaries provide a mapping between names and objects. You can apply the following operations to dictionaries:

Operation	Description
$x = d[k]$	Indexing by key.
$d[k] = x$	Key assignment.
del $d[k]$	Delete an item by key.
len(d)	Number of items in the dictionary.

Key values can be any immutable object, such as strings, numbers, and tuples.

The Attribute (.) Operator

The dot (.) operator is used to access the attributes of an object. For example,

```
foo.x = 3
print foo.y
a = foo.bar(3,4,5)
```

More than one dot operator can appear in a single expression, such as in `foo.y.a.b`. The dot operator can also be applied to the intermediate results of functions, as in `a = foo.bar(3,4,5).spam`.

Type Conversion

Sometimes it's necessary to perform conversions between the built-in types. The following built-in functions perform explicit type conversions:

Function	Description
int(x)	Converts x to an integer.
long(x)	Converts x to a long integer.
float(x)	Converts x to a floating-point number.
complex($real$ [,$imag$])	Creates a complex number.
str(x)	Converts object x to a string representation.

Function	Description
repr(x)	Converts object x to an expression string.
eval(str)	Evaluates a string and returns an object.
tuple(s)	Converts sequence s to a tuple.
list(s)	Converts sequence s to a list.
chr(x)	Converts an integer to a character.
ord(x)	Converts a single character to its integer value.
hex(x)	Converts an integer to a hexadecimal string.
oct(x)	Converts an integer to an octal string.

You also can write the repr(x) function using backquotes as `x`. Note that the str() and repr() functions may return different results. repr() typically creates an expression string that can be evaluated with eval() to re-create the object. On the other hand, str() produces a concise or nicely formatted representation of the object (and is used by the print statement).

To convert strings back into numbers and other objects, use the int(), long(), and float() functions. The eval() function can also convert a string containing a valid expression to a Python object. For example:

```
a = int("34")              # a = 34
b = float("3.1415926")     # b = 3.1415926
c = eval("3, 5, 6")        # c = (3,5,6)
```

Alternatively, these functions in the string module convert strings into numbers:

Function	Description
string.atoi(s)	Converts string s to an integer.
string.atol(s)	Converts string s to a long integer.
string.atof(s)	Converts string s to a floating point.

Boolean Expressions and Truth Values

The and, or, and not keywords can form Boolean expressions. The behavior of these operators is as follows:

Operator	Description
x or y	If x is false, return y. Otherwise, return x.
x and y	If x is false, return x. Otherwise, return y.
not x	If x is false, return 1. Otherwise, return 0.

When you use an expression to determine a true or false value, any nonzero number or nonempty string, list, tuple, or dictionary is taken to be true. Zero, None, and empty lists, tuples, and dictionaries evaluate as false. Boolean expressions are evaluated from left to right and consume the right operand only if it's needed to determine the final value. For example, a and b evaluates b only if a is true.

Object Equality and Identity

The equality operator (*x* == *y*) tests the values of *x* and *y* for equality. In the case of lists and tuples, all the elements are compared and evaluated as true if they're of equal value. For dictionaries, a true value is returned only if *x* and *y* have exactly the same set of keys and all the objects with the same key have equal values.

The identity operators (*x* is *y* and *x* is not *y*) test two objects to see whether they refer to the same object in memory. In general, it may be the case that *x* == *y*, but *x* is not *y*.

Comparison between objects of non-compatible types such as a file and a floating-point number are legal, but the outcome is arbitrary and may not make any sense. In addition, extension modules may choose to raise an exception for invalid comparisons involving extension types.

Order of Evaluation

Table 4.2 lists the order of operation (precedence rules) for Python operators. All operators except the power (**) operator are evaluated from left to right and are listed in the table from highest to lowest precedence. That is, operators listed first in the table are evaluated before
operators listed later. (*Note:* Operators included together within subsections—such as *x* * *y*, *x* / *y*, and *x* % *y*—have equal precedence.)

Table 4.2   Order of Evaluation (Highest to Lowest)

Operator	Name
(...), [...], {...}	Tuple, list, and dictionary creation.
` ... `	String conversion.
s[i], s[i:j] s.attr f(...)	Indexing and slicing, Attributes, and Function calls.
+x, -x, ~x	Unary operators.
x ** y	Power (right associative).
x * y, x / y, x % y	Multiplication, division, modulo.
x + y, x - y	Addition, subtraction.
x << y, x >> y	Bit shifting.
x & y	Bitwise and.
x ^ y	Bitwise exclusive or.

Operator	Name
$x < y$, $x <= y$, $x > y$, $x >= y$, $x == y$, $x != y$ $x <> y$ x is y, x is not y x in s, x not in s	Comparison, identity, and sequence membership tests.
not x	Logical negation.
x and y	Logical and.
x or y	Logical or.
lambda $args$: $expr$	Anonymous function.

5

Control Flow

This chapter describes statements related to the control flow of a program. Topics include conditionals, loops, and exceptions.

Conditionals

The `if`, `else`, and `elif` statements control conditional code execution. The general format of a conditional statement is as follows:

```
if expression:
    statements
elif expression:
    statements
elif expression:
    statements
...
else:
    statements
```

If no action is to be taken, you can omit both the `else` and `elif` clauses of a conditional. Use the `pass` statement if no statements exist for a particular clause. For example,

```
if expression:
    pass            # Do nothing
else:
    statements
```

Loops

You implement loops using the `for` and `while` statements. For example:

```
while expression:
    statements

for i in s:
    statements
```

The `while` statement executes statements until the associated expression evaluates to false. The `for` statement iterates over all the elements in a sequence until no more elements are available. If the elements of the sequence are tuples, each of identical size, the following variation of the `for` statement can be used:

```
for x,y,z in s:
    statements
```

In this case, s must be a sequence of tuples, each with three elements. On each iteration, the contents of the variables x, y, and z are assigned to the contents of the corresponding tuple.

To break out of a loop, use the `break` statement. For example, the following function reads lines of text from the user until an empty line of text is entered:

```
while 1:
    cmd = raw_input('Enter command > ')
    if not cmd:
        break              # No input, stop loop
    # process the command
    ...
```

To jump to the next iteration of a loop (skipping the remainder of the loop body), use the `continue` statement. This statement tends to be used less often, but is sometimes useful when the process of reversing a test and indenting another level would make the program too deeply nested or unnecessarily complicated. As an example, the following loop prints only the non-negative elements of a list:

```
for a in s:
    if a < 0:
        continue       # Skip negative elements
    print a
```

The `break` and `continue` statements apply only to the innermost loop being executed. If it's necessary to break out of a deeply nested loop structure, you can use an exception. Python doesn't provide a goto statement.

The `else` statement can also be attached to loop constructs, as in the following example:

```
# while-else
while i < 10:
    do something
    i = i + 1
else:
    print 'Done'

# for-else
for a in s:
    if a == 'Foo':
        break
else:
    print 'Not found!'
```

The `else` clause of a loop executes only if the loop runs to completion. This either occurs immediately (if the loop wouldn't execute at all) or after the last iteration. On the other hand, if the loop is terminated early using the `break` statement, the `else` clause is skipped.

Exceptions

Exceptions indicate errors and break out of the normal control flow of a program. An exception is raised using the `raise` statement. The general format of the `raise` statement is `raise Exception [, value]` where `Exception` is the exception type and `value` is an optional value giving specific details about the exception. For example:

```
raise RuntimeError, 'Unrecoverable Error'
```

If the `raise` statement is used without any arguments, the last exception generated is raised again (although this works only while handling a previously raised exception).

To catch an exception, use the `try` and `except` statements, as shown here:

```
try:
    f = open('foo')
except IOError, e:
    print "Unable to open 'foo': ", e
```

When an exception occurs, the interpreter stops executing statements in the try block and looks for an except clause that matches the exception that has occurred. If found, control is passed to the first statement in the except clause. Otherwise, the exception is propagated up to the block of code in which the try statement appeared. This code may itself be enclosed in a try-except that can handle the exception. If an exception works its way up to the top level of a program without being caught, the interpreter aborts with an error message.

The optional second argument to the except statement is the name of a variable in which the argument supplied to the raise statement is placed if an exception occurs. Exception handlers can examine this value to find out more about the cause of the exception.

Multiple exception-handling blocks are specified using multiple except clauses, such as in the following example:

```
try:
    do something
except IOError, e:
    # Handle I/O Error
    ...
except TypeError, e:
    # Handle Type error
    ...
except NameError, e:
    # Handle Name error
    ...
```

A single handler can catch multiple exception types like this:

```
try:
    do something
except (IOError, TypeError, NameError), e:
    # Handle I/O, Type, or Name errors
    ...
```

To ignore an exception, use the pass statement as follows:

```
try:
    do something
except IOError:
    pass            # Do nothing (oh well).
```

To catch all exceptions, omit the exception name and value:

```
try:
    do something
except:
    print 'An error occurred'
```

The `try` statement also supports an `else` clause, which must follow the last `except` clause. This code is executed if the code in the `try` block doesn't raise an exception. Here's an example:

```
try:
    f = open('foo', 'r')
except IOError:
    print 'Unable to open foo'
else:
    data = f.read()
    f.close()
```

The `finally` statement defines a cleanup action for code contained in a `try` block. For example:

```
f = open('foo','r')
try:
    # Do some stuff
    ...
finally:
    f.close()
    print "File closed regardles of what happened."
```

The `finally` clause isn't used to catch errors. Rather, it's used to provide code that must always be executed, regardless of whether or not an error occurs. If no exception is raised, the code in the `finally` clause is executed immediately after the code in the try block. If an exception does occur, control is first passed to the first statement of the `finally` clause. After this code has executed, the exception is re-raised to be caught by another exception handler. The `finally` and `except` statements cannot appear together within a single `try` statement.

Python defines the built-in exceptions listed in the following table. (For specific details about these exceptions, see Appendix A, "The Python Library.")

Exception	Description
Exception	The root of all exceptions.
StandardError	Base for all built-in exceptions.
ArithmeticError	Base for arithmetic exceptions.
FloatingPointError	Failure of a floating-point operation.
OverflowError	Arithmetic overflow.
ZeroDivisionError	Division or modulus operation with 0.
AssertionError	Raised by the `assert` statement.
AttributeError	Raised when an attribute name is invalid.
EnvironmentError	Errors that occur externally to Python.
IOError	I/O or file-related error.
OSError	Operating system error.
EOFError	Raised when the end of file is reached.

Exception	Description
ImportError	Failure of the import statement.
KeyboardInterrupt	Generated by the interrupt key (usually Ctrl+C).
LookupError	Indexing and key errors.
IndexError	Out-of-range sequence offset.
KeyError	Nonexistent dictionary key.
MemoryError	Out of memory.
NameError	Failure to find local or global name.
RuntimeError	A generic catch-all error.
SyntaxError	Parsing error.
SystemError	Nonfatal system error in the interpreter.
SystemExit	Generated by sys.exit().
TypeError	Passing an inappropriate type to an operation.
ValueError	Invalid type.

All the exceptions in a particular group can be caught by specifying the group name in an except clause. For example,

```
try:
    statements
except LookupError:      # Catch IndexError or KeyError
    statements
```

or

```
try:
    statements
except StandardError:   # Catch any built-in exception
    statements
```

Defining New Exceptions

All the built-in exceptions are defined in terms of classes. To create a new exception, create a new class definition that inherits from exceptions.Exception such as the following:

```
import exceptions
# Exception class
class NetworkError(exceptions.Exception):
    def __init__(self,args=None):
        self.args = args

# Raises an exception
def error1():
    raise NetworkError, 'Bad hostname'

# Catches an exception
try:
    error1()
except NetworkError, e:
    print e.args           # Prints error message from above
```

When an exception is raised, the optional value supplied in the `raise` statement is used as the argument to the exception's class constructor. If the constructor for an exception requires more than one argument, it can be raised in two ways:

```
import exceptions
# Exception class
class NetworkError(exceptions.Exception):
    def __init__(self,errno,msg):
        self.errno = errno
        self.errmsg = msg

# Raises an exception (multiple arguments)
def error2():
    raise NetworkError(1, 'File not found')

# Raises an exception (multiple arguments)
def error3():
    raise NetworkError, (1, 'File not found')
```

Class-based exceptions enable you to create hierarchies of exceptions. For instance, the `NetworkError` exception defined earlier could serve as a base class for a variety of more specific errors. For example:

```
class HostnameError(NetworkError):
    pass

class TimeoutError(NetworkError):
    pass

def error3():
    raise HostnameError

def error4():
    raise TimeoutError

try:
    error3()
except NetworkError:
    import sys
    print sys.exc_type    # Prints exception type
```

In this case, the `except NetworkError` statement catches any exception derived from `NetworkError`. To find the specific type of error that was raised, examine the variable `sys.exc_type`. Similarly, the `sys.exc_value` variable contains the value of the last exception. Alternatively, the `sys.exc_info()` function can be used to retrieve exception information in a manner that doesn't rely on global variables and is thread-safe.

Older versions of Python supported user-defined exceptions in the form of strings. For example:

```
NetworkError = "NetworkError"

def error5():
    raise NetworkError, 'Bad hostname'
```

Although string-based exceptions are still supported (and are syntactically indistinguishable from class-based exceptions), they're considered a Python anachronism.

Assertions and __debug__

The `assert` statement can introduce debugging code into a program. The general form of `assert` is

```
assert test [, data]
```

where *test* is an expression that should evaluate to true or false. If *test* evaluates to false, `assert` raises an `AssertionError` exception with the optional *data* supplied to the assert statement. For example:

```
def divide(a,b):
    assert b != 0, "Can't divide by zero"
    q = a/b
    r = a - q*b
    return (q,r)
```

Internally, the `assert` statement is translated into the following code:

```
if __debug__:
    if not (test):
        raise AssertionError, data
```

`__debug__` is a built-in name that's set to 1 unless the interpreter is running in optimized mode (specified with the -O option). Although `__debug__` is used by assertions, you also can use it to include any sort of debugging code. Its value can also be modified by the user if necessary.

6

Functions and Functional Programming

Most substantial programs are broken up into functions for better modularity and ease of maintenance. Python makes it easy to define functions, but borrows a number of ideas from functional programming languages that simplify certain tasks. This chapter describes functions, anonymous functions, and functional programming features as well as the eval() and execfile() functions and the exec() statement.

Functions

Functions are defined with the def statement:

```
def add(x,y):
    return x+y
```

Invoke the function by writing the function name followed by a tuple of function arguments, such as a = add(3,4). The order and number of arguments must match those given in the function definition. If a mismatch exists, a TypeError exception is raised.

By assigning values, you can attach default arguments to function parameters. For example:

```
def foo(x,y,z = 42):
```

When a function defines a parameter with a default value, that parameter and all the parameters that follow are optional. If values are not assigned to all the optional parameters in the function definition, a SyntaxError exception is raised.

Default parameter values are always set to the objects that were supplied as values when the function was defined. For example:

```
a = 10
def foo(x = a):
    print x

a = 5               # Reassign 'a'.
foo()               # Prints '10' (default value not changed)
```

However, the use of mutable objects as default values can lead to unintended behavior. For example:

```
a = [10]
def foo(x = a):
    print x
a.append(20)
foo()              # Prints '[10, 20]'
```

A function can accept a variable number of parameters if an asterisk (*) is added to the last parameter name:

```
def fprintf(file, fmt, *args):
    file.write(fmt % args)

# Use fprintf. args gets (42,"hello world", 3.45)
fprintf(out,"%d %s %f", 42, "hello world", 3.45)
```

In this case, all the remaining arguments are placed into the *args* variable as a tuple. To pass *args* to another function, use the apply() function, as shown here:

```
def printf(fmt, *args):
        # Create a new set of arguments and pass them on
        apply(fprintf, (sys.stdout, fmt) + args)
```

You can also pass function arguments by explicitly naming each parameter and specifying a value as follows:

```
def foo(w,x,y,z):
    print w,x,y,z

# Keyword invocation
foo(x=3, y=22, w='hello', z=[1,2])
```

With keyword arguments, the order of the parameters doesn't matter. However, unless you're using default values, you must explicitly name all the function parameters. If you omit any of the required parameters or if the name of a keyword doesn't match any of the parameter names in the function definition, a TypeError exception is raised.

Positional arguments and keyword arguments can appear in the same function call, provided that all the positional arguments appear first. For example:

```
foo('hello',3, z=[1,2], y=22)
```

If the last argument of a function definition begins with **, all the additional keyword arguments (those that don't match any of the parameter names) are placed in a dictionary and passed to the function. For example:

```
def spam(**parms):
    print "You supplied the following args:"
    for k in parms.keys():
        print "%s = %s" % (k, str(parms[k]))

spam(x=3, a="hello", foobar=(2,3))
```

You can combine extra keyword arguments with variable-length argument lists, as long as the ** parameter appears last:

```
# Accept variable number of positional or keyword arguments
def spam(x, *args, **keywords):
    print x, args, keywords
```

Keywords arguments can also be used with the `apply()` function as an optional third argument. For example, the following two statements perform the same operation:

```
foo('hello',3, z = [1,2], y=22)
apply(foo, ('hello',3), {'z':[1,2], 'y':22})
```

Parameter Passing and Return Values

When a function is invoked, its parameters are passed by reference. If a mutable object (such as a list or dictionary) is passed to a function where it's then modified, those changes will be reflected in the caller. For example:

```
a = [1,2,3,4,5]
def foo(x):
    x[3] = -55    # Modify an element of x

foo(a)            # Pass a
print a           # Produces [1,2,3,-55,5]
```

The `return` statement returns a value from a function. If no value is specified or if you omit the `return` statement, the `None` object is returned. To return multiple values, place them in a tuple:

```
def factor(a):
    d = 2
    while (d < (a/2)):
        if ((a/d)*d == a):
            return ((a/d),d)
        d = d + 1
    return (a,1)
```

Multiple return values returned in a tuple can be assigned to individual variables as follows:

```
x,y = factor(1243)     # Return values placed in x and y.
(x,y) = factor(1243)   # Alternate version. Same behavior.
```

Scoping Rules

Each time a function executes, a new local namespace is created. This namespace contains the names of the function parameters, as well as the names of variables that are assigned inside the function body. When resolving names, the interpreter first searches the local namespace. If no match exists, it searches the global namespace. The global namespace for a function is always the module in which the function was defined. If the interpreter finds no match in the global namespace, it makes a final check in the built-in namespace. If this fails, a `NameError` exception is raised.

One peculiarity of namespaces is the manipulation of global variables from within a function. For example, consider the following code:

```
a = 42
def foo():
    a = 13
foo()
print a
```

When executed, the value 42 prints, despite the appearance that we might be modifying the variable a inside the function foo. When variables are assigned in a function, they're always bound to the function's local namespace; as a result, the variable a in the function body refers to an entirely new object containing the value 13. To alter this behavior, use the global statement. global simply marks a list of names as belonging to the global namespace, and is necessary only when global variables will be modified. It can be placed anywhere in a function body and used repeatedly. For example:

```
a = 42
def foo():
    global a      # 'a' is in global namespace
    a = 13
foo()
print a
```

Python allows nested function definitions. However, nested functions don't provide nested scopes. As a result, a program using a nested function might not work as you expect. For example, the following program is legal, but doesn't execute properly:

```
def bar():
    x = 10
    def spam():            # Nested function definition
        print 'x is ', x   # Looks for x in global scope of bar()
    while x > 0:
        spam()             # Fails with a NameError on 'x'
        x = x - 1
```

When the nested function spam() executes, its global namespace is the same as the global namespace for bar() (the module in which the function is defined). As a result, spam() is unable to resolve any symbols in the namespace of bar() and fails with a NameError. In practice, nested functions are used only in special situations such as cases where a program may want to define a function differently based on the result of a conditional.

The apply() Function

The apply(*funcname*, [, *args* [, *kwargs*]]) function is used to invoke a function indirectly where the arguments have been constructed in the form of a tuple or dictionary. *args* is a tuple containing the positional argument to be supplied to the function. If omitted, no arguments are passed. *kwargs* is a dictionary containing keyword arguments. The following statements produce identical results:

```
foo(3,"x", name='Dave', id=12345)
apply(foo, (3,"x"), { 'name': 'Dave', 'id': 12345 })
```

The lambda Operator

To create an anonymous function in the form of an expression, use the lambda statement:

```
lambda args : expression
```

args is a comma-separated list of arguments and *expression* is an expression involving those arguments. For example:

```
a = lambda x,y : x+y
print a(2,3)                # produces '5'
```

The code defined with lambda must be a valid expression. Multiple statements and other nonexpression statements such as print, for, and while cannot appear in a lambda statement. lambda expressions follow the same scoping rules as functions.

map(), reduce(), and filter()

The *t* = map(*func*, *s*) function applies the function *func* to each of the elements in *s* and returns a new list *t*. Each element of *t* is *t[i]* = *func*(*s[i]*). The function given to map() should require only one argument. For example:

```
a = [1, 2, 3, 4, 5, 6]
def foo(x):
    return 3*x

b = map(foo,a)     # b = [3, 6, 9, 12, 15, 18]
```

Alternatively, this could be calculated using an anonymous function as follows:

```
b = map(lambda x: 3*x, a)     # b = [3, 6, 9, 12, 15, 18]
```

The map() function can also be applied to multiple lists such as *t* = map(*func*, *s1*, *s2*, ..., *sn*). In this case, each element of *t* is *t[i]* = *func*(*s1[i]*, *s2[i]*, ..., *sn[i]*), and the function given to map() must accept the same number of arguments as the number of lists given. The result has the same number of elements as the longest list in *s1*, *s2*, ... *sn*. During the calculation, short lists are extended with values of None to match the length of the longest list, if necessary.

If the function is set to None, the identity function is assumed. If multiple lists are passed to map(None, *s1*, *s2*, ... *sn*), the function returns a list of tuples where each tuple contains an element from each list. For example:

```
a = [1,2,3,4]
b = [100,101,102,103]
c = map(None, a, b)    # c = [(1,100), (2,101), (3,102), (4,103)]
```

The reduce(*func*, *s*) function collects information from a sequence and returns a single value (for example, a sum, maximum value, and so on). reduce() works by applying the function *func* to the first two elements of *s*. This value is then combined with the third element to yield a new value. This result is then combined with the fourth element, and so forth until the end of the sequence. The function *func* must accept two arguments and return a single value. For example:

```
def sum(x,y):
    return x+y

b = reduce(sum, a)    # b = (((1+2)+3)+4) = 10
```

The `filter(func,s)` function filters the elements of *s* using a filter function `func()` that returns true or false. A new sequence is returned consisting of all elements *x* of *s* for which `func(x)` is true. For example:

```
c = filter(lambda x: x < 4, a)    # c = [1, 2, 3]
```

If *func* is set to `None`, the identity function is assumed and `filter()` returns all elements of *s* that evaluate to true.

eval(), exec, execfile(), and compile()

The `eval(str [,globals [,locals]])` function executes an expression string and returns the result. For example:

```
a = eval('3*math.sin(3.5+x) + 7.2')
```

Similarly, the exec statement executes a string containing arbitrary Python code. The code supplied to exec is executed within the namespace of the caller as if the code actually appeared in place of the exec statement. For example:

```
a = [3, 5, 10, 13]
exec "for i in a: print i"
```

Finally, the `execfile(filename [,globals [,locals]])` function executes the contents of a file. For example:

```
execfile("foo.py")
```

All these functions execute within the namespace of the caller (which is used to resolve any symbols that appear within a string or file). Optionally, eval(), exec, and execfile() can accept one or two dictionaries that serve as the global and local namespaces for the code to be executed, respectively. For example:

```
globals = {'x': 7,
           'y': 10,
           'names': ['Dave', 'Mark', 'Michelle' ]
          }

locals = { }

# Execute using the above dictionaries as the global and local namespace
a = eval("3*x + 4*y", globals, locals)
exec "for n in names: print n" in globals, locals    # Note unusual syntax.
execfile("foo.py", globals, locals)
```

If one or both namespaces are omitted, the current values of the global and local namespaces are used.

It should also be noted that the syntax of the exec statement in the example is different from that of eval() and execfile(). exec is a statement (much like print or while), whereas eval() and execfile() are built-in functions.

When a string is passed to exec, eval(), or execfile(), the parser first compiles it into bytecode. Because this process is expensive, it may be better to precompile the code and reuse the bytecode on subsequent calls if the code is going to be executed multiple times.

The `compile(str,filename,kind)` function compiles a string into bytecode where *str* is a string containing the code to be compiled and *filename* is the file in which the string is defined (for use in traceback generation). The *kind* argument specifies the type of code being compiled—'single' for a single statement, 'exec' for a set of statements, or 'eval' for an expression. The code object returned by the compile() function can also be passed to the eval() function and exec statement. For example:

```
str = "for i in range(0,10): print i"
c = compile(str,'','exec')        # Compile into a code object
exec c                            # Execute it

str2 = "3*x + 4*y"
c2 = compile(str2, '', 'eval')    # Compile into an expression
result = eval(c2)                 # Execute it
```

7

Classes and Object-Oriented Programming

Classes are the primary mechanism used to create data structures and new kinds of objects. This chapter covers the details of classes, but is not intended to be an introduction to object-oriented programming and design. It is assumed that the reader has prior experience with data structures and object-oriented programming in other languages such as C, C++, or Java. (Chapter 3, "Types and Objects," contains additional information about the terminology and internal implementation of objects.)

The class statement

A *class* defines a set of attributes that are associated with a collection of objects known as *instances*. These attributes typically include variables that are known as *class variables* and functions that are known as *methods*.

Classes are defined using the class statement. The body of a class contains a series of statements that are executed when the class is first defined. For example:

```
class Account:
    "A simple class"
    account_type = "Basic"
    def __init__(self,name,balance):
        "Initialize a new Account instance"
        self.name = name
        self.balance = balance
    def deposit(self,amt):
        "Add to the balance"
        self.balance = self.balance + amt
    def withdraw(self,amt):
        "Subtract from the balance"
        self.balance = self.balance - amt
    def inquiry(self):
        "Return the current balance"
        return self.balance
```

The objects created during the execution of the class body are placed into a class object that serves as a namespace. For example, the members of the Account class are accessible as follows:

```
Account.account_type
Account.__init__
Account.deposit
Account.withdraw
Account.inquiry
```

It's important to note that a class statement doesn't create any instances of a class (for example, no accounts are actually created in the above example). Rather, a class only defines the set of attributes that are shared by all of the instances that will be created.

The functions defined within a class (methods) always operate on a class instance that's passed as the first argument. By convention, this argument is called "self", although any legal identifier name can be used. Class variables such as "account_type" are shared among all instances of a class (that is, they're not individually assigned to each instance).[1]

Although a class defines a namespace, this namespace is not a scope for code appearing inside the class body. Thus, references to other attributes of a class must use a fully qualified name. For example:

```
class Foo:
    def bar(self):
        print "bar!"
    def spam(self):
        bar(self)      # Incorrect! 'bar' generates a NameError
        Foo.bar(self) # This works
```

Finally, it's not possible to define class methods that don't operate on instances. For example:

```
class Foo:
    def add(x,y):
        return x+y

a = Foo.add(3,4)      # TypeError.  Need class instance as first argument
```

Class Instances

Instances of a class are created by calling a class object as a function. This creates a new instance and calls the __init__() method of the class (if defined). For example:

```
# Create a few accounts
a = Account("Guido", 1000.00)      # Invokes Account.__init__(a,"Guido",1000.00)
b = Account("Bill", 100000000000L)
```

---

1. *For Java and C++ programmers, class variables have the same behavior as static member variables.*

Once created, the attributes and methods of the newly created instances are accessible using the dot (.) operator as follows:

```
a.deposit(100.00)        # Calls Account.deposit(a,100.00)
b.withdraw(sys.maxint)   # Calls Account.withdraw(b,sys.maxint)
name = a.name            # Get account name
print a.account_type     # Print account type
```

Internally, each instance is implemented using a dictionary that's accessible as the instance's __dict__ attribute (described in detail in Chapter 3). This dictionary contains the information that's unique to each instance. For example:

```
>>> print a.__dict__
{'balance': 1100.0, 'name': 'Guido'}
>>> print b.__dict__
{'balance': 97852516353L, 'name': 'Bill'}
```

Whenever the attributes of an instance are modified, these changes are made to the instance's local dictionary. Within methods defined in the class, attributes are changed through assignment to the 'self' variable as shown in the __init__(), deposit(), and withdraw() methods of Account. However, new attributes can be added to an instance at any time. For example:

```
a.number = 123456    # Add 'number' to a.__dict__
```

Although the assignment of attributes is always performed on the local dictionary of an instance, attribute access is somewhat more complicated. Whenever an attribute is accessed, the interpreter first searches the dictionary of the instance. If no match is found, the intepreter searches the dictionary of the class object used to create the instance. If this fails, a search of base classes is performed. If this fails, a final attempt to find the attribute is made by attempting to invoke the __getattr__() method of the class (if defined). If this fails, an AttributeError exception is raised.

Reference Counting and Instance Destruction

All instances have a reference count. If the reference count reaches zero, the instance is destroyed. When the instance is about to be destroyed, the interpreter looks for a __del__() method associated with the object and calls it. In practice, it's rarely necessary for a class to define a __del__() method. The only exception is when the destruction of an object requires a cleanup action such as closing a file, shutting down a network connection, or releasing other system resources. Even in these cases, it's dangerous to rely on __del__() for a clean shutdown, as there's no guarantee that this method will be called when the interpreter exits. A better approach may be to define a method such as close() that a program can use to explicitly perform a shutdown.

Occasionally, a program will use the del statement to delete a reference to an object. If this causes the reference count of the object to reach zero, the __del__() method is called. However, in general, the del statement doesn't directly call __del__().

Inheritance

Inheritance is a mechanism for creating a new class that specializes or modifies the behavior of an existing class. The original class is called a *base class* or a *superclass*. The new class is called a *derived class* or a *subclass*. When a class is created via inheritance, it "inherits" the attributes defined by its base classes. However, a derived class may redefine any of these attributes and add new attributes of its own.

Inheritance is specified with a comma-separated list of base-class names in the class statement. For example:

```
class A:
    varA = 42
    def method1(self):
        print "Class A : method1"

class B:
    varB = 37
    def method1(self):
        print "Class B : method1"
    def method2(self):
        print "Class B : method2"

class C(A,B):        # Inherits from A and B
    varC = 3.3
    def method3(self):
        print "Class C : method3"

class D: pass
class E(C,D): pass
```

When searching for an attribute defined in a base class, the base classes are searched using a depth-first search algorithm in the same order as specified in the class definition. For example, in class E in the preceding example, base classes are searched in the order C, A, B, D. In the event that multiple base classes define the same symbol, the first symbol encountered in the search process is used. For example:

```
c = C()            # Create a 'C'
c.method3()        # Invokes C.method3(c)
c.method1()        # Invokes A.method1(c)
c.varB             # Access B.varB
```

If a derived class defines an attribute with the same name as an attribute in a base class, instances of the derived class use the attributes in the derived class. If it's ever necessary to access the original attribute, a fully qualified name can be used as follows:

```
class D(A):
    def method1(self):
        print "Class D : method1"
        A.method1(self)          # Invoke base class method
```

One notable use of this is in the initialization of class instances. When an instance is created, the __init__() methods of base classes are not invoked. Thus, it's up to a derived class to perform the proper initialization of its base classes, if necessary. For example:

```
class D(A):
    def __init__(self, args1):
        # Initialize the base class
        A.__init__(self)
        # Initialize myself
        ...
```

Similar steps may also be necessary when defining cleanup actions in the __del__()
method.

Information Hiding

By default, all attributes are "public." This means that all attributes of a class instance
are accessible without any restrictions. It also implies that everything defined in a base
class is inherited and accessible within a derived class. This behavior is often undesirable in object-oriented applications because it exposes the internal implementation of
an object and it can lead to namespace conflicts between objects defined in a derived
class and those defined in a base class.

To fix this, all names in a class that start with a double underscore, such as __Foo, are
mangled to form a new name of the form _Classname__Foo. This effectively provides a
way for a class to have private attributes, since private names used in a derived class
won't collide with the same private names used in a base class. For example:

```
class A:
    def __init__(self):
        self.__X = 3          # Mangled to self._A__X

class B(A):
    def __init__(self):
        A.__init__(self)
        self.__X = 37         # Mangled to self._B__X
```

Although this scheme provides the illusion of data hiding, there's no strict mechanism
in place to prevent access to the "private" attributes of a class. In particular, if the name
of the class and corresponding private attribute are known, they can be accessed using
the mangled name.

Operator Overloading

User-defined objects can be made to work with all of Python's built-in operators
by adding implementations of the special methods described in Chapter 3 to a class.
For example, the following class implements the complex numbers with some of the
standard mathematical operators and type coercion to allow complex numbers to be
mixed with integers and floats:

```
class Complex:
    def __init__(self,real,imag=0):
        self.real = float(real)
        self.imag = float(imag)
    def __repr__(self):
        return "Complex(%s,%s)" % (self.real, self.imag)
    def __str__(self):
        return "(%g+%gj)" % (self.real, self.imag)
    # self + other
    def __add__(self,other):
        return Complex(self.real + other.real, self.imag + other.imag)
    # self - other
    def __sub__(self,other):
        return Complex(self.real - other.real, self.imag - other.imag)
```

continues >>

>>continued

```
# -self
def __neg__(self):
    return Complex(-self.real, -self.imag)
# other + self
def __radd__(self,other):
    return Complex.__add__(other,self)
# other - self
def __rsub__(self,other):
    return Complex.__sub__(other,self)
# Coerce other numerical types to complex
def __coerce__(self,other):
    if isinstance(other,Complex):
        return self,other
    try:    # See if it can be converted to float
        return self, Complex(float(other))
    except ValueError:
        pass
```

In this example, there are a few items of interest:

- First, the normal behavior of `__repr__`() is to create a string that can be evaluated to re-create the object. In this case, a string of the form `"Complex(r,i)"` is created. On the other hand, the `__str__`() method creates a string that's intended for nice output formatting (this is the string that would be produced by the `print` statement).

- Second, to handle operators in which complex numbers appear on both the left and right side of operators, both the `__op__`() and `__rop__`() methods for each operation must be provided.

- Finally, the `__coerce__` method is used to handle operations involving mixed types. In this case, other numeric types are converted to complex numbers so that they can be used in the complex arithmetic methods.

Classes, Types, and Membership Tests

Currently, there's a separation between types and classes. In particular, built-in types such as lists and dictionaries cannot be specialized via inheritance, nor does a class define a new type. In fact, all class definitions have a type of `ClassType`, while all class instances have a type of `InstanceType`. Thus, the expression

```
type(a) == type(b)
```

is true for any two objects that are instances of a class (even if they were created by different classes).

To test for membership in a class, the built-in function `isinstance(obj,cname)` can be used. This function returns true if an object *obj* belongs to the class *cname* or any class derived from *cname*. For example:

```
class A: pass
class B(A): pass
class C: pass

a = A()        # Instance of 'A'
b = B()        # Instance of 'B'
c = C()        # Instance of 'C'
```

```
isinstance(a,A)   # Returns 1
isinstance(b,A)   # Returns 1, B derives from A
isinstance(b,C)   # Returns 0, C not derived from A
```

Similarly, the built-in function `issubclass(A,B)` returns true if the class *A* is a subclass of class *B*. For example:

```
issubclass(B,A)   # Returns 1
issubclass(C,A)   # Returns 0
```

It should also be noted that the `isinstance()` function can be used to perform type checking against any of the built-in types. For example:

```
import types
isinstance(3, types.IntType)     # Returns 1
isinstance(3, types.FloatType)   # Returns 0
```

This is the recommended way to perform type checking with the built-in types, as the distinction between types and classes may disappear in a future release.

8

Modules and Packages

Large Python programs are often organized as a package of modules. In addition, a large number of modules are included in the Python library. This chapter describes the module and package system in more detail.

Modules

You can turn any valid source file into a module by loading it with the `import` statement. For example, consider the following code:

```
# file : spam.py
a = 37                  # A variable
def foo:                # A function
    print "I'm foo"
class bar:              # A class
    def grok(self):
        print "I'm bar.grok"
b = bar()               # Create an instance
```

To load this code as a module, you use the statement `import spam`. The first time `import` is used to load a module, it does three things:

- First, it creates a new namespace that serves as a namespace to all the objects defined in the corresponding source file. This is the namespace accessed when functions and methods defined within the module use the `global` statement.

- Second, `import` executes the code contained in the module within the newly created namespace.

- Finally, `import` creates a name within the caller that refers to the module namespace. This name matches the name of the module and is used as follows:

```
import spam             # Loads and executes the module 'spam'
print spam.a            # Accesses a member of module 'spam'
spam.foo()
c = spam.bar()
...
```

To import multiple modules, supply import with a comma-separated list of module names, like this:

```
import string, os, regex    # Imports 'string', 'os', and 'regex'
```

Use the from statement to load specific definitions within a module into the current namespace. The from statement is identical to import except that instead of creating a name referring to the newly created module namespace, references to one or more of the objects defined in the module are placed into the current namespace. For example:

```
from string import atoi    # Imports 'string'
                           # Places atoi in current namespace

print atoi("12345")        # Invokes 'atoi' without module name
string.atoi("45")          # NameError: string
```

The from statement also accepts a comma-separated list of object names. The asterisk (*) wildcard character can also be used to load all the definitions in a module except those that start with an underscore. For example:

```
from string import atoi,atol,atof
from string import *  # Load all definitions into current namespace
```

The import statement can appear at any point in a program. However, the code in each module is loaded and executed only once, regardless of how often you use the import statement. Subsequent import statements simply create a reference to the module namespace created on a previous import. You can find a dictionary containing all currently loaded modules in the variable sys.modules, which is a dictionary mapping module names to module objects. The contents of this dictionary are used to determine whether import loads a fresh copy of a module.

Each module defines a variable __name__ that contains the module name. Programs can examine this variable to determine the module in which they're executing. The top-level module of the interpreter is named __main__. Programs specified on the command line or entered interactively run inside the __main__ module. Sometimes, a program may alter its behavior depending on whether it has been imported as a module or is running in __main__. This can be done as follows:

```
# Check if running as a program
if __name__ == '__main__':
    # Yes.
    statements
else:
    # No. I must have been imported as a module
    statements
```

The Module Search Path

When loading modules, the interpreter searches the list of directories in sys.path. The following is a typical value of sys.path:

```
['', '/usr/local/lib/python1.5/',
 '/usr/local/lib/python1.5/test',
 '/usr/local/lib/python1.5/plat-sunos5',
 '/usr/local/lib/python1.5/lib-tk',
 '/usr/local/lib/python1.5/lib-dynload',
 '/usr/local/lib/site-python']
```

The empty string ' ' refers to the current directory.

To add new directories to the search path, simply append them to this list.

Module Loading and Compilation

So far, this chapter has presented modules as files containing Python code. However, modules loaded with `import` really fall into four general categories:

- Programs written in Python (.py files).

- C or C++ extensions that have been compiled into shared libraries or DLLs.

- Packages containing a collection of modules.

- Built-in modules written in C and linked into the Python interpreter.

When looking for a module `foo`, the interpreter searches each of the directories in `sys.path` for the following files (listed in search order):

1. A directory `foo` defining a package.

2. `foo.so`, `foomodule.so`, `foomodule.sl`, or `foomodule.dll` (compiled extensions).

3. `foo.pyo` (only if the -0 option has been used).

4. `foo.pyc`.

5. `foo.py`.

Packages are described shortly; compiled extensions are described in Appendix B, "Extending and Embedding Python." For .py files, when a module is first imported, it's compiled into bytecode and written back to disk as a .pyc file. On subsequent imports, the interpreter loads this precompiled bytecode unless the modification date of the .py file is more recent (in which case, the .pyc file is regenerated). .pyo files are used in conjunction with the interpreter's -0 option. These files contain bytecode stripped of line numbers, assertions, and other debugging information. As a result, they're somewhat smaller and allow the interpreter to run slightly faster. If none of these files exist in any of the directories in `sys.path`, the interpreter checks whether the name corresponds to a built-in module name. If no match exists, an `ImportError` exception is raised.

The compilation of files into .pyc and .pyo files occurs only in conjunction with the `import` statement. Programs specified on the command line or standard input don't produce such files.

Module Reloading

The built-in function `reload()` can be used to reload and execute the code contained within a module previously loaded with `import`. It accepts a module name as a single argument. For example:

```
import foo
... some code ...
reload(foo)          # Reloads foo
```

All operations involving the module after the execution of `reload()` will utilize the newly loaded code. However, `reload()` doesn't retroactively update objects created using the old module. Thus, it's possible for references to coexist for objects in both the old and new versions of a module. Furthermore, compiled extensions written in C or C++ cannot be reloaded using `reload()`.

As a general rule, avoid module reloading except during debugging and development.

Packages

Packages allow a collection of modules to be grouped under a common package name. This technique helps resolve namespace conflicts between module names used in different applications. A package is defined by creating a directory with the same name as the package and creating a file `__init__.py` in that directory. You can then place additional source files, compiled extensions, and subpackages in this directory as needed. For example, a package might be organized as follows:

```
Graphics/
    __init__.py
    Primitive/
        __init__.py
        lines.py
        fill.py
        text.py
        ...
    Graph2d/
        __init__.py
        plot2d.py
        ...
    Graph3d/
        __init__.py
        plot3d.py
        ...
    Formats/
        __init__.py
        gif.py
        png.py
        tiff.py
        jpeg.py
```

The `import` statement is used to load modules from a package in a number of ways:

- `import Graphics.Primitive.fill`

  This loads the submodule `Graphics.Primitive.fill`. The contents of this module have to be explicitly named, such as
  `Graphics.Primitive.fill.floodfill(img,x,y,color)`.

- `from Graphics.Primitive import fill`

  This loads the submodule `fill` but makes it available without the package prefix; for example, `fill.floodfill(img,x,y,color)`.

■ `from Graphics.Primitive.fill import floodfill`

This loads the submodule `fill` but makes the `floodfill` function directly accessible; for example, `floodfill(img,x,y,color)`.

Whenever any part of a package is imported, the code in the file `__init__.py` is executed. Minimally, this file may be empty, but it can also contain code to perform package-specific initializations. All the `__init__.py` files encountered during an import are executed. Thus, the statement `import Graphics.Primitive.fill` shown earlier would execute the `__init__.py` files in both the Graphics directory and the Primitive directory.

One peculiar problem with packages is the handling of the statement

`from Graphics.Primitive import *`

The intended outcome of this statement is to import all the modules associated with a package into the current namespace. However, because filename conventions vary from system to system (especially with regard to case sensitivity), Python cannot accurately determine what modules those might be. As a result, this statement just imports all the references defined in the `__init__.py` file in the Primitive directory. This behavior can be modified by defining a list `__all__` that contains all the module names associated with the package. This list should be defined in the package `__init__.py` file. For example:

```
# Graphics/Primitive/__init__.py
__all__ = ["lines","text","fill",...]
```

Now when the user issues a `from Graphics.Primitive import *` statement, all the listed submodules are loaded as expected.

Importing a package name alone doesn't import all the submodules contained in the package. For example, the following code doesn't work:

```
import Graphics
Graphics.Primitive.fill.floodfill(img,x,y,color)  # Fails!
```

However, because the `import Graphics` statement executes the `__init__.py` file in the Graphics directory, it could be modified to import all the submodules automatically as follows:

```
# Graphics/__init__.py
import Primitive, Graph2d, Graph3d
```

```
# Graphics/Primitive/__init__.py
import lines, fill, text, ...
```

Now the `import Graphics` statement imports all the submodules and makes them available using their fully qualified names.

The modules contained within the same directory of a package can refer to each other without supplying a full package name. For example, the `Graphics.Primitive.fill` module could import the `Graphics.Primitive.lines` module simply by using `import lines`. However, if a module is located in a different subdirectory, its full package name must be used. For example, if the `plot2d` module of `Graphics.Graph2d` needs to use the `lines` module of `Graphics.Primitive`, it must use a statement such as `from Graphics.Primitive import lines`. If necessary, a module can examine its `__name__` variable to find its fully qualified module name. For example, the following code imports a module from a sibling subpackage knowing only the name of the sibling (and not that of its top-level package):

```
# Graphics/Graph2d/plot2d.py

# Determine the name of the package where my package is located
import string
base_package = string.join(string.split(__name__,'.')[:-2],'.')

# Import the ../Primitive/fill.py module
exec "from %s.Primitive import fill" % (base_package,)
```

Finally, when Python imports a package, it defines a special variable __path__ that contains a list of directories that are searched when looking for package submodules (__path__ is a package-specific version of the sys.path variable). __path__ is accessible to the code contained in __init__.py files and initially contains a single item with the directory name of the package. If necessary, a package can add additional directories to the __path__ list to alter the search path used for finding submodules.

9

Input and Output

This chapter describes the details of Python I/O, including command-line options, environment variables, file I/O, and object persistence.

Reading Options and Environment Variables

When the interpreter starts, command-line options are placed in the list sys.argv. The first element is the name of the program. Subsequent elements are the options presented on the command line *after* the program name. The following program shows how to access command-line options:

```
# printopt.py
# Print all of the command line options
import sys
for i in range(len(sys.argv)):
    print "sys.argv[%d] = %s" % (i, sys.argv[i])
```

Running the program produces the following:

```
% python printopt.py foo bar -p
sys.argv[0] = printopt.py
sys.argv[1] = foo
sys.argv[2] = bar
sys.argv[3] = -p
%
```

Environment variables are accessed in the dictionary os.environ. For example:

```
import os
path = os.environ["PATH"]
user = os.environ["USER"]
editor = os.environ["EDITOR"]
... etc ...
```

The environment variables can also be modified for later accesses and for use by child processes.

Files

The built-in function open(*name* [,*mode*]) opens and creates files, as shown here:

```
f = open("foo")          # Opens 'foo' for reading
f = open("foo","w")      # Open for writing
```

The file mode is "r" for read, "w" for write, or "a" for append. The mode character can be followed by "b" for binary data, such as "rb" or "wb". In addition, a file can be opened for updates by supplying a plus (+) character, such as "r+" or "w+". When a file is opened for update, you can perform both input and output, as long as all output operations flush their data before any subsequent input operations. If a file is opened using "w+" mode, its length is first truncated to zero.

open() returns a file object that supports the methods shown in Table 9.1.

Table 9.1   File Methods

Method	Description
f.read([*n*])	Reads at most *n* bytes.
f.readline()	Reads a single line of input up to *n* characters. If *n* is omitted, reads the entire line.
f.readlines()	Reads all the lines and returns a list.
f.write(*S*)	Writes string *S*.
f.writelines(*L*)	Writes all strings in list *L*.
f.close()	Closes the file.
f.tell()	Returns the current file pointer.
f.seek(*offset* [, *where*])	Seeks to a new file position.
f.isatty()	Returns 1 if *f* is an interactive terminal.
f.flush()	Flushes the output buffers.
f.truncate([*size*])	Truncates the file to at most *size* bytes.
f.fileno()	Returns an integer file descriptor.
f.readinto(*buffer*,*nbytes*)	Read *nbytes* of data from the file into a writable buffer object. This is currently an undocumented and unsupported feature in Python 1.5.2.

The read() method returns the entire file as a string unless an optional length parameter is given specifying the maximum number of bytes. The readline() method returns the next line of input, including the terminating newline; the readlines() method returns all the input lines as a list of strings. Both the readline() and readlines() methods are platform-aware and handle different representations of newlines properly (for example, '\n' versus '\r\n').

The write() method writes a string to the file, and the writelines() method writes a list of strings to the file. In all these cases, the string may contain binary data, including embedded NULL characters.

The seek() method is used to randomly access parts of a file given an *offset* and a placement rule in *where*. If *where* is 0 (the default), seek() assumes that *offset* is relative to the start of the file. If *where* is 1, the position is moved relative to the

current position, and if *where* is 2, the offset is taken from the end of the file. The
fileno() method returns the integer file-descriptor for a file and is sometimes used in
low-level I/O operations in certain library modules. The readinto() method is
currently unsupported and reserved for future releases.

File objects also have the following data attributes:

Attribute	Description
f.closed	Boolean value indicates the file state: 0 if the file is open, 1 if closed.
f.mode	The I/O mode for the file.
f.name	Name of the file if created using open(). Otherwise, it will be a string indicating the source of the file.
f.softspace	Boolean value indicating whether a space character needs to be printed before another value when using the print statement. Classes that emulate files must provide a writable attribute of this name that's initially initialized to zero.

Standard Input, Output, and Error

The interpreter provides three standard file objects, known as *standard input*, *standard
output*, and *standard error*, which are available in the sys module as sys.stdin,
sys.stdout, and sys.stderr, respectively. stdin is a file object corresponding to
the stream of input characters supplied to the interpreter. stdout is the file object
that receives output produced by print. stderr is a file that receives error messages.
More often than not, stdin is mapped to the user's keyboard, while stdout and stderr
produce text onscreen.

The methods described in the preceding section can be used to perform raw I/O
with the user. For example, the following function reads a line of input from standard
input:

```
def gets():
    text = ""
    while 1:
        c = sys.stdin.read(1)
        text = text + c
        if c == '\n': break
    return text
```

Alternatively, the built-in function raw_input(*prompt*) can read a line of text from
stdin:

```
s = raw_input("type something : ")
print "You typed '%s'" % (s,)
```

Finally, keyboard interrupts (often generated by Ctrl+C) result in a KeyboardInterrupt
exception that can be caught using an exception handler.

The print Statement

The print statement produces output on the file contained in sys.stdout. print accepts a comma-separated list of objects such as the following:

```
print "The values are", x, y, z
```

For each object, the str() function is invoked to produce an output string. These output strings are then joined and separated by a single space to produce the final output string. The output is terminated by a newline unless a trailing comma is supplied to the print statement. In this case, only a trailing space is printed. For example:

```
print "The values are ", x, y, z, w
# Print the exact same text, using two print statements
print "The values are ", x, y,    # Omits trailing newline
print z, w
```

To produce formatted output, use the string-formatting operator (%) as described in Chapter 4, "Operators and Expressions." For example:

```
print "The values are %d %7.5f %s" % (x,y,z) # Formatted I/O
```

You can change the destination of the print statement by modifying the value of sys.stdout. Here's an example:

```
import sys
sys.stdout = open("output","w")
print "hello world"
...
sys.stdout.close()
```

Should it ever be necessary to restore the original value of sys.stdout, it should be saved beforehand. The original values of sys.stdout, sys.stdin, and sys.stderr at interpreter startup are also available in sys.__stdout__, sys.__stdin__, and sys.__stderr__, respectively.

Persistence

It's often necessary to save and restore the contents of an object to a file. One approach to this problem is to write a pair of functions that read and write data from a file in a special format. An alternative approach is to use the pickle and shelve modules.

The pickle module serializes an object into a stream of bytes that can be written to a file. For example, the following code writes an object to a file:

```
import pickle
object = someObject()
f = open(filename,'w')
pickle.dump(object, f)      # Save object
```

To restore the object, you can use the following code:

```
import pickle
f = open(filename,'r')
object = pickle.load(f)    # Restore the object
```

The shelve module is similar, but saves objects in a dictionary-like database. For example:

```
import shelve
object = someObject()
dbase = shelve.open(filename)     # Open a database
dbase['key'] = object             # Save object in database
...
object = dbase['key']             # Retrieve it
dbase.close()                     # Close the database
```

In both cases, only serializable objects can be saved to a file. Most Python objects can be serialized, but special-purpose objects such as files maintain an internal state that cannot be saved and restored in this manner. For more details about the pickle and shelve modules, see Appendix A, "The Python Library."

10
Execution
Environment

This chapter describes the environment in which Python programs are executed. The goal is to describe the runtime behavior of the interpreter, including program startup, site configuration, and program termination.

Interpreter Options and Environment

The interpreter has a number of options that control its runtime behavior and environment. On Unix and Windows, options are given to the interpreter in the form of command-line options such as the following:

```
python [options] [-c cmd ¦ filename ¦ - ] [args]
```

On the Macintosh, options to the Python interpreter are set using a separate program, EditPythonPrefs.

The following command-line options are available:

Option	Description
-d	Generates parser debugging information.
-i	Enters interactive mode after program execution.
-O	Optimized mode.
-S	Prevents inclusion of the site initialization module.
-t	Reports warnings about inconsistent tab usage.
-u	Unbuffered binary stdout and stdin.
-v	Verbose mode.
-x	Skips the first line of the source program.
-X	Disables class-based exceptions.
-c cmd	Executes cmd as a string.

The -d option debugs the interpreter and is of limited use to most programmers. -i starts an interactive session immediately after a program has finished execution, and is useful for debugging. The -O option applies some optimization to byte-compiled files, and is described in Chapter 8, "Modules and Packages." The -S option omits the site initialization module described in the later section "Site Configuration Files." The -t and -v options report additional warnings and debugging information. -x ignores the first line of a program in the event that it's not a valid Python statement (for example, when the first line starts the Python interpreter in a script). Finally, the -X option provides backward compatibility with older programs that rely on string-based exceptions.

The program name appears after all the interpreter options. If no name is given, or the hyphen (-) character is used as a filename, the interpreter reads the program from standard input. If standard input is an interactive terminal, a banner and prompt will be presented. Otherwise, the interpreter opens the specified file and executes its statements until an end-of-file marker is reached. The -c option can be used to execute short programs in the form of a command-line option.

Command-line options appearing after the program name or - are passed to the program in sys.argv, as described in the section "Reading Options and Environment Variables" in Chapter 9, "Input and Output."

Additionally, the interpreter reads the following environment variables:

Variable	Description
PYTHONPATH	Colon-separated module search path.
PYTHONSTARTUP	File executed on interactive startup.
PYTHONHOME	Location of the Python installation.
PYTHONINSPECT	Implies the -i option.
PYTHONUNBUFFERED	Implies the -u option.

PYTHONPATH sets the module search path sys.path, which is described in Chapter 8. PYTHONSTARTUP specifies a file to execute when the interpreter runs in interactive mode. The PYTHONHOME variable is used to set the location of the Python installation. If a single directory such as /usr/local is given, the interpreter expects to find all files in that location. If two directories are given, such as /usr/local:/usr/local/sparc-solaris-2.6, the interpreter searches for platform-independent files in the first directory and platform-dependent files in the second. PYTHONHOME has no effect if no valid Python installation exists at the specified location.

On Windows, some of the environment variables such as PYTHONPATH are read from registry entries found in HKEY_LOCAL_MACHINE/Software/Python. On the Macintosh, these settings can be adjusted using the EditPythonPrefs program.

Interactive Sessions

If no program name is given and the standard input to the interpreter is an interactive terminal, Python starts in interactive mode. In this mode, a banner message is printed and the user is presented with a prompt. In addition, the interpreter evaluates the script contained in the PYTHONSTARTUP environment variable (if set). This script is evaluated as if part of the input program (that is, it isn't loaded using an import statement). One application of this script might be to read a user configuration file such as .pythonrc.

When accepting interactive input, two user prompts appear. The >>> prompt appears at the beginning of a new statement; the ... prompt indicates a statement continuation. For example:

```
Python 1.5.2 (#1, Jun 27 1999, 15:39:11)  [GCC 2.7.2.3] on linux2
Copyright 1991-1995 Stichting Mathematisch Centrum, Amsterdam
>>> for i in range(0,4):
...     print i
...
0
1
2
3
>>>
```

In customized applications, you can change the prompts by modifying the values of sys.ps1 and sys.ps2, respectively.

On some systems, Python may be compiled to use the GNU readline library. If enabled, this library provides command histories, completion, and other additions to Python's interactive mode.

Launching Python Applications

In most cases, you'll want programs to start the interpreter automatically, rather than first having to start the interpreter manually. On Unix, this is done using shell scripts by setting the first line of a program to something like this:

```
#!/usr/local/bin/python
# Python code from this point on...
import string
print "Hello world"
...
```

On Windows, double-clicking a .py, .pyw, .wpy, or .pyc file automatically launches the interpreter. Normally, programs will run in a console window unless they're renamed with a .pyw suffix (in which case the program will run silently). If it's necessary to supply options to the interpreter, Python can also be started from a .bat file.

On the Macintosh, clicking a .py file normally launches the editor that was used to create the file. However, two special programs in the Macintosh distribution can be used to build applications. Dropping a .py file on the BuildApplet program converts the program into a file that automatically launches the Python interpreter when opened. The BuildApplication program converts a Python program into a standalone application that can be distributed and executed on machines that don't have a Python installation.

Site Configuration Files

A typical Python installation may include a number of third-party modules and packages. To configure these packages, the interpreter first imports the module site. The role of site is to search for package files and to add additional directories to the module search path sys.path. For details on the site module, see Appendix A, "The Python Library."

Program Termination

A program terminates when no more statements exist to execute in the input program, when an uncaught `SystemExit` exception is raised (as generated by `sys.exit()`), or when the interpreter receives a `SIGTERM` or `SIGHUP` signal (on Unix). On exit, the interpreter decrements the reference count of all objects in all the currently known namespaces (and destroys each namespace as well). If the reference count of an object reaches zero, the object is destroyed using its `__del__()` method. It's important to note that in some cases the destructor of an object might not be invoked at program termination. This can occur if circular references exist between objects (in which case, objects may be allocated, but accessible from no known namespace).

Because there's no guarantee that an object's destructor will be invoked at termination, it may be a good idea to explicitly clean up certain objects, such as open files and network connections. To accomplish this, add specialized cleanup methods (for example `close()`) to user-defined objects. Another possibility is to write a termination function and assign it to `sys.exitfunc`. When a program terminates, the interpreter first tries to execute the function assigned to `sys.exitfunc`. This can be set by the user as follows:

```
import sys
connection = open_connection("bigserver.com")

oldexitfunc = getattr(sys, 'exitfunc', None)
def cleanup(last_exit = oldexitfunc):
    print "Going away..."
    close_connection(connection)
    if last_exit: last_exit ()

sys.exitfunc = cleanup
```

When setting `sys.exitfunc`, it's good practice to call any previously defined exit function, as shown in the example.

One final peculiarity about program termination is that the destructors for some objects may try to access global data or methods defined in other modules. Since these objects may have already been destroyed, a `NameError` exception occurs in the destructor, and you may get an error such as the following:

```
Exception exceptions.NameError: 'c' in <method Bar.__del__ \
of Bar instance at c0310> ignored
```

If this occurs, it means the destructor has aborted prematurely. It also implies that a destructor may have failed in an attempt to perform an important operation (such as cleanly shutting down a server connection). If this is a concern, it's probably a good idea to perform an explicit shutdown step in your code, rather than relying on the interpreter to destroy objects cleanly at program termination. The peculiar `NameError` exception can also be eliminated by declaring default arguments in the declaration of the `__del__()` method. For example:

```
import foo
class Bar:
    def __del__(self, foo=foo):
        foo.bar()         # Use something in module foo
```

A

The Python Library

Python is bundled with a large collection of modules that provide a wide range of services ranging from interacting with the operating system to multimedia support. These modules are collectively known as the *Python library*. Currently, the library consists of approximately 180 modules that have been contributed by dozens of users.

This appendix describes most of the more frequently used modules in the Python library, with a focus on built-in functions, Python services, string processing, operating system interfaces, threads, and network programming. A brief overview of background material is introduced as necessary, but the reader is assumed to be reasonably familiar with basic operating system and programming concepts. Furthermore, because much of the library is based on C programming APIs, a good C programming book may help with some of the finer points of some modules. Extensive online documentation for the library is also available at http://www.python.org/doc/lib.

This appendix is largely based on the contents of the online library documentation as of Python version 1.5.2. However, a number of substantial modifications have been made:

- The library reference has been abridged to fit into a more compact format.

- Additional reference material has been added to better describe certain modules—especially with respect to operating system interfaces and network programming.

- Several modules require significant understanding of outside topics such as low-level network protocols and data formats. In these cases, only a brief description is given, along with references to related information.

- Special-purpose modules applicable to a single platform are omitted (for instance, multimedia extensions for the SGI).

- Large frameworks such as Tkinter and the Win32 extensions are omitted because they're beyond the scope of this book (and are covered in books of their own).

- Obsolete modules are omitted, even though these modules are still included in the standard distribution.

It's also important to note that the Python library is always being improved and extended with new functionality. Although the modules covered here are the most stable, their contents are still likely to change slightly over time. When in doubt, it's always best to consult the online documentation.

Finally, a few words on notational conventions. The compatibility and availability of each module and certain functions in the following sections are often indicated through the use of the following letters:

A	All versions of Python
J	JPython
M	Macintosh
W	Windows
U	Unix

It should also be noted that JPython was in beta release as this book went to press. Wherever possible, I have tried to indicate JPython compatibility, with the unfortunate knowledge that this information may be somewhat inaccurate or out of date in future releases of JPython. JPython users will almost certainly want to consult http://www.jpython.org for the most up-to-date compatibility information.

Built-in Functions and Exceptions

This section describes Python's built-in functions and exceptions. Much of this material is covered less formally in the chapters of this book. Additional details and some of the more subtle aspects of many built-in functions can be found here.

Built-in Functions

The functions in this section are always available to the interpreter and are contained within the __builtin__ module. In addition, the __builtins__ attribute of each module usually refers to this module (except when running in a restricted execution environment as described in the "Restricted Execution" section).

__import__(*name* [, *globals* [, *locals* [, *fromlist*]]])

This function is invoked by the import statement to load a module. *name* is a string containing the module name, *globals* is an optional dictionary defining the global namespace, *locals* is a dictionary defining the local namespace, and *fromlist* is a list of targets given to the from statement. For example, the statement import spam results in a call to __import__("spam", globals(), locals(), []), while the statement from spam import foo results in a call __import__ ("spam", globals(), locals(), ['foo']). If the module name is prefixed by a package name such as foo.bar and *fromlist* is empty, the corresponding module object is returned. If *fromlist* is not empty, only the top-level package is returned.

This function is intended to be a low-level interface to the module loader. It doesn't perform all the steps performed by an import statement (in particular, the local namespace is not updated with names referring to objects contained within the module). This function can be redefined by the user to implement new behaviors for import. The default implementation doesn't even look at the *locals* parameter, while *globals* is only used to determine package context (these parameters are supplied so that alternative implementations of __import__() have full access to the global and local namespace information where import statements appear).

abs(*x*)

Returns the absolute value of *x*.

apply(*func* [, *args* [, *keywords*]])

Performs a function call operation on a callable object *func*. *args* is a tuple containing positional arguments and *keywords* is a dictionary containing keyword arguments.

buffer(*object* [, *offset*[, *size*])

Creates a new buffer object. This is an undocumented function in Python 1.5.2. Please refer to the online documentation for more details.

callable(*object*)

Returns 1 if *object* is a callable object, 0 otherwise.

chr(*i*)

Converts an ASCII integer value *i*, 0 <= *i* <= 255, into a one-character string.

cmp(*x*, *y*)

Compares *x* and *y* and returns a negative number if *x* < *y*, 0 if *x* == *y*, and a positive number if *x* > *y*. Any two objects can be compared, although the result may be meaningless if the two objects have no meaningful comparison method defined (for example, comparing a number with a file object).

coerce(*x*, *y*)

Returns a tuple containing the values of *x* and *y* converted to a common type. See the section "Mathematical Operations" in Chapter 3, "Types and Objects."

compile(*string*, *filename*, *kind*)

Compiles *string* into a code object for use with exec or eval(). *filename* is a string containing the name of the file in which the string was defined. *kind* is 'exec' for a sequence of statements, 'eval' for a single expression, or 'single' for a single executable statement.

complex(*real* [, *imag*])

Creates a complex number.

delattr(*object*, *attr*)

Deletes an attribute of an object. *attr* is a string. This is the same as del *object*.*attr*.

dir([*object*])

Returns a sorted list of attribute names. These are taken from the object's __dict__, __methods__, and __members__ attributes. If no argument is given, the names in the current local symbol table are returned.

divmod(*a*, *b*)

Returns the quotient and remainder of long division as a tuple. For integers, the value (*a* / *b*, *a* % *b*) is returned. For floats, (math.floor(*a* / *b*), *a* % *b*) is returned.

eval(*expr* [, *globals* [, *locals*]])

Evaluates an expression. *expr* is a string or a code object created by compile(). *globals* and *locals* define the global and local namespaces for the operation. If omitted, the expression is evaluated in the namespace of the caller.

execfile(*filename* [, *globals* [, *locals*]])

Executes the statements in the file *filename*. *globals* and *locals* define the global and local namespaces in which the file is executed. If omitted, the file's contents are executed in the namespace of the caller.

filter(*function, list*)

Creates a new list consisting of the objects from *list* for which *function* evaluates to true. If *function* is None, the identity function is used and all the elements of *list* that are false are removed.

float(*x*)

Converts *x* to a floating-point number.

getattr(*object, name*)

Returns an attribute of an object. *name* is a string. Same as *object.name*.

globals()

Returns a dictionary corresponding to the global namespace of the caller.

hasattr(*object, name*)

Returns 1 if *name* is the name of an attribute of *object*, 0 otherwise. *name* is a string.

hash(*object*)

Returns an integer hash value for an object (if possible). The hash value is the same for any two objects that compare as equals. Mutable objects don't define a hash value.

hex(*x*)

Converts *x* to a hexadecimal string.

id(*object*)

Returns the unique integer identity of *object*.

input([*prompt*])

Same as eval(raw_input(*prompt*)).

intern(*string*)

Checks to see whether *string* is contained in an internal table of strings. If found, a copy of the internal string is returned. If not, *string* is added to the internal table and returned. This function is primarily used to get better performance in operations involving dictionary lookups. Interned strings are never garbage collected.

isinstance(*object, classobj*)

Returns true if *object* is an instance of *classobj* or a subclass of *classobj*. Can also be used for type checking if *classobj* is a type object.

issubclass(*class1, class2*)

Returns true if *class1* is a subclass of (derived from) *class2*. *Note:* issubclass (A, A) is true.

len(*s*)

Returns the number of items contained in *s*.

list(*s*)

Returns a new list consisting of the items in the sequence *s*.

locals()

Returns a dictionary corresponding to the local namespace of the caller.

long(*x*)

Converts a number or string *x* to a long integer.

map(*function*, *list*, ...)

Applies *function* to every item of *list* and returns a list of results. If multiple lists are supplied, *function* is assumed to take that many arguments, with each argument taken from a different list. If *function* is None, the identity function is assumed. If None is mapped to multiple lists, a list of tuples is returned, wherein each tuple contains an element from each list. Short lists are extended with values of None to match the length of the longest list, if necessary.

max(*s* [, *args*, ...])

For a single argument *s*, returns the maximum value of the sequence *s*. For multiple arguments, returns the largest of the arguments.

min(*s* [, *args*, ...])

For a single argument *s*, returns the minimum value of the sequence *s*. For multiple arguments, returns the smallest of the arguments.

oct(*x*)

Converts an integer *x* to an octal string.

open(*filename* [, *mode* [, *bufsize*]])

Opens the file *filename* and returns a new file object (see Chapter 10, "Execution Environment"). *mode* indicates how the file should be opened: 'r' for reading, 'w' for writing, and 'a' for appending. An optional '+' can be added to the mode to open the file for updating (which allows both reading and writing). A mode of 'w+' truncates the file to zero length if it already exists. A mode of 'r+' or 'a+' opens the file for both reading and writing, but leaves the original contents intact when the file is opened. Append 'b' to the mode to indicate binary mode. If the mode is omitted, a mode of 'r' is assumed. The *bufsize* argument specifies the buffering behavior, where 0 is unbuffered, 1 is line buffered, and any other positive number indicates an approximate buffer size in bytes. A negative number indicates that the system default should be used (this is the default behavior).

ord(*c*)

Returns the integer ASCII value of a single character *c*.

pow(*x*, *y* [, *z*])

Returns *x* ** *y*. If *z* is supplied, returns (*x* ** *y*) % *z*.

range([*start*,] *stop* [, *step*])

Creates a list of integers from *start* to *stop*. *step* indicates a stride and is set to 1 if omitted. If *start* is omitted, it defaults to 0. A negative *step* creates a list of numbers in descending order.

▶ **See Also** xrange (p. 93).

raw_input([*prompt*])

Reads a line of input from standard input (sys.stdin) and returns it as a string. If *prompt* is supplied, it's first printed to standard output (sys.stdout). Trailing newlines are stripped and an EOFError exception is raised if an EOF is read. If the readline module is loaded, this function will use it to provide advanced line-editing and command-completion features.

reduce(*func*, *seq* [, *initializer*])

Applies a function *func* cumulatively to the items in the sequence *seq* and returns a single value. *func* is expected to take two arguments and is first applied to the first two items of *seq*. This result and subsequent elements of *seq* are then combined one at a time in a similar manner, until all elements of *seq* have been consumed. *initializer* is an optional starting value used in the first computation and when *seq* is empty.

reload(*module*)

Reloads an already imported module. *module* must refer to an existing module object. The use of this function is discouraged except for debugging. Keep the following issues in mind:

- When a module is reloaded, the dictionary defining its global namespace is retained. Thus, definitions in the old module that aren't part of the newly reloaded module are retained. Modules can exploit this to see if they have been previously loaded.

- It's usually illegal to reload dynamically loaded modules written in C or C++.

- If any other modules have imported this module by using the **from** statement, they'll continue to use the definitions in the previously imported module. This problem can be avoided by either reissuing the **from** statement or using fully qualified names such as *module.name*.

- If there are any object instances created by classes in the old module, they'll continue to use methods defined in the old module.

repr(*object*)

Returns a string representation of *object*. This is the same string generated by backquotes (` `` `). In most cases, the returned string is an expression that can be passed to eval() to re-create the object.

round(*x* [, *n*])

Rounds the result of rounding the floating-point number *x* to the closest multiple of 10 to the power *n*. If *n* is omitted, it defaults to 0. If two multiples are equally close, rounding is done away from 0 (for example, 0.5 is rounded to 1.0 and -0.5 is rounded to -1.0).

setattr(*object*, *name*, *value*)

Sets an attribute of an object. *name* is a string. Same as *object.name* = *value*.

slice([*start*,] *stop* [, *step*])

Returns a slice object representing integers in the specified range. Slice objects are also generated by extended slice syntax. See the section "Sequence and Mapping Methods" in Chapter 3 for details.

str(*object*)

Returns a string representing the printable form of an object. This is the same string as would be produced by the print statement.

tuple(*s*)

Creates a tuple whose items are taken from the sequence *s*. If *s* is already a tuple, it's returned unmodified.

type(*object*)

Returns the type of *object*. The type is returned as a type object as defined in the types module.

vars([object])

Returns the symbol table of *object* (usually found in its __dict__ attribute). If no argument is given, a dictionary corresponding to the local namespace is returned.

xrange([start,] stop [, step])

Works exactly like range() except that an XRangeType object is returned. This object produces the same values as stored in the list created by range(), but without actually storing them. This is useful when working with very large ranges of integers that would consume a large amount of memory.

Built-in Exceptions

Built-in exceptions are contained in the exceptions module, which is always loaded prior to the execution of any program. Exceptions are defined as classes. The following exceptions serve as base classes for all the other exceptions:

Exception

The root class for all exceptions. All built-in exceptions are derived from this class. User-defined exceptions are encouraged to use this as a base class.

StandardError

The base class for all built-in exceptions.

ArithmeticError

Base class for arithmetic exceptions, including OverflowError, ZeroDivisionError, and FloatingPointError.

LookupError

Base class for indexing and key errors, including IndexError and KeyError.

EnvironmentError

Base class for errors that occur outside Python, including IOError and OSError.

The preceding exceptions are never raised explicitly. However, they can be used to catch certain classes of errors. For instance, the following code would catch any sort of numerical error:

```
try:
    # Some operation
    ...
except ArithmeticError, e:
    # Math error
```

When an exception is raised, an instance of an exception class is created. This instance is placed in the optional variable supplied to the except statement. For example:

```
except IOError, e:
    # Handle error
    # 'e' has an instance of IOError
```

Most exceptions have an associated value that can be found in the args attribute of the exception instance ('e.args' in the preceding example). In most cases, this is a string describing the error. For EnvironmentError exceptions, the value is a 2-tuple or 3-tuple containing an integer error number, string error message, and an optional filename.

The following exceptions are raised by programs:

AssertionError

Failed assert statement.

AttributeError

Failed attribute reference or assignment.

EOFError

End of file. Generated by the built-in functions input() and raw_input(). *Note:* A number of I/O methods such as read() and readlines() return an empty string for EOF.

FloatingPointError

Failed floating-point operation.

IOError

Failed I/O operation. The value is a tuple (*errno, errmsg* [, *filename*]) containing an integer error number *errno*, an error message *errmsg*, and an optional filename *filename*.

ImportError

Raised when an import statement can't find a module or when from can't find a name in a module.

IndexError

Sequence subscript out of range.

KeyError

Key not found in a dictionary.

KeyboardInterrupt

Raised when the user hits the interrupt key (usually Ctrl+C).

MemoryError

Recoverable out-of-memory error.

NameError

Name not found in local or global namespaces.

NotImplementedError

Unimplemented feature. Can be raised by base classes that require derived classes to implement certain methods.

OSError

Operating system error. Primarily raised by functions in the os module. The value is the same as for IOError.

OverflowError

Result of arithmetic operation is too large to be represented.

RuntimeError

A generic error not covered by any of the other categories.

SyntaxError

Parser syntax error. Instances have the attributes filename, lineno, offset, and text that can be used to gather more information.

SystemError

Internal error in the interpreter. The value is a string indicating the problem.

SystemExit

Raised by the sys.exit() function. The value is an integer indicating the return code. If it's necessary to exit immediately, os._exit() can be used.

TypeError

Operation or function applied to an object of inappropriate type.

ValueError

Generated when the argument to a function or operation is the right type, but of inappropriate value.

ZeroDivisionError

Dividing by zero.

Python Services

The modules in this section are primarily used to interact with the Python interpreter and its environment.

copy

Availability: A

The copy module provides functions for making shallow and deep copies of compound objects, including lists, tuples, dictionaries, and class instances.

copy(x)

Makes a shallow copy of x by creating a new compound object and duplicating the members of x by reference.

deepcopy(x [, visit])

Makes a deep copy of x by creating a new compound object and recursively duplicating all the members of x. visit is an optional dictionary that's used internally to detect and avoid cycles in recursively defined data structures.

A class can implement its own copy methods by implementing the methods __copy__(self) and __deepcopy__(self, visit). Both methods should return a copy of the object. In addition, the __deepcopy__() method must accept a dictionary visit as described for the deepcopy() function. When writing __deepcopy__(), it's not necessary to modify visit. However, visit should be passed to subsequent calls to deepcopy() (if any) performed inside the __deepcopy__() method.

Notes

- This module can be used with simple types such as integers and strings, but there's little need to do so.

- The copy functions don't work with modules, class objects, functions, methods, tracebacks, stack frames, files, sockets, or other similar types.

- The copy_reg module is not used by this module.

▶ **See Also** pickle (p. 99).

copy_reg

Availability: A

The `copy_reg` module extends the capabilities of the `pickle` and `cPickle` modules to handle the serialization of objects described by extension types (as defined in C extension modules). To do this, extension writers use this module to register reduction and construction functions that are used to serialize and unserialize an object, respectively.

constructor(*cfunc*)

Declares *cfunc* to be a valid constructor function. *cfunc* must be a callable object that accepts the tuple of values returned by the reduction function given to the `pickle()` function.

pickle(*type*, *rfunc* [, *cfunc*])

Registers *rfunc* as a reduction function for objects of type *type*. *rfunc* is a function that takes an object of the specified type and returns a tuple containing the constructor function and a tuple of arguments to pass to that function in order to reassemble the object. If supplied, *cfunc* is the constructor function that's registered using the `constructor()` function.

Example

The following example shows how this module would be used to pickle complex numbers. (*Note:* Because complex numbers are already pickleable, this example is only intended to illustrate the use of this module.)

```
# Register a method for pickling complex numbers
import copy_reg

# Create a complex number from two reals
def construct_complex(real,imag):
    return complex(real,imag)        # Built-in function

# Take a complex number 'c' and turn it into a tuple of floats
def reduce_complex(c):
    return construct_complex, (c.real, c.imag)

# Register our handler
copy_reg.pickle(type(1j),reduce_complex, construct_complex)
```

When complex numbers are pickled, the `reduce_complex()` function is called. When the object is later unpickled, the function `construct_complex()` is called, using the tuple of values originally returned by `reduce_complex()`.

Notes

- `copy_reg` is a misnomer—this module isn't used by the `copy` module.
- It's not necessary to use this module when pickling instances of user-defined classes.

▶ **See Also** `pickle` (p. 99).

marshal

Availability: A

The `marshal` module is used to serialize Python objects. `marshal` is similar to the `pickle` and `shelve` modules, but is less powerful and intended for use only with simple objects. It shouldn't be used to implement persistent objects in general (use `pickle` instead).

dump(*value*, *file*)

Writes the object value to the open file object *file*. If *value* is an unsupported type, a ValueError exception is raised.

dumps(*value*)

Returns the string written by the dump() function. If *value* is an unsupported type, a ValueError exception is raised.

load(*file*)

Reads and returns the next value from the open file object *file*. If no valid value is read, an EOFError, ValueError, or TypeError exception will be raised.

loads(*string*)

Reads and returns the next value from the string *string*.

Notes

- Data is stored in a binary architecture-independent format.

- Only None, integers, long integers, floats, complex numbers, strings, tuples, lists, dictionaries, and code objects are supported. Lists, tuples, and dictionaries can only contain supported objects. Class instances and recursive references in lists, tuples, and dictionaries are not supported.

- marshal is significantly faster than pickle, but isn't as flexible.

▶ **See Also** pickle (p. 99), shelve (p. 124).

new

Availability: U, W, M

The new module is used to create various types of objects used by the interpreter. The primary use of this module is by applications that need to create objects in a non-regular manner (such as when unmarshalling data).

instance(*class*, *dict*)

Creates a class instance of *class* with dictionary *dict* without calling the __init__() method.

instancemethod(*function*, *instance*, *class*)

Creates a method object, bound to *instance*. *function* must be a callable object. If *instance* is None, an unbound instance is created.

function(*code*, *globals* [, *name* [, *argdefs*]])

Creates a function object with the given *code* object and global namespace. *name* is the name of the function or None (in which case the function name is taken from *code*.co_name). *argdefs* is a tuple containing default parameter values.

code(*argcount*, *nlocals*, *stacksize*, *flags*, *codestring*, *constants*, *names*, ➡*varnames*, *filename*, *name*, *firstlineno*, *lnotab*)

Creates a new Code object. See the section "Code Objects" in Chapter 3 for a description of the arguments.

module(*name*)

Creates a new module object. *name* is the module name.

classobj(*name, baseclasses, dict*)

Creates a new class object. *name* is the class name, *baseclasses* is a tuple of base classes, and *dict* is a dictionary defining the class namespace.

▶ **See Also** Chapter 3.

operator

Availability: A

The operator module provides functions that access the built-in operators and special methods of the interpreter described in Chapter 3. For example, add(3, 4) is the same as 3 + 4. When the name of a function matches the name of a special method, it can also be invoked using its name with double underscores—for example, __add__(3, 4).

Function	Description
add(a, b)	Returns a + b for numbers.
sub(a, b)	Returns a - b.
mul(a, b)	Returns a * b for numbers.
div(a, b)	Returns a / b.
mod(a, b)	Returns a % b.
neg(a)	Returns -a.
pos(a)	Returns +a.
abs(a)	Returns the absolute value of a.
inv(a)	Returns the inverse of a.
lshift(a, b)	Returns a << b.
rshift(a, b)	Returns a >> b.
and_(a, b)	Returns a & b (bitwise and).
or_(a, b)	Returns a ¦ b (bitwise or).
xor(a, b)	Returns a ^ b (bitwise xor).
not_(a)	Returns not a.
truth(a)	Returns 1 if a is true, 0 otherwise.
concat(a, b)	Returns a + b for sequences.
repeat(a, b)	Returns a * b for a sequence a and integer b.
contains(a, b)	Returns the result of b in a.
sequenceIncludes(a, b)	Returns the result of b in a.
countOf(a, b)	Returns the number of occurrences of b in a.
indexOf(a, b)	Returns the index of the first occurrence of b in a.
getitem(a, b)	Returns a [b].
setitem(a, b, c)	a [b] = c.
delitem(a, b)	del a [b].
getslice(a, b, c)	Returns a[b:c].
setslice(a, b, c, v)	Sets a[b:c] = v.
delslice(a, b, c)	del a[b:c].

▶ **See Also** "Special Methods" in Chapter 3.

pickle and cPickle

Availability: A

The pickle and cPickle modules and cPickle are used to serialize Python objects into a stream of bytes suitable for storing in a file, transferring across a network, or placing in a database. This process is sometimes called *pickling, serializing, marshalling,* or *flattening.* The resulting byte stream can also be converted back into a series of Python objects using an *unpickling* process.

The pickling and unpickling process is controlled by using Pickler and Unpickler objects as created by the following two functions:

Pickler(*file* [, *bin*])

Creates a pickling object that writes data to the file object *file. bin* specifies that data should be written in binary format. By default, a less efficient—but readable—text format is used.

Unpickler(*file*)

Creates an unpickling object that reads data from the file object *file.* The unpickler automatically detects whether the incoming data is in binary or text format.

To serialize an object *x* onto a file *f*, the dump() method of the pickler object is used. For example:

```
p = pickle.Pickler(f)      # Send pickled data to file f
p.dump(x)                  # Dump x
```

To later unpickle the object from the file, do the following:

```
u = pickle.Unpickler(f)
x = u.load()               # Restore x from file f
```

Multiple calls to the dump() and load() methods are allowed, provided that the sequence of load() calls used to restore a collection of previously stored objects matches the sequence of dump() calls used during the pickling process.

The following functions are available as shortcuts to common pickling operations:

dump(*object, file* [, *bin*])

Dumps a pickled representation of *object* to the file object *file.* Same as Pickler(*file, bin*).dump(*object*).

dumps(*object* [, *bin*])

Same as dump(), but returns a string containing the pickled data.

load(*file*)

Loads a pickled representation of an object from the file object *file.* Same as Unpickler(*file*).load().

loads(*string*)

Same as load(), but reads the pickled representation of an object from a string.

The following objects can be pickled:

■ None.

■ Integers, long integers, floating-point, and complex numbers.

■ Tuples, lists, and dictionaries containing only pickleable objects.

- Classes defined at the top level of a module.
- Instances of classes defined at the top level of a module.

When class instances are pickled, their corresponding class definition must appear at the top level of a module (that is, no nested classes). When instances are unpickled, the module in which their class definition appeared is automatically imported. In addition, when instances are re-created, their `__init__()` method is not invoked. If it's necessary to call `__init__()` when unpickling, the class must define a special method `__getinitargs__()` that returns a tuple of arguments to be supplied to `__init__()`. If present, `pickle` will call this function and encode the constructor arguments in the byte stream for use when unpickling.

It's also worth noting that when pickling class instances in which the corresponding class definition appears in `__main__`, that class definition must be manually reloaded prior to unpickling a saved object (because there's no way for the interpreter to know how to automatically load the necessary class definitions back into `__main__` when unpickling).

A class can define customized methods for saving and restoring its state by implementing the special methods `__getstate__()` and `__setstate__()`. The `__getstate__()` method must return a pickleable object (such as a string) representing the state of the object. The `__setstate__()` method accepts the pickled object and restores its state. If no `__getstate__()` method is found, `pickle` simply pickles an object's `__dict__` attribute.

Exception

PicklingException

Raised on attempts to pickle unsupported object types.

Notes

- Recursive objects (objects containing references to themselves) and object sharing are handled correctly. However, if the same object is dumped to a `Pickler` object more than once, only the first instance is saved (even if the object has changed between dumps).

- When class instances are pickled, their class definitions and associated code for methods are not saved. This allows classes to be modified or upgraded while still being able to read data saved from older versions.

- `pickle` defines `Pickler` and `Unpickler` as classes that can be subclassed if necessary.

- The `cPickle` module is up to 1,000 times faster than `pickle`, but doesn't allow subclassing of the `Pickler` and `Unpickler` objects.

- The data format used by `pickle` is Python specific and shouldn't be assumed to be compatible with any external standards (such as XDR).

- Any object that provides `write()`, `read()`, and `readline()` methods can be used in place of a file.

- The `copy_reg` module is used to register new types with the `pickle` module.
  ▶ **See Also** `shelve` (p. 124), `marshal` (p. 96), `copy_reg` (p. 96).

site

Availability: U, W, M

The site module is automatically imported when the interpreter starts and is used to perform site-wide initialization of packages. The module works by first creating a list of up to four directory names created from the values of sys.prefix and sys.exec_prefix. On Windows or Macintosh platforms, the list of directories is as follows:

```
[ sys.prefix,
    sys.exec_prefix ]
```

On Unix, the directories are as follows:

```
[ sys.prefix + 'lib/pythonvers/site-packages',
    sys.prefix + 'lib/site-python',
    sys.exec_prefix + 'lib/pythonvers/site-packages',
    sys.exec_prefix + 'lib/site-python' ]
```

For each directory in the list, a check is made to see whether the directory exists. If so, it's added to the sys.path variable. Next, a check is made to see whether it contains any path configuration files (files with a .pth suffix). A path configuration file contains a list of directories relative to the location of the path file that should be added to sys.path. For example:

```
# foo package configuration file 'foo.pth'
foo
bar
```

Each directory in the path configuration file must be listed on a separate line. Comments and blank lines are ignored. When the site module loads the file, it checks to see whether each directory exists. If so, the directory is added to sys.path. Duplicated items are added to the path only once.

After all paths have been added to sys.path, an attempt is made to import a module named sitecustomize. The purpose of this module is to perform any additional (and arbitrary) site customization. If the import of sitecustomize fails with an ImportError, the error is silently ignored.

▶ **See Also** sys (p. 101), Chapter 8, "Modules and Packages," Chapter 10, "Execution Environment."

sys

Availability: A

The sys module contains variables and functions that pertain to the operation of the interpreter and its environment. The following variables are defined:

Variable	Description
argv	List of command-line options passed to a program. argv[0] is the name of the program.
builtin_module_names	Tuple containing names of modules built into the Python executable.

continues >>

>>continued

Variable	Description
copyright	String containing copyright message.
exec_prefix	Directory where platform-dependent Python files are installed.
executable	String containing the name of the interpreter executable.
exitfunc	Function object that's called when the interpreter exits. It can be set to a function taking no parameters. By default, exitfunc is not defined. See Chapter 10, p. 86.
last_type, last_value, last_traceback	These variables are set when an unhandled exception is encountered and the interpreter prints an error message. last_type is the last exception type, last_value is the last exception value, and last_traceback is a stack trace. *Note:* The use of these variables is not thread-safe. sys.exc_info() should be used instead.
maxint	Largest integer supported by the integer type.
modules	Dictionary mapping module names to module objects.
path	List of strings specifying the search path for modules. See Chapter 8.
platform	Platform identifier string, such as 'linux-i386'.
prefix	Directory where platform-independent Python files are installed.
ps1, ps2	Strings containing the text for the primary and secondary prompts of the interpreter. Initially, ps1 is set to '>>> ' and ps2 is set to '... '. The str() method of whatever object is assigned to these values is evaluated to generate the prompt text.
stdin, stdout, stderr	File objects corresponding to standard input, standard output, and standard error. stdin is used for the raw_input() and input() functions. stdout is used for print and the prompts of raw_input() and input(). stderr is used for the interpreter's prompts and error messages. These variables can be assigned to any object that supports a write() method operating on a single string argument.
__stdin__, __stdout__, __stderr__	File objects containing the values of stdin, stdout, and stderr at the start of the interpreter.
tracebacklimit	Maximum number of levels of traceback information printed when an unhandled exception occurs. The default value is 1000. A value of 0 suppresses all traceback information and causes only the exception type and value to be printed.
version	Version string.

The following functions are available:

exc_info()

Returns a tuple (*type*, *value*, *traceback*) containing information about the exception that's currently being handled. *type* is the exception type, *value* is the exception parameter passed to raise, and *traceback* is a traceback object containing the call stack at the point where the exception occurred. Returns None if no exception is currently being handled.

exit([*n*])

Exits from Python by raising the SystemExit exception. *n* is an integer exit code indicating a status code. A value of 0 is considered normal (the default); nonzero values are considered abnormal. If a noninteger value is given to *n*, it's printed to sys.stderr and an exit code of 1 is used.

getrefcount(*object*)

Returns the reference count of *object*. (Not available in JPython.)

setcheckinternal(*n*)

Sets the number of virtual instructions that must be executed by the interpreter before it checks for periodic events such as signals and thread context switches. The default value is 10. (Not available in JPython.)

setprofile(*pfunc*)

Sets the system profile function that can be used to implement a source code profiler. See the later section "The Python Profiler" for information about the Python profiler.

settrace(*tfunc*)

Sets the system trace function, which can be used to implement a debugger. See the later section "The Python Debugger" for information about the Python debugger.

traceback

Availability: A

The traceback module is used to gather and print stack traces of a program after an exception has occurred. The functions in this module operate on traceback objects such as the third item returned by the sys.exc_info() function.

print_tb(*traceback* [, *limit* [, *file*]])

Prints up to *limit* stack trace entries, from *traceback* to the file *file*. If *limit* is omitted, all the entries are printed. If *file* is omitted, the output is sent to sys.stderr.

print_exception(*type*, *value*, *traceback* [, *limit* [, *file*]])

Prints exception information and a stack trace to *file*. *type* is the exception type and *value* is the exception value. *limit* and *file* are the same as in print_tb().

print_exc([*limit* [, *file*]])

The same as print_exception() applied to the information returned by the sys.exc_info() function.

print_last([*limit* [, *file*]])

The same as print_exception(sys.last_type, sys.last_value, sys.last_traceback, *limit*, *file*).

print_stack([*frame* [, *limit* [, *file*]]])

Prints a stack trace from the point at which it's invoked. *frame* specifies an optional stack frame from which to start. *limit* and *file* have the same meaning as for print_tb().

extract_tb(*traceback* **[,** *limit***])**

Extracts the stack trace information used by print_tb().

extract_stack([*frame* **[,** *limit***]])**

Extracts the stack trace information used by print_stack().

format_list(*list***)**

Formats stack trace information for printing.

format_exception_only(*type, value***)**

Formats exception information for printing.

format_exception(*type, value, traceback* **[,** *limit***])**

Formats an exception and stack trace for printing.

format_tb(*traceback* **[,** *limit***])**

Same as format_list(extract_tb(*traceback, limit*)).

format_stack([*frame* **[,** *limit***]])**

Same as format_list(extract_stack(*frame, limit*)).

tb_lineno(*traceback***)**

Returns the line number set in a traceback object.

Notes

Additional details are available in the online documentation.

> ▶ **See Also** sys (p. 101), "The Python Debugger" (p. 237), Chapter 3, and http://www.python.org/doc/lib/module-traceback.html.

types

Availability: A

The types module defines names for all the built-in object types. The contents of this module are often used in conjunction with the built-in isinstance() function and other type-related operations. The module defines the following variables:

Variable	Description
BuiltinFunctionType	Type of built-in functions.
CodeType	Code object.
ComplexType	Complex numbers.
ClassType	User-defined class.
DictType	Dictionaries.
DictionaryType	Alternative name for dictionaries.
EllipsisType	Type of Ellipsis.
FileType	Files.
FloatType	Floating-point numbers.
FrameType	Execution frame object.
FunctionType	User-defined functions and lambdas.
InstanceType	Instance of a user-defined class.

Variable	Description
IntType	Integers.
LambdaType	Alternative name for FunctionType.
ListType	Lists.
LongType	Long integers.
MethodType	User-defined class method.
ModuleType	Modules.
NoneType	Type of None.
SliceType	Extended slice object. Returned by slice().
StringType	Strings.
TracebackType	Traceback objects.
TupleType	Tuples.
TypeType	Type of type objects.
UnboundMethodType	Alternative name for MethodType.
XRangeType	Object created by using xrange().

Example

```
from types import *
if isinstance(s,ListType):
    print 'Is a list'
else:
    print 'Is not a list'
```

▶ **See Also** Chapter 3.

UserDict and UserList

Availability: A

The UserDict and UserList modules provide class wrappers around the built-in dictionary and list types. These wrappers can be used as a base class for classes that want to override or add new methods to these types. Each module defines a single class UserDict and UserList, respectively:

UserDict()

Returns a class instance that simulates a dictionary.

UserList([*list*])

Returns a class instance that simulates a list. *list* is an optional list that will be used to set the initial value. If omitted, the list will be set to [ ].

In both cases, the real dictionary or list object can be accessed in the data attribute of the instance.

Example

```
# A dictionary with case-insensitive keys
from UserDict import UserDict
import string
```

```
class MyDict(UserDict):
    # Perform a case-insensitive lookup
    def __getitem__(self,key):
        return self.data[string.lower(key)]
    def __setitem__(self,key,value):
        self.data[string.lower(key)] = value
    def __delitem__(self,key):
        del self.data[string.lower(key)]

# Use new dictionary-like class
d = MyDict()
d['Content-Type'] = 'text/html'
print d['content-type']      # Returns 'text/html'
```

Mathematics

The modules in this section provide a variety of mathematical functions.

array

Availability: U, W, M

The array module defines a new object type ArrayType that works almost exactly like other sequence types except that its contents are constrained to a single type. The type of an array is determined at the time of creation, using one of the following typecodes:

Type Code	Description	C Type	Minimum Size (in Bytes)
'c'	8-bit character	char	1
'b'	8-bit integer	signed char	1
'B'	8-bit unsigned integer	unsigned char	1
'h'	16-bit integer	short	2
'H'	16-bit unsigned integer	unsigned short	2
'i'	integer	int	4 or 8
'I'	unsigned integer	unsigned int	4 or 8
'l'	long integer	long	4 or 8
'L'	unsigned long integer	unsigned long	4 or 8
'f'	single-precision float	float	4
'd'	double-precision float	double	8

The representation of integers and long integers is determined by the machine architecture (they may be 32 or 64 bits). When values stored as 'L' or 'I' are returned, they're returned as Python long integers.

The module defines the following function:

array(*typecode* [, *initializer*])

Creates an array of type *typecode*. *initializer* is a string or list of values used to initialize values in the array. The following attributes and methods apply to an array object *a*:

Item	Description
a.typecode	Typecode character used to create the array.
a.itemsize	Size of *items* stored in the array (in bytes).
a.append(*x*)	Appends *x* to the end of the array.
a.buffer_info()	Returns (*address*, *length*) giving the memory location and length of the buffer used to store the array.
a.byteswap()	Swaps the byte ordering of all items in the array from big-endian to little-endian or vice versa. This is only supported for integer values.
a.fromfile(*f*, *n*)	Reads *n* items (in binary format) from the file object *f* and appends to the end of the array. *f* must be a file object. Raises EOFError if fewer than *n* items can be read.
a.fromlist(*list*)	Appends items from *list* to the end of the array.
a.fromstring(*s*)	Appends items from string *s* where *s* is interpreted as a string of binary values—same as would have been read using fromfile().
a.insert(*i*, *x*)	Inserts *x* before position *i*.
a.reverse()	Reverses the order of the array.
a.tofile(*f*)	Writes all items to file *f*. Data is saved in native binary format.
a.tolist()	Converts the array to an ordinary list of values.
a.tostring()	Converts to a string of binary data—the same data as would be written using tofile().

Exception

When items are inserted into an array, a TypeError exception is generated if the type of the item doesn't match the type used to create the array.

Notes

- This module is used to create large lists in a storage-efficient manner. The resulting arrays are not suitable for numeric work. For example, the addition operator doesn't add the corresponding elements of the arrays; it appends one array to the other. To create storage- and calculation-efficient arrays, use the Numeric extension available at ftp-icf.llnl.gov/pub/python. Note that the Numeric API is completely different.
- The type of an array object is array.ArrayType.

▶ **See Also** struct (p. 118), xdrlib (p. 226).

cmath

Availability: U, W, M

The cmath module provides mathematical functions for complex numbers. All functions accept and return complex numbers.

Function	Description
acos(x)	Returns the arccosine of x.
acosh(x)	Returns the arc hyperbolic cosine of x.
asin(x)	Returns the arcsine of x.
asinh(x)	Returns the arc hyperbolic sine of x.
atan(x)	Returns the arctangent of x.
atanh(x)	Returns the arc hyperbolic tangent of x.
cos(x)	Returns the cosine of x.
cosh(x)	Returns the hyperbolic cosine of x.
exp(x)	Returns e ** x.
log(x)	Returns the natural logarithm of x.
log10(x)	Returns the base-10 logarithm of x.
sin(x)	Returns the sine of x.
sinh(x)	Returns the hyperbolic sine of x.
sqrt(x)	Returns the square root of x.
tan(x)	Returns the tangent of x.
tanh(x)	Returns the hyperbolic tangent of x.

The following constants are defined:

Constant	Description
pi	Mathematical constant pi, as a real.
e	Mathematical constant e, as a real.

▶ **See Also** math (p. 108).

math

Availability: A

The math module defines standard mathematical functions. These functions operate on integers and floats, but don't work with complex numbers.

Function	Description
acos(x)	Returns the arccosine of x.
asin(x)	Returns the arcsine of x.
atan(x)	Returns the arctangent of x.
atan2(y, x)	Returns the atan(y / x).
ceil(x)	Returns the ceiling of x.
cos(x)	Returns the cosine of x.
cosh(x)	Returns the hyperbolic cosine of x.
exp(x)	Returns e ** x.
fabs(x)	Returns the absolute value of x.
floor(x)	Returns the floor of x.
fmod(x, y)	Returns x % y.

Function	Description
frexp(x)	Returns the positive mantissa and exponent of x.
hypot(x, y)	Returns the Euclidean distance, sqrt(x * x + y * y).
ldexp(x, i)	Returns x * (2 ** i).
log(x)	Returns the natural logarithm of x.
log10(x)	Returns the base-10 logarithm of x.
modf(x)	Returns the fractional and integer parts of x. Both have the same sign as x.
pow(x, y)	Returns x ** y.
sin(x)	Returns the sine of x.
sinh(x)	Returns the hyperbolic sine of x.
sqrt(x)	Returns the square root of x.
tan(x)	Returns the tangent of x.
tanh(x)	Returns the hyperbolic tangent of x.

The following constants are defined:

Constant	Description
pi	Mathematical constant pi.
e	Mathematical constant e.

▶ **See Also** cmath (p. 107).

random

Availability: A

The random module implements a number of pseudo–random-number generators for various distributions on the real numbers. The module also exports the choice(), randint(), random(), and uniform() functions from the whrandom module. The following functions all return real values and use argument names that correspond to names in the distribution's standard mathematical equation.

betavariate(alpha, beta)

Returns a value between 0 and 1 from the Beta distribution. alpha > -1 and beta > -1.

cunifvariate(mean, arc)

Circular uniform distribution. mean is the mean angle and arc is the range of the distribution, centered around the mean angle. Both of these values must be specified in radians in the range between 0 and pi. Returned values are in the range (mean - arc/2, mean + arc/2).

expovariate(lambd)

Exponential distribution. lambd is 1.0 divided by the desired mean. Returns values in the range (0, +∞).

gamma(alpha, beta)

Gamma distribution. alpha > -1, beta > 0.

gauss(*mu*, *sigma*)

Gaussian distribution with mean *mu* and standard deviation *sigma*. Slightly faster than normalvariate().

lognormvariate(*mu*, *sigma*)

Log normal distribution. Taking the natural logarithm of this distribution results in a normal distribution with mean *mu*, standard deviation *sigma*.

normalvariate(*mu*, *sigma*)

Normal distribution with mean *mu* and standard deviation *sigma*.

paretovariate(*alpha*)

Pareto distribution with shape parameter *alpha*.

vonmisesvariate(*mu*, *kappa*)

mu is the mean angle in radians between 0 and 2 * pi, *kappa* is a non-negative concentration factor. If *kappa* is zero, the distribution reduces to a uniform random angle over the range 0 to 2 * pi.

weibullvariate(*alpha*, *beta*)

Weibull distribution with scale parameter *alpha* and shape parameter *beta*.

Note

The Numeric extension also provides a number of efficient generators for large samples.

▶ **See Also** whrandom (p. 110).

whrandom

Availability: A

The whrandom module provides a floating-point pseudo–random-number generator using the Wichmann-Hill algorithm. When the module is first imported, a random number generator is created and seeded with values derived from the current time. The following functions are available.

choice(*seq*)

Returns a random element from the nonempty sequence *seq*.

randint(*a*, *b*)

Returns a random integer N, $a <= N <= b$.

random()

Returns the next random number in the range (0.0, 1.0).

seed(*x*, *y*, *z*)

Initializes the random number generator from integers *x*, *y*, and *z*. If $x = y = z$, the current time is used as a seed.

The module also defines a class whrandom that can be used to create multiple random number generators. The preceding functions are also methods of instances of this class.

Example

```
g = whrandom.whrandom()
g.seed(1,2,3)
n = g.random()
```

▶ **See Also** random (p. 109).

String Handling

The modules in this section are used for string processing.

re

Availability: A

The re module is used to perform regular-expression pattern matching and replacement in strings. Regular expression patterns are specified as strings containing a mix of text and special-character sequences. Since patterns often make extensive use of special characters and the backslash, they're usually written as "raw" strings such as r'(?P<int>\d+)\.(\d*)'. For the remainder of this section, all regular expression patterns are denoted using the raw string syntax.

The following special-character sequences are recognized in regular expression patterns:

Character(s)	Description
text	Matches the literal string *text*.
.	Matches any character except newline.
^	Matches the start of a string.
$	Matches the end of the string.
*	Matches zero or more repetitions of the preceding expression, matching as many repetitions as possible.
+	Matches one or more repetitions of the preceding expression, matching as many repetitions as possible.
?	Matches zero or one repetitions of the preceding expression.
*?	Matches zero or more repetitions of the preceding expression, matching as few repetitions as possible.
+?	Matches one or more repetitions of the preceding expression, matching as few repetitions as possible.
??	Matches zero or one repetitions of the preceding expression, matching as few repetitions as possible.
{*m*, *n*}	Matches from *m* to *n* repetitions of the preceding expression, matching as many repetitions as possible.
{*m*, *n*}?	Matches from *m* to *n* repetitions of the preceding expression, matching as few repetitions as possible.
[...]	Matches a set of characters such as r'[abcdef]' or r'[a-zA-z]'. Special characters such as * are not active inside a set.
[^...]	Matches the characters not in the set, such as r'[^0-9]'.
A¦B	Matches either *A* or *B* where *A* and *B* are both regular expressions.
(...)	Matches the regular expression inside the parentheses as a group and saves the matched substring.

continues >>

	Character(s)	Description
>>continued	(?iLmsx)	Interprets the letters "i", "L", "m", "s", and "x" as flag settings corresponding to the re.I, re.L, re.M, re.S, re.X flag settings given to re.compile().
	(?:...)	Matches the regular expression inside the parentheses, but discards the matched substring.
	(?P<name>...)	Matches the regular expression in the parentheses and creates a named group. The group name must be a valid Python identifier.
	(?P=name)	Matches the same text that was matched by an earlier named group.
	(?#...)	A comment. The contents of the parentheses are ignored.
	(?=...)	Matches the preceding expression only if followed by the pattern in the parentheses. For example, r'Hello (?=World)' matches 'Hello ' only if followed by 'World'.
	(?!...)	Matches the preceding expression only if it's not followed by the pattern in parentheses. For example, r'Hello (?!World)' only matches 'Hello ' if it's not followed by 'World'.

Special characters can be matched by preceding them with a backslash. For example, r'*' matches the character *. In addition, a number of backslash sequences have special meanings:

Character(s)	Description
\number	Matches the text that was matched by a previous group number. Groups are numbered from 1 to 99 starting from the left.
\A	Matches only at the start of the string.
\b	Matches the empty string at the beginning or end of a word. A word is a sequence of alphanumeric characters terminated by whitespace or any other non-alphanumeric character.
\B	Matches the empty string not at the beginning or end of a word.
\d	Matches any decimal digit. The same as r'[0-9]'.
\D	Matches any non-digit character. The same as r'[^0-9]'.
\s	Matches any whitespace character. The same as r'[\t\n\r\f\v]'.
\S	Matches any non-whitespace character. The same as r'[^ \t\n\r\f\v]'.
\w	Matches any alphanumeric character.
\W	Matches any character not contained in the set defined by \w.
\Z	Matches only at the end of the string.
\\	Matches a literal backslash.

The following functions are used to perform pattern matching and replacement.

compile(str [, flags])

Compiles a regular-expression pattern string into a regular-expression object. This object can be passed as the pattern argument to all of the functions that follow. *flags* is the bitwise-or of the following:

Flag	Description
I or IGNORECASE	Performs non–case-sensitive matching.
L or LOCALE	Uses locale settings for \w, \W, \b, and \B.
M or MULTILINE	Makes ^ and $ apply to each line. Normally ^ and $ apply to the beginning and end of an entire string.
S or DOTALL	Makes the . character match all characters, including the newline.
X or VERBOSE	Ignores unescaped whitespace and comments.

search(*pattern*, *string* [, *flags*])

Searches *string* for the first match of *pattern*. *flags* has the same meaning as for compile(). Returns a MatchObject on success, None if no match was found.

match(*pattern*, *string* [, *flags*])

Checks whether zero or more characters at the beginning of *string* match *pattern*. Returns a MatchObject on success, or None.

split(*pattern*, *string* [, *maxsplit* = 0])

Splits *string* by the occurrences of *pattern*. Returns a list of strings including the text matched by any groups in the pattern. *maxsplit* is the maximum number of splits to perform.

findall(*pattern*, *string*)

Returns a list of all non-overlapping matches of *pattern* in *string*, including empty matches. If the pattern has groups, a list of the text matched by the groups is returned. If more than one group is used, each item in the list is a tuple containing the text for each group.

sub(*pattern*, *repl*, *string* [, *count* = 0])

Replaces the leftmost non-overlapping occurrences of *pattern* in *string* by the replacement *repl*. *repl* can be a string or a function. If it's a function, it's called with a MatchObject and should return the replacement string. If *repl* is a string, back references such as "\6" are used to refer to groups in the pattern. The sequence "\g<*name*>" is used to refer to a named group. *count* is the maximum number of substitutions to perform.

subn(*pattern*, *repl*, *string* [, *count* = 0])

Same as sub(), but returns a tuple containing the new string and the number of substitutions.

escape(*string*)

Returns a string with all non-alphanumerics backslashed.

A compiled regular-expression object *r* created by the compile() function has the following methods and attributes:

r.search(*string* [, *pos*] [, *endpos*])

Searches *string* for a match. *pos* and *endpos* specify the starting and ending positions for the search. Returns a MatchObject for a match, None otherwise.

r.match(*string* [, *pos*] [, *endpos*])

Checks whether zero or more characters at the beginning of *string* match. *pos* and *endpos* specify the range of *string* to be searched. Returns a MatchObject for a match, None otherwise.

r.split(*string* [, *maxsplit* = 0])

Identical to the split() function.

r.findall(*string*)

Identical to the findall() function.

r.sub(*repl*, *string* [, *count* = 0])

Identical to the sub() function.

r.subn(*repl*, *string* [, *count* = 0])

Identical to the subn() function.

r.flags

The flags argument used when the regular expression object was compiled, or 0.

r.groupindex

A dictionary mapping symbolic group names defined by r'(?P<*id*>)' to group numbers.

r.pattern

The pattern string from which the regular expression object was compiled.

The MatchObject instances returned by search() and match() contain information about the contents of groups as well as positional data about where matches occurred. A MatchObject instance *m* has the following methods and attributes:

m.group([*group1*, *group2*, ...])

Returns one or more subgroups of the match. The arguments specify group numbers or group names. If no group name is given, the entire match is returned. If only one group is given, a string containing the text matched by the group is returned. Otherwise, a tuple containing the text matched by each of the requested groups is returned. An IndexError is raised if an invalid group number or name is given.

m.groups([*default*])

Returns a tuple containing the text matched by all groups in a pattern. *default* is the value returned for groups that didn't participate in the match (the default is None).

m.groupdict([*default*])

Returns a dictionary containing all the named subgroups of the match. *default* is the value returned for groups that didn't participate in the match (the default is None).

m.start([*group*])
m.end([*group*])

Returns the indices of the start and end of the substring matched by a group. If *group* is omitted, the entire matched substring is used. Returns None if the group exists but didn't participate in the match.

m.span([*group*])

Returns a 2-tuple (*m*.start(*group*), *m*.end(*group*)). If *group* didn't contribute to the match, this returns (None, None). If *group* is omitted, the entire matched substring is used.

m.pos

The value of pos passed to the search() or match() function.

m.endpos

The value of endpos passed to the search() or match() function.

m.re

The regular-expression object whose match() or search() method produced this MatchObject instance.

m.string

The string passed to match() or search().

Exception

The only exception is error, which is raised when a pattern string is not a valid regular expression.

Example

```
import re
s = open("foo").read()          # Read some text

# Replace all occurrences of "foo" with "bar"
t = re.sub("foo","bar",s)

# Get the title of an HTML document
tmatch = re.search(r'<title>(.*?)</title>',s, re.IGNORECASE)
if tmatch: title = tmatch.group(1)

# Extract a list of possible e-mail addresses from s
pat = re.compile(r'([a-zA-Z][\w-]*@[\w-]+(?:\.[\w-]+)*)')
addrs = re.findall(pat,s)

# Replace strings that look like URLs such as "http://www.python.org" with
# an HTML anchor tag of the form
# <a href="http://www.python.org">http://www.python.org</a>

pat = re.compile(r'((ftp|http)://[\w-]+(?:\.[\w-]+)*(?:/[\w-]*)*)')
t = pat.sub('<a href="\\1">\\1</a>', s)
```

Notes

- Detailed information about the theory and implementation of regular expressions can be found in textbooks on compiler construction. The book *Mastering Regular Expressions* by Jeffrey Friedl (O'Reilly & Associates, 1997, ISBN 1-56592-257-3) may also be useful.

- The re module is 8-bit clean and can process strings that contain null bytes and characters whose high bit is set. Regular expression patterns cannot contain null bytes, but can specify the null bytes as '\000'.

- Two obsolete modules, regex and regsub, perform similar operations. Refer to the online documentation for details.

▶ **See Also** string (p. 115).

string

Availability: A

The string module contains a number of useful constants and functions for manipulating strings. The following constants are defined:

Constant	Description
`digits`	The string `'0123456789'`.
`hexdigits`	The string `'0123456789abcdefABCDEF'`.
`letters`	Concatenation of `lowercase` and `uppercase`.
`lowercase`	String containing all lowercase letters.
`octdigits`	The string `'01234567'`.
`uppercase`	String containing all uppercase letters.
`whitespace`	String containing all whitespace characters. This usually includes space, tab, linefeed, return, formfeed, and vertical tab.

The following functions are available:

`atof(s)`

Converts string *s* to a floating-point number.

`atoi(s [, base])`

Converts string *s* to an integer `base` is an optional base.

`atol(s [, base])`

Converts string *s* to a long integer `base` is an optional base.

`capitalize(s)`

Capitalizes the first character of *s*.

`capwords(s)`

Capitalizes the first letter of each word in *s*, replaces repeated whitespace characters with a single space, and removes leading and trailing whitespace.

`count(s, sub [, start [, end]])`

Counts the number of non-overlapping occurrences of *sub* in *s*[*start*:*end*].

`expandtabs(s [, tabsize=8])`

Expands tabs in string *s* with whitespace. *tabsize* specifies the number of characters between tab stops.

`find(s, sub [, start [, end]])`
`index(s, sub [, start [, end]])`

Returns the first index in *s*[*start*:*end*] where the substring *sub* is found. If *start* and *end* are omitted, the entire string is searched. `find()` returns `-1` if not found, while `index()` raises a `ValueError` exception.

`rfind(s, sub [, start [, end]])`
`rindex(s, sub [, start [, end]])`

Like `find()` and `index()`, but finds the highest index.

`lower(s)`

Converts all uppercase characters in *s* to lowercase.

`maketrans(from, to)`

Creates a translation table that maps each character in *from* to the character in the same position in *to*. *from* and *to* must be the same length.

split(s [, sep [, maxsplit]])
splitfields(s [, sep [, maxsplit]])

Returns a list of words in s. If sep is omitted, the words are separated by white-space. Otherwise, the string in sep is used as a delimiter. maxsplit specifies the maximum number of splits that can occur. The remainder of the string will be returned as the last element.

join(words [, sep])
joinfields(words [, sep])

Concatenates a sequence of words into a string, with words separated by the string in sep. If omitted, the words are separated by whitespace.

lstrip(s)
rstrip(s)
strip(s)

Strips leading and/or trailing whitespace from s.

swapcase(s)

Changes uppercase to lowercase and lowercase to uppercase in s.

translate(s, table [, delchars])

Deletes all characters from s that are in delchars and translates the remaining characters using table. table must be a 256-character string mapping characters to characters as created by maketrans().

upper(s)

Converts all lowercase characters in s to uppercase.

ljust(s, width)
rjust(s, width)
center(s, width)

Left-aligns, right-aligns, or centers s in a field of width width.

zfill(s, width)

Pads a numeric string on the left with 0 digits up to the given width.

replace(str, old, new [, max])

Replaces max occurrences of old with new in str. If max is omitted, all occurrences are replaced.

▶ **See Also** re (p. 111).

StringIO and cStringIO

Availability: A

The StringIO and cStringIO modules define an object that behaves like a file but reads and writes data from a string buffer.

StringIO([buffer])

Creates a new StringIO object. buffer is an initial value (by default, the empty string).

A StringIO object supports all the standard file operations—read(), write(), and so on—and the following methods:

s.getvalue()

Returns the contents of the string buffer before close() is called.

s.close()

Releases the memory buffer.

Note

The `StringIO` module defines `StringIO` as a class. `cStringIO` defines it as an extension type and provides significantly faster performance.

▶ **See Also** Chapter 9, "Input and Output,"
the section "Files" (for file methods).

struct

Availability: A

The `struct` module is used to convert data between Python and binary data structures (represented as Python strings). These data structures are often used when interacting with functions written in C or with binary network protocols.

pack(*fmt*, *v1*, *v2*, ...)

Packs the values *v1*, *v2*, and so on into a string according to the format string in *fmt*.

unpack(*fmt*, *string*)

Unpacks the contents of *string* according to the format string in *fmt*. Returns a tuple of the unpacked values.

calcsize(*fmt*)

Calculates the size in bytes of the structure corresponding to a format string *fmt*.

The format string is a sequence of characters with the following interpretations:

Format	C Type	Python Type
'x'	pad byte	No value.
'c'	char	String of length 1.
'b'	signed char	Integer.
'B'	unsigned char	Integer.
'h'	short	Integer.
'H'	unsigned short	Integer.
'i'	int	Integer.
'I'	unsigned int	Integer.
'l'	long	Integer.
'L'	unsigned long	Integer.
'f'	float	Float.
'd'	double	Float.
's'	char[]	String.
'p'	char[]	String with length encoded in the first byte.
'P'	void *	Integer.

Each format character can be preceded by an integer to indicate a repeat count (for example, '4i' is the same as 'iiii'). For the 's' format, the count represents the maximum length of the string, so '10s' represents a 10-byte string. A format of '0s' indicates a string of zero length. The 'p' format is used to encode a string in which the length appears in the first byte, followed by the string data. This is useful when dealing with Pascal code, as is sometimes necessary on the Macintosh. *Note:* The length of the string in this case is limited to 255 characters.

When the 'I' and 'L' formats are used to unpack a value, the return value is a Python long integer. In addition, the 'P' format may return an integer or long integer, depending on the word size of the machine.

The first character of each format string can also specify a byte ordering and alignment of the packed data, as shown in the following table.

Format	Byte Order	Size and Alignment
'@'	Native	Native
'='	Native	Standard
'<'	Little-endian	Standard
'>'	Big-endian	Standard
'!'	Network (big-endian)	Standard

Native byte ordering may be little- or big-endian, depending the machine architecture. The native sizes and alignment correspond to the values used by the C compiler and are implementation specific. The standard alignment assumes that no alignment is needed for any type. The standard size assumes that short is 2 bytes, int is 4 bytes, long is 4 bytes, float is 32 bits, and double is 64 bits. The 'P' format can only use native byte ordering.

Note

Sometimes it's necessary to align the end of a structure to the alignment requirements of a particular type. To do this, end the structure format string with the code for that type with a repeat count of zero. For example, the format 'llh0l' specifies a structure that ends on a four-byte boundary (assuming longs are aligned on four-byte boundaries). In this case, two pad bytes would be inserted after the short value specified by the 'h' code. This only works when native size and alignment are being used—standard size and alignment don't enforce alignment rules.

▶ **See Also** array (p. 106), xdrlib (p. 226).

Data Management and Object Persistence

The modules in this section are used to store data in a variety of DBM-style database formats. These databases operate like a large disk-based hash table in which objects are stored and retrieved using unique key strings.

All the databases are opened using a variation of the open() function (defined in each database module):

```
open(filename [, flag [, mode]])
```

Opens the database file *filename* and returns a database object. *flag* is 'r' for read-only access, 'w' for read-write access, 'c' to create the database if it doesn't exist, or 'n' to force the creation of a new database. *mode* is the file access mode (the default is 0666 on Unix).

The object returned by the open() function supports the following dictionary-like operations:

Operation	Description
d[*key*] = *value*	Inserts *value* into the database.
value = *d*[*key*]	Gets data from the database.
del *d*[*key*]	Removes a database entry.
d.close()	Closes the database.
d.has_key(*key*)	Tests for a key.
d.keys()	Returns a list of keys.

In all cases *key* must be a string. In addition, *value* must be a string for all the database modules except the shelve module.

Note

Most of the database packages described rely upon third-party libraries that must be installed in addition to Python.

anydbm

Availability: A

The anydbm module provides a generic interface that's used to open a database without knowing which of the lower-level database packages are actually installed and available. When imported, it looks for one of the bsddb, gdbm, or dbm modules. If none are installed, the dumbdbm module is loaded.

A database object is created using the open() function:

```
open(filename [, flag [, mode]])
```

Opens the database file *filename* and returns a database object. If the database already exists, the whichdb module is used to determine its type and the corresponding database module to use. If the database doesn't exist, an attempt is made to create it using the first installed module in the above list of database modules. *flags* and *mode* are as described in the introduction to this section, "Data Management and Object Persistence" (p. 119).

Exception

error

A tuple containing the exceptions that can be raised by each of the supported database modules.

Programs wishing to catch errors should use this tuple as an argument to except. For example:

```
try:
    d = anydbm.open("foo","r")
except anydbm.error:
    # Handle error
```

Note

If the dumbdbm module is the only installed database module, attempts to reopen a previously created database with anydbm will fail. Use dumbdbm.open() instead.

▶ **See Also** dumbdbm (p. 123), whichdb (p. 124).

bsddb

Availability: Optional, U, W

The bsddb module provides an interface to the Berkeley DB library. Hash, btree, or record-based files can be created using the appropriate open() call:

hashopen(*filename* [, *flag* [, *mode*]])

Opens the hash format file named *filename*.

btopen(*filename* [, *flag* [, *mode*]])

Opens the btree format file named *filename*.

rnopen(*filename* [, *flag* [, *mode*]])

Opens a DB record format file named *filename*.

Databases created by this module behave like dictionaries as described in the introduction to this section and additionally provide methods for moving a "cursor" through records:

Method	Description
d.set_location(*key*)	Sets the cursor to the item indicated by the key and returns it.
d.first()	Sets the cursor to the first item in the database and returns it.
d.next()	Sets the cursor to the next item in the database and returns it.
d.previous()	Sets the cursor to the previous item in the DB file and returns it. Not supported on hashtable databases.
d.last()	Sets the cursor to the last item in the DB file and returns it. Not supported on hashtable databases.
d.sync()	Synchronizes the database on disk.

Exception

`error`

Exception raised on non–key-related database errors.

Notes

- This module uses the version 1.85 API of the Berkley DB package available at `http://www.sleepycat.com`.

- All the `open()` functions accept additional optional arguments that are rarely used. Consult the online documentation for details.

▶ See Also dbhash (p. 122),
`http://www.python.org/doc/lib/module-bsddb.html`.

dbhash

Availability: Optional, U, W

The `dbhash` module is used to open databases using the `bsddb` module, but with an interface that closely matches the interface of the other database modules.

`open(filename, flag [, mode])`

Opens a DB database and returns the database object.

A database object *d* returned by `open()` provides the following methods:

Method	Description
d.first()	Returns the first key in the database.
d.last()	Returns the last key in a database traversal.
d.next(*key*)	Returns the next key following *key* in the database.
d.previous(*key*)	Returns the item that comes before *key* in a forward traversal of the database.
d.sync()	Writes unsaved data to the disk.

Exception

`error`

Exception raised on database errors other than `KeyError`. Same as `bsddb.error`.

Note

The `bsddb` module must be installed.

▶ See Also bsddb (p. 121).

dbm

Availability: Optional, U

The `dbm` module provides an interface to the Unix dbm library.

`open(filename [, flag [, mode]])`

Opens a dbm database and returns a dbm object. *filename* is the name of the database file (without the `.dir` or `.pag` extension). The returned object behaves like a dictionary, as described in the section introduction ("Data Management and Object Persistence," p. 119).

Exception

error

Exception raised for dbm-specific errors other than KeyError.

▶ **See Also** anydbm (p. 120), gdbm (p. 123).

dumbdbm

Availability: A

The dumbdbm module is a simple DBM-style database implemented in Python. It should only be used when no other DBM database modules are available.

open(*filename* [, *flag* [, *mode*]])

Opens the database file *filename*. *filename* shouldn't include any suffixes such as .dat or .dir. The returned database object behaves like a dictionary, as described in the section introduction ("Data Management and Object Persistence," p.119).

Exception

error

Exception raised for database-related errors other than KeyError.

▶ **See Also** anydbm (p. 120), whichdb (p. 124).

gdbm

Availability: Optional, U, W

The gdbm module provides an interface to the GNU DBM library.

open(*filename* [, *flag* [, *mode*]])

Opens a gdbm database with filename *filename*. Appending "f" to the flag opens the database in fast mode. In this mode, altered data is not automatically written to disk after every change, resulting in better performance. If used, the sync() method should be used to force unwritten data to be written to disk on program termination.

A gdbm object *d* behaves like a dictionary as described in the section introduction ("Data Management and Object Persistence," p. 119), but also supports the following methods:

Method	Description
d.firstkey()	Returns the starting key in the database.
d.nextkey(*key*)	Returns the key that follows *key* in a traversal of the database.
d.reorganize()	Reorganizes the database and reclaims unused space. This can be used to shrink the size of the gdbm file after a lot of deletions have occurred.
d.sync()	Forces unwritten data to be written to disk.

Exception

error

    Exception raised for gdbm-specific errors.

Note

The GNU DBM library is available at www.gnu.org/software/gdbm/gdbm.html.
▶ See Also anydbm (p. 120), whichdb (p. 124).

shelve

Availability: A

The shelve module provides support for persistent objects using a special "shelf" object. This object behaves like a dictionary except that all the objects it contains are stored on disk using a database such as dbm or gdbm. A shelf is created using the shelve.open() function.

open(*filename*)

    Opens a shelf file. If the file doesn't exist, it's created. *filename* should be the database filename and not include a suffix. Returns a shelf object.

Once opened, the following dictionary operations can be performed on a shelf:

Operation	Description
d[*key*] = *data*	Stores data at *key*. Overwrites existing data.
data = d[*key*]	Retrieves data at *key*.
del *d*[*key*]	Deletes data at *key*.
d.has_key(*key*)	Tests for the existence of *key*.
d.keys()	Returns all keys.
d.close()	Closes the shelf.

The key values for a shelf must be strings. The objects stored in a shelf must be serializable using the pickle module.

Note

The shelve module differs from other database modules in that it allows almost any Python object to be stored.
▶ See Also pickle (p. 99), Chapter 9.

whichdb

Availability: A

The whichdb module provides a function that attempts to guess which of the several simple database modules (dbm, gdbm, or dbhash) should be used to open a database file.

whichdb(*filename*)

filename is a filename without any suffixes. Returns None if the file can't be opened because it's unreadable or doesn't exist. Returns the empty string if the file format can't be guessed. Otherwise, a string containing the required module name is returned, such as 'dbm' or 'gdbm'.

Notes

- This module may not work correctly with newer versions of the Berkeley DB.
- Databases created using the dumbdbm module are not recognized.

▶ **See Also** anydbm (p. 120).

Operating System Services

The modules in this section provide access to a wide variety of operating system services with an emphasis on file, process, and terminal management.

Note: A general familiarity with basic operating system concepts is assumed in this section. Furthermore, a number of modules provide advanced functionality that's beyond the scope of this book to introduce, but which is presented for readers who know what they're doing.

Most of Python's operating system modules are based on POSIX interfaces. POSIX is a standard that defines a core set of operating system interfaces. Most Unix systems support POSIX, and other platforms such as Windows and Macintosh support large portions of the interface.

Readers may want to supplement the material presented here with additional references. *The C Programming Language, Second Edition* by Brian W. Kernighan and Dennie M. Ritchie (Prentice Hall, 1989, ISBN 0-13-110362-8) provides a good overview of files, file descriptors, and the low-level interfaces on which many of the modules in this section are based. More advanced readers may want to consult a book such as W. Richard Stevens' *Advanced Programming in the Unix Environment* by (Addison Wesley, 1992, ISBN 0-201-56317-7). Background material regarding operating system concepts can be found in a text such as *Operating Systems Concepts, 5th Edition* by Abraham Silberschatz and Peter Baer Galvin (Addison Wesley, 1998, ISBN 0-201-59113-8). Threads and network programming are presented in separate sections of this appendix.

cmp

Availability: U, W, M

The cmp module is used to efficiently compare the contents of two files.

cmp(*filename1*, *filename2*)

Compares two files. Files are considered to be equivalent if they have identical types, sizes, and modification times. The contents of the files are not examined.

▶ **See Also** stat (p. 164).

commands

Availability: U

The commands module is used to execute system commands as a string and return their output as a string.

getoutput(*cmd*)

Executes *cmd* in a shell and returns a string containing both the standard output and standard error streams of the command.

getstatus(*filename*)

Returns the output of "ls -ld *filename*" as a string.

getstatusoutput(*cmd*)

Like getoutput() except that a 2-tuple (*status*, *output*) is returned, where *status* is the exit code as returned by the os.wait() function and *output* is the string returned by getoutput().

mkarg(*str*)

Turns *str* into an argument that can be safely used within a command string (using quoting rules of the shell).

Notes

■ The os.popen2() call is used to execute commands.

■ The returned output strings don't include a trailing newline.

▶ **See Also** os (p. 145), popen2 (p. 156).

crypt

Availability: U

The crypt module provides an interface to the Unix crypt() routine that's used to encrypt passwords.

crypt(*word*, *salt*)

Encrypts *word* using a modified DES algorithm. *salt* is a two-character seed used to initialize the algorithm. Returns the encrypted word as a string. Only the first eight characters of *word* are significant.

Example

The following code reads a password from the user and compares it against the value in the system password database:

```
import getpass
import pwd
import crypt
uname = getpass.getuser()         # Get username from environment
pw    = getpass.getpass()         # Get entered password
realpw = pwd.getpwnam(uname)[1]   # Get real password
entrpw = crypt.crypt(pw,realpw[:2])  # Encrypt
if realpw == entrpw:              # Compare
        print "Password Accepted"
else:
        print "Get lost."
```

▶ **See Also** pwd (p. 157), getpass (p. 136).

errno

Availability: U, W, M

The errno module defines symbolic names for the integer error codes returned by various operating system calls. These codes are typically found in the errno attribute of an OSError or IOError exception. The os.strerror() function can be used to translate an error code into a string error message. The following dictionary can also be used to translate an integer error code into its symbolic name:

errorcode

Dictionary mapping errno integers to symbolic names (such as 'EPERM').

The following list shows the POSIX symbolic names for many system error codes. Not all names are available on all machines. Some platforms may define additional codes. The codes U, W, M, and A are used to indicate availability of the following codes for Unix, Windows, Macintosh, and all platforms, respectively (doesn't include JPython):

Error Code	Platform	Description
E2BIG	A	Arg list too long.
EACCES	A	Permission denied.
EADDRINUSE	A	Address already in use.
EADDRNOTAVAIL	A	Cannot assign requested address.
EADV	U	Advertise error.
EAFNOSUPPORT	A	Address family not supported by protocol.
EAGAIN	A	Try again.
EALREADY	A	Operation already in progress.
EBADE	U	Invalid exchange.
EBADF	A	Bad file number.
EBADFD	U	File descriptor in bad state.
EBADMSG	U	Not a data message.
EBADR	U	Invalid request descriptor.
EBADRQC	U	Invalid request code.
EBADSLT	U	Invalid slot.
EBFONT	U	Bad font file format.
EBUSY	A	Device or resource busy.
ECHILD	A	No child processes.
ECHRNG	U	Channel number out of range.
ECOMM	U	Communication error on send.
ECONNABORTED	A	Software caused connection abort.
ECONNREFUSED	A	Connection refused.
ECONNRESET	A	Connection reset by peer.
EDEADLK	A	Resource deadlock would occur.
EDEADLOCK	U, W	File-locking deadlock error.

continues >>

>>continued

Error Code	Platform	Description
EDESTADDRREQ	A	Destination address required.
EDOM	A	Math argument out of domain of func.
EDOTDOT	U	RFS-specific error.
EDQUOT	A	Quota exceeded.
EEXIST	A	File exists.
EFAULT	A	Bad address.
EFBIG	A	File too large.
EHOSTDOWN	A	Host is down.
EHOSTUNREACH	A	No route to host.
EIDRM	U	Identifier removed.
EILSEQ	U	Illegal byte sequence.
EINPROGRESS	U, W	Operation now in progress.
EINTR	A	Interrupted system call.
EINVAL	A	Invalid argument.
EIO	A	I/O error.
EISCONN	A	Transport endpoint is already connected.
EISDIR	A	Is a directory.
EISNAM	U	Is a named type file.
EL2HLT	U	Level 2 halted.
EL2NSYNC	U	Level 2 not synchronized.
EL3HLT	U	Level 3 halted.
EL3RST	U	Level 3 reset.
ELIBACC	U	Cannot access a needed shared library.
ELIBBAD	U	Accessing a corrupted shared library.
ELIBEXEC	U	Cannot exec a shared library directly.
ELIBMAX	U	Attempting to link in too many shared libraries.
ELIBSCN	U	.lib section in a.out corrupted.
ELNRNG	U	Link number out of range.
ELOOP	A	Too many symbolic links encountered.
EMFILE	A	Too many open files.
EMLINK	U	Too many links.
EMSGSIZE	U	Message too long.
EMULTIHOP	U	Multihop attempted.
ENAMETOOLONG	U	Filename too long.
ENAVAIL	U	No XENIX semaphores available.
ENETDOWN	U	Network is down.
ENETRESET	U	Network dropped connection because of reset.

Error Code	Platform	Description
ENETUNREACH	U	Network is unreachable.
ENFILE	U	File table overflow.
ENOANO	U	No anode.
ENOBUFS	A	No buffer space available.
ENOCSI	U	No CSI structure available.
ENODATA	U	No data available.
ENODEV	A	No such device.
ENOENT	A	No such file or directory.
ENOEXEC	A	exec format error.
ENOLCK	A	No record locks available.
ENOLINK	U	Link has been severed.
ENOMEM	A	Out of memory.
ENOMSG	U	No message of desired type.
ENONET	U	Machine is not on the network.
ENOPKG	U	Package not installed.
ENOPROTOOPT	A	Protocol not available.
ENOSPC	A	No space left on device.
ENOSR	U	Out of streams resources.
ENOSTR	U	Device not a stream.
ENOSYS	A	Function not implemented.
ENOTBLK	U, M	Block device required.
ENOTCONN	A	Transport endpoint is not connected.
ENOTDIR	A	Not a directory.
ENOTEMPTY	A	Directory not empty.
ENOTNAM	U	Not a XENIX named type file.
ENOTSOCK	A	Socket operation on non-socket.
ENOTTY	A	Not a terminal.
ENOTUNIQ	U	Name not unique on network.
ENXIO	A	No such device or address.
EOPNOTSUPP	A	Operation not supported on transport endpoint.
EOVERFLOW	U	Value too large for defined data type.
EPERM	A	Operation not permitted.
EPFNOSUPPORT	A	Protocol family not supported.
EPIPE	A	Broken pipe.
EPROTO	U	Protocol error.
EPROTONOSUPPORT	A	Protocol not supported.
EPROTOTYPE	A	Protocol wrong type for socket.

continues >>

>>continued

Error Code	Platform	Description
ERANGE	A	Math result not representable.
EREMCHG	U	Remote address changed.
EREMOTE	U, M	Object is remote.
EREMOTEIO	U	Remote I/O error.
ERESTART	U	Interrupted system call should be restarted.
EROFS	U, M	Read-only file system.
ESHUTDOWN	U, M	Cannot send after transport endpoint shutdown.
ESOCKTNOSUPPORT	U, M	Socket type not supported.
ESPIPE	A	Illegal seek.
ESRCH	A	No such process.
ESRMNT	U	srmount error.
ESTALE	A	Stale NFS file handle.
ESTRPIPE	U	Streams pipe error.
ETIME	U	Timer expired.
ETIMEDOUT	A	Connection timed out.
ETOOMANYREFS	A	Too many references: Cannot splice.
ETXTBSY	U, M	Text file busy.
EUCLEAN	U	Structure needs cleaning.
EUNATCH	U	Protocol driver not attached.
EUSERS	A	Too many users.
EWOULDBLOCK	A	Operation would block.
EXDEV	A	Cross-device link.
EXFULL	U	Exchange full.
WSAEACCES	W	Permission denied.
WSAEADDRINUSE	W	Address already in use.
WSAEADDRNOTAVAIL	W	Cannot assign requested address.
WSAEAFNOSUPPORT	W	Address family not supported by protocol family.
WSAEALREADY	W	Operation already in progress.
WSAEBADF	W	Invalid file handle.
WSAECONNABORTED	W	Software caused connection abort.
WSAECONNREFUSED	W	Connection refused.
WSAECONNRESET	W	Connection reset by peer.
WSAEDESTADDRREQ	W	Destination address required.
WSAEDISCON	W	Remote shutdown.

Error Code	Platform	Description
WSAEDQUOT	W	Disk quota exceeded.
WSAEFAULT	W	Bad address.
WSAEHOSTDOWN	W	Host is down.
WSAEHOSTUNREACH	W	No route to host.
WSAEINPROGRESS	W	Operation now in progress.
WSAEINTR	W	Interrupted system call.
WSAEINVAL	W	Invalid argument.
WSAEISCONN	W	Socket already connected.
WSAELOOP	W	Cannot translate name.
WSAEMFILE	W	Too many open files.
WSAEMSGSIZE	W	Message too long.
WSAENAMETOOLONG	W	Name too long.
WSAENETDOWN	W	Network is down.
WSAENETRESET	W	Network dropped connection on reset.
WSAENETUNREACH	W	Network is unreachable.
WSAENOBUFS	W	No buffer space is available.
WSAENOPROTOOPT	W	Bad protocol option.
WSAENOTCONN	W	Socket is not connected.
WSAENOTEMPTY	W	Cannot remove non-empty directory.
WSAENOTSOCK	W	Socket operation on non-socket.
WSAEOPNOTSUPP	W	Operation not supported.
WSAEPFNOSUPPORT	W	Protocol family not supported.
WSAEPROCLIM	W	Too many processes.
WSAEPROTONOSUPPORT	W	Protocol not supported.
WSAEPROTOTYPE	W	Protocol wrong type for socket.
WSAEREMOTE	W	Item not available locally.
WSAESHUTDOWN	W	Cannot send after socket shutdown.
WSAESOCKTNOSUPPORT	W	Socket type not supported.
WSAESTALE	W	File handle no longer available.
WSAETIMEDOUT	W	Connection timed out.
WSAETOOMANYREFS	W	Too many references to a kernel object.
WSAEUSERS	W	Quota exceeded.
WSAEWOULDBLOCK	W	Resource temporaily unavailable.
WSANOTINITIALISED	W	Successful WSA Startup not performed.
WSASYSNOTREADY	W	Network subsystem not available.
WSAVERNOTSUPPORTED	W	Winsock.dll version out of range.

▶ **See Also** os (p. 145).

fcntl

Availability: U

The fcntl module performs file and I/O control on Unix file descriptors. File descriptors can be obtained using the fileno() method of a file or socket object. This module relies on a large number of constants defined in the FCNTL module (that should also be imported).

fcntl(fd, cmd [, arg])

Performs command *cmd* on an open file descriptor *fd*. *cmd* is an integer command code. *arg* is an optional argument that's either an integer or a string. If *arg* is passed as an integer, the return value of this function is an integer. If *arg* is a string, it's interpreted as a binary data structure, and the return value of the call is the contents of the buffer converted back into a string object. The following commands are available (these constants are defined in the FCNTL module):

Command	Description
F_DUPFD	Duplicates a file descriptor. *arg* is the lowest number that the new file descriptor can assume. Similar to the os.dup() system call.
F_SETFD	Sets the close-on-exec flag to *arg* (0 or 1). If set, the file is closed on an exec() system call.
F_GETFD	Returns the close-on-exec flag.
F_SETFL	Sets status flags to *arg*, which is the bitwise-or of the following: O_NDELAY—Nonblocking I/O (System V only). O_APPEND—Append mode (System V only). O_SYNC—Synchronous write (System V only). FNDELAY—Nonblocking I/O (BSD only). FAPPEND—Append mode (BSD only). FASYNC—Sends SIGIO signal to process group when I/O is possible (BSD only).
F_GETFL	Gets status flags as set by F_SETFL.
F_GETOWN	Gets process ID or process group ID set to receive SIGIO and SIGURG signals (BSD only).
F_SETOWN	Sets process ID or process group ID to receive SIGIO and SIGURG signals (BSD only).
F_GETLK	Returns flock structure used in file locking operations.
F_SETLK	Locks a file returning -1 if the file is already locked.
F_SETLKW	Locks a file, but waits if the lock can't be acquired.

An IOError exception is raised if the fcntl() function fails. The F_GETLK and F_SETLK commands are supported through the lockf() function.

ioctl(fd, op, arg)

This function is identical to the fcntl() function, except that the operations are defined in the library module IOCTL. The IOCTL module may be unavailable on some platforms.

flock(*fd*, *op*)

Performs a lock operation *op* on file descriptor *fd*. *op* is the bitwise-or of the following:

Item	Description
LOCK_EX	Exclusive lock.
LOCK_NB	Don't lock when locking.
LOCK_SH	Shared lock.
LOCK_UN	Unlock.

In non-blocking mode, an IOError exception is raised if the lock can't be acquired.

lockf(*fd*, *op* [, *len* [, *start* [, *whence*]]])

Performs record or range locking on part of a file. *op* is the same as for the flock() function. *len* is the number of bytes to lock. *start* is the starting position of the lock relative to the value of *whence*. *whence* is 0 for the beginning of the file, 1 for the current position, and 2 for the end of the file.

Examples

```
import fcntl, FCNTL

# Set the close-on-exec bit for a file object f
fcntl.fcntl(f.fileno(), FCNTL.F_SETFD, 1)

# Lock a file (blocking)
fcntl.flock(f.fileno(), FCNTL.LOCK_EX)

# Lock the first 8192 bytes of a file (non-blocking)
try:
    fcntl.lockf(f.fileno(), FCNTL.LOCK_EX ¦ FCNTL.LOCK_NB, 8192, 0, 0)
except IOError,e:
    print "Unable to acquire lock", e
```

Notes

- The set of available fcntl() commands and options is system-dependent.

- Many of the functions in this module can also be applied to the file descriptors of sockets (see socket, p. 202).

▶ **See Also** os (p. 145).

fileinput

Availability: A

The fileinput module iterates over a list of input files and reads their contents line by line. The main interface to the module is the following function:

input([*files* [, *inplace* [, *backup*]]])

Creates an instance of the FileInput class. *files* is an optional list of filenames to be read (a single filename is also permitted). If omitted, the filenames are read from the command line in sys.argv[1:]. An empty list implies input from stdin as does a filename of ' - '. If *inplace* is set to 1, each input file is moved to a backup file and `sys.stdout` is redirected to overwrite the original input file. The *backup* file is then removed when the output is closed. The backup option specifies a filename extension such as `.bak` that is appended to each filename in order to create the names of backup files. When given, the backup files are not deleted. By default, *backup* is the empty string and no backup files are created.

All `FileInput` instances have the following methods. These methods are also available as functions (which apply to the last instance created by the `input()` function).

Method	Description
`filename()`	Returns the name of the file currently being read.
`lineno()`	Returns the cumulative line number just read.
`filelineno()`	Returns the line number in the current file.
`isfirstline()`	Returns true if the line just read was the first line of a file.
`isstdin()`	Returns true if the input is `stdin`.
`nextfile()`	Closes the current file and skips to the next file.
`close()`	Closes the file sequence.

In addition, the `FileInput` instance returned by `input()` can be used as an iterator for reading all input lines.

Example

The following code reads and prints all the input lines from a list of files supplied on the command line:

```
import fileinput
for line in fileinput.input():
    print '%5d %s' % (fileinput.lineno(), line),
```

Notes

- All files opened by this module are opened in text mode.
- An `IOError` is raised if a file can't be opened.
- Empty files are opened and closed immediately.
- All lines returned include trailing newlines unless the last line of an input file doesn't include a newline.
- MS-DOS/Windows short filenames (eight characters plus a three-letter suffix) aren't supported.

▶ **See Also** `glob` (p. 137), `fnmatch` (p. 135).

findertools

Availability: M

The `findertools` module is used to access some of the functionality in the Macintosh finder. All file and folder parameters can be specified either as full pathname strings or as `FSSpec` objects as created using the `macfs` module.

launch(*file*)

Launches a file either by launching an application or by opening a document in the correct application.

Print(*file*)

Prints a file.

copy(*file*, *destdir*)

Copies *file* to the folder *destdir*.

move(*file*, *destdir*)

Moves *file* to the folder *destdir*.

sleep()

Puts the Macintosh to sleep (if supported).

restart()

Restarts the machine.

shutdown()

Shuts down the machine.

▶ **See Also** macfs (p. 140), macostools (p. 143).

fnmatch

Availability: A

The fnmatch module provides support for matching filenames using Unix shell-style wildcard characters:

Character(s)	Description
*	Matches everything.
?	Matches any single character.
[*seq*]	Matches any character in *seq*.
[!*seq*]	Matches any character not in *seq*.

The following functions can be used to test for a wildcard match:

fnmatch(*filename*, *pattern*)

Returns true or false depending on whether *filename* matches *pattern*. Case sensitivity depends on the operating system (and may be non–case-sensitive on certain platforms such as Windows).

fnmatchcase(*filename*, *pattern*)

Performs a case-sensitive comparison of *filename* against *pattern*.

Examples

```
fnmatch("foo.gif", "*.gif")        # Returns true
fnmatch("part37.html", "part3[0-5].html") # Returns false
```

▶ **See Also** glob (p. 137).

getopt

Availability: A

The getopt module is used to parse command-line options (typically passed in sys.argv).

getopt(args, options [, long_options])

Parses the command-line options supplied in the list *args*. *options* is a string of letters corresponding to the single-letter options that a program wants to recognize (for example, '-x'). If an option requires an argument, the option letter must be followed by a colon. If supplied, *long_options* is a list of strings corresponding to long option names. When supplied in *args*, these options are always preceded by a double hyphen (--) such as in '--exclude' (the leading -- is not supplied in *long_options*). Long option names requiring an argument should be followed by an equal sign (=). The function returns a list of (*option*, *value*) pairs matched and a list of program arguments supplied after all of the options. The options are placed in the list in the same order in which they were found. Long and short options can be mixed. Option names are returned with the leading hyphen (-) or double hyphen (--).

Exception

error

Exception raised when an unrecognized option is found or when an option requiring an argument is given none. The exception argument is a string indicating the cause of the error.

Example

```
>>> import getopt
>>> args = ['-a', '-b', 'foo', '--exclude','bar', 'x1', 'x2']
>>> opts, pargs = getopt.getopt(args, 'ab:', ['exclude='])
>>> opts
[('-a', ''), ('-b', 'foo'), ('--exclude', 'bar')]
>>> pargs
['x1', 'x2']
>>>
```

Note

Only single-letter command-line options can be recognized with a single hyphen (-). For example, '-a 3' is legal, but '-aa=3' isn't.

▶ **See Also** sys (p. 101).

getpass

Availability: U

The getpass module provides support for reading passwords and usernames.

getpass([prompt])

Prompts the user for a password without echoing. The default prompt is 'Password: '. Returns the entered password as a string.

getuser()

Returns the login name of the user by first checking the environment variables $LOGNAME, $USER, $LNAME, and $USERNAME and then checking the system password database. Raises a KeyError exception if no name can be found. Unix and Windows.

Notes

- An example of getpass is shown in the documentation for the crypt module.
- The getpass module depends on the termios module, which is disabled by default on some systems.

▶ **See Also** pwd (p. 157), crypt (p. 126).

glob

Availability: A

The glob module returns all filenames in a directory that match a pattern specified using the rules of the Unix shell (as described in the fnmatch module).

glob(*pattern*)

Returns a list of pathnames that match *pattern*.

Example

```
glob("*.html")
glob("image[0-5]*.gif")
```

Note

Tilde (~) and shell variable expansion is not performed. Use os.path.expanduser() and os.path.expandvars() to perform these expansions prior to calling glob().

▶ **See Also** fnmatch (p. 135), os.path (p. 154).

grp

Availability: U

The grp module provides access to the Unix group database.

getgrgid(*gid*)

Returns the group database entry for a group ID as a 4-tuple (*gr_name*, *gr_passwd*, *gr_gid*, *gr_mem*):

- *gr_name* is the group name.
- *gr_passwd* is the group password (if any)
- *gr_gid* is the integer group ID.
- *gr_mem* is a list of usernames in the group.

Raises KeyError if the group doesn't exist.

getgrnam(*name*)

Same as getgrgid(), but looks up a group by name.

getgrall()

Returns all available group entries as a list of tuples as returned by getgrgid().

▶ **See Also** pwd (p. 157).

gzip

Availability: Optional, U, W, M

The gzip module provides a class GzipFile that can be used to read and write files compatible with the GNU gzip program. GzipFile objects work like ordinary files except that data is automatically compressed or decompressed.

GzipFile([*filename* [, *mode* [, *compresslevel* [, *fileobj*]]]])

Opens a GzipFile. *filename* is the name of a file and *mode* is one of 'r', 'rb', 'a', 'ab', 'w', or 'wb'. The default is 'rb'. *compresslevel* is an integer from 1 to 9 that controls the level of compression. 1 is the fastest and produces the least compression. 9 is the slowest and produces the most compression (the default). *fileobj* is an existing file object that should be used. If supplied, it's used instead of the file named by *filename*.

open(*filename* [, *mode* [, *compresslevel*]])

Same as GzipFile(*filename, mode, compresslevel*). The default mode is 'rb'. The default *compresslevel* is 9.

Notes

- Calling the close() method of a GzipFile object doesn't close files passed in *fileobj*. This allows additional information to be written to a file after the compressed data.

- Files produced by the Unix compress program are not supported.

- This module requires the zlib module.

▶ **See Also** zlib (p. 173).

locale

Availability: U

The locale module provides access to the POSIX locale database, which allows programmers to handle certain cultural issues in an application without knowing all of the specifics of each country where the software is executed. A "locale" defines a set of parameters that describe the representation of strings, time, numbers, and currency. These parameters are grouped into the following category codes:

Category	Description
LC_CTYPE	Character conversion and comparison.
LC_COLLATE	String sorting. Affects strcoll() and strxfrm().
LC_TIME	Time formatting. Affects time.strftime().
LC_MONETARY	Formatting of monetary values.

Category	Description
LC_MESSAGES	Message display. This may affect error messages returned by functions such as os.strerror().
LC_NUMERIC	Number formatting. Affects format(), atoi(), atof(), and str().
LC_ALL	A combination of all locale settings.

The following functions are available:

setlocale(*category* [, *locale*])

If *locale* is specified, this function changes the locale setting for a particular category. *locale* is a string that specifies the locale name. If set to "C", the portable locale is selected (the default). If the empty string, the default locale from the user's environment is selected. If *locale* is omitted, a string representing the setting for the given category is returned. Raises the exception locale.Error on failure.

localeconv()

Returns the database of local conventions as a dictionary.

strcoll(*string1*, *string2*)

Compares two strings according to the current LC_COLLATE setting. Returns a negative, positive, or zero value depending on whether *string1* collates before or after *string2* or is equal to it.

strxfrm(*string*)

Transforms a string to one that can be used for the built-in function cmp() and still return locale-aware results.

format(*format*, *val* [, *grouping* = 0])

Formats a number *val* according to the current LC_NUMERIC setting. The *format* follows the conventions of the % operator. For floating-point values, the decimal point is modified if appropriate. If *grouping* is true, the locale grouping is taken into account.

str(*float*)

Formats a floating-point number using the same format as the built-in function str(float), but takes the decimal point into account.

atof(*string*)

Converts a string to a floating-point number according to the LC_NUMERIC settings.

atoi(*string*)

Converts a string to an integer according to the LC_NUMERIC conventions.

Exception

Error

Raised on failure of the setlocale() function.

Note

Additional information is available in the online library reference.

▶ **See Also** http://www.python.org/doc/lib/module-locale.html.

macfs

Availability: M

The macfs module is used to manipulate files and aliases on the Macintosh. For any function or method that expects a file argument, the argument may be a full or partial Macintosh pathname string, an FSSpec object, or a 3-tuple (wdRefNum, parID, name).

FSSpec(file)

Creates an FSSpec object for the specified file.

RawFSSpec(data)

Creates an FSSpec object given the raw data for the underlying FSSpec C data structure as a string.

RawAlias(data)

Creates an Alias object given the raw data for the underlying alias C data structure as a string.

FInfo()

Creates a zero-filled FInfo object.

ResolveAliasFile(file)

Resolves an alias file. Returns a 3-tuple (fsspec, isfolder, aliased) where fsspec is the resulting FSSpec object, isfolder is true if fsspec points to a folder, and aliased is true if the file was an alias.

StandardGetFile([type1 [, type2 [, ...]]])

Presents an "open input file" dialog and requests the user to select a file. Up to four four-character file types can be passed to limit the types of files from which the user can choose. Returns a tuple containing an FSSpec object and a flag indicating whether the user completed the dialog without canceling.

PromptGetFile(prompt [, type1 [, type2, ...]])

Similar to StandardGetFile() but allows a prompt to be specified.

StandardPutFile(prompt [, default])

Presents an "open output file" dialog and requests the user to select a filename. prompt is a prompt string and default is the default filename. Returns a tuple containing an FSSpec object and a flag indicating whether the user completed the dialog without canceling.

GetDirectory([prompt])

Presents a "select a directory" dialog. prompt is a prompt string. Returns a tuple containing an FSSpec object and a success indicator.

SetFolder([fsspec])

Sets the folder that's initially presented to the user when one of the file selection dialogs is presented. fsspec should point to a file in the folder, not the folder itself (the file need not exist, though). If no argument is passed, the folder will be set to the current directory.

FindFolder(where, which, create)

Locates a special Macintosh folder such as the Trash or Preferences folder. where is the disk to search and is typically set to MACFS.kOnSystemDisk, which is a four-character string specifying the folder to locate (these strings are often specified using one of the symbols in the following table), and *create*, if set to 1, causes the folder to be created if it doesn't exist. Returns a tuple (vrefnum, dirid). The contents of this tuple can be used as the first two elements of the 3-tuple (vrefnum,dirid,name) suitable for use as a filename.

The following list shows the symbolic names in the MACFS module used for the *which* parameter of FindFolder():

kALMLocationsFolderType	kMacOSReadMesFolderType
kALMModulesFolderType	kModemScriptsFolderType
kALMPreferencesFolderType	kOpenDocEditorsFolderType
kAppleExtrasFolderType	kOpenDocFolderType
kAppleMenuFolderType	kOpenDocLibrariesFolderType
kApplicationAliasType	kOpenDocShellPlugInsFolderType
kApplicationSupportFolderType	kPreferencesFolderType
kApplicationsFolderType	kPrintMonitorDocsFolderType
kAssistantsFolderType	kPrinterDescriptionFolderType
kChewableItemsFolderType	kPrinterDriverFolderType
kColorSyncProfilesFolderType	kScriptingAdditionsFolderType
kContextualMenuItemsFolderType	kSharedLibrariesFolderType
kControlPanelDisabledFolderType	kShutdownItemsDisabledFolderType
kControlPanelFolderType	kStartupFolderType
kControlStripModulesFolderType	kStartupItemsDisabledFolderType
kDesktopFolderType	kStationeryFolderType
kDocumentsFolderType	kSystemExtensionDisabledFolderType
kEditorsFolderType	kSystemFolderType
kExtensionDisabledFolderType	kTemporaryFolderType
kExtensionFolderType	kTextEncodingsFolderType
kFavoritesFolderType	kThemesFolderType
kFontsFolderType	kTrashFolderType
kGenEditorsFolderType	kUtilitiesFolderType
kHelpFolderType	kVoicesFolderType
kInternetPlugInFolderType	kVolumeRootFolderType
	kWhereToEmptyTrashFolderType

NewAliasMinimalFromFullPath(*pathname*)

Returns a minimal alias object that points to the given file, which must be specified as a full pathname. This is the only way to create an alias pointing to a nonexisting file.

FindApplication(*creator*)

Locates the application with the four-character creator code *creator*. The function returns an FSSpec object pointing to the application.

An instance *f* of an FSSpec object has the following attributes and methods:

f.data

The raw data from the underlying FSSpec object.

f.as_pathname()

Returns the full pathname.

f.as_tuple()

Returns the (*wdRefNum*, *parID*, *name*) tuple of the file.

f.NewAlias([*file*])

Creates an Alias object pointing to the file described by *f*. If the optional *file* parameter is given, the alias is created relative to that file; otherwise, it's absolute.

f.NewAliasMinimal()

Creates a minimal alias pointing to this file.

f.GetCreatorType()

Returns the four-character creator code and file type.

f.SetCreatorType(*creator*, *type*)

Sets the four-character *creator* and *type* of the file.

f.GetFInfo()

Returns a FInfo object describing the finder information for the file.

f.SetFInfo(*finfo*)

Sets the finder info for the file to the values in the FInifo object *finfo*.

f.GetDates()

Returns a tuple with three floating-point values representing the creation date, modification date, and backup date of the file.

f.SetDates(*crdate*, *moddate*, *backupdate*)

Sets the creation, modification, and backup dates of the file.

An Alias object *a* has the following attributes and methods:

a.data

The raw data for the Alias record as a binary string.

a.Resolve([*file*])

Resolves the alias and returns a tuple containing the FSSpec for the file pointed to and a flag indicating whether the Alias object was modified during the search process. If the file doesn't exist but the path leading up to it does, a valid *fsspec* is returned. *file* is an optional file that must be supplied if the alias was originally created as a relative alias.

a.GetInfo(*index*)

Retrieves alias information. *index* is an integer code that specifies the information to retrieve, and is one of the following values:

Value	Description
-3	Zone name.
-2	Server name.
-1	Volume name.
0	Target name.
1	Parent directory name.

a.Update(*file* [, *file2*])

Updates the alias to point to *file*. If *file2* is present, a relative alias will be created.

An FInfo object *finfo* has the following attributes:

finfo.Creator

The four-character creator code of the file.

finfo.Type

The four-character type code of the file.

***finfo*.Flags**

The finder flags for the file as 16-bit integers. The bit values in Flags are defined by the following constants defined in the module MACFS: kHasBeenInited, kHasBundle, kHasCustomIcon, kIsAlias, kIsInvisible, kIsOnDesk, kIsShared, kIsStationary, kNameLocked.

***finfo*.Location**

A pointer giving the position of the file's icon in its folder.

***finfo*.Fldr**

The folder the file is in (as an integer).

> ▶ **See Also** macostools (p. 143), findertools (p. 134),
> http://www.python.org/doc/mac (Macintosh Library Reference).

macostools

Availability: M

The macostools module contains functions for file manipulation on the Macintosh.

copy(*src, dst* [, *createpath* [, *copytimes*]])

Copies file *src* to *dst*. If *createpath* is nonzero, *dst* must be a pathname, and the folders leading to the destination are created if necessary. By default, the data and resource forks are copied in addition to some finder information. If *copytimes* is nonzero, the creation, modification, and backup times are copied as well. Custom icons, comments, and icon positions are not copied. If *src* is an alias, the original to which the alias points is copied, not the alias file.

copytree(*src, dst*)

Recursively copies a file tree from *src* to *dst*, creating folders as needed. *src* and *dst* must be pathname strings.

mkalias(*src, dst*)

Creates a finder alias *dst* pointing to *src*.

touched(*dst*)

Tells the finder that the finder information of *dst* has changed and that the finder should update the file's icon and other currently viewable information.

BUFSIZ

The buffer size used for copying (in bytes). The default is 1 megabyte.

Note

Except for copytree(), filenames can be specified as strings or as FSSpec objects created by the macfs module.

> ▶ **See Also** macfs (p. 140).

msvcrt

Availability: W

The msvcrt module provides access to a number of useful functions in the Microsoft Visual C++ runtime library.

getch()

Reads a keypress and returns the resulting character. This call blocks if a keypress is not available. If the pressed key was a special function key, the call returns '\000' or '\xe0' and the next call returns the keycode. This function doesn't echo characters to the console, nor can the function be used to read Ctrl+C.

getche()

The same as getch() except that characters are echoed (if printable).

get_osfhandle(fd)

Returns the file handle for the file descriptor fd. Raises IOError if fd is not recognized.

heapmin()

Forces the internal Python memory manager to return unused blocks to the operating system. It works only on Windows NT and raises IOError on failure.

kbhit()

Returns true if a keypress is waiting to be read.

locking(fd, mode, nbytes)

Locks part of a file given a file descriptor from the C runtime. nbytes is the number of bytes to lock relative to the current file pointer. mode is one of the following integers:

Setting	Description
0	Unlocks the file region (LK_UNLCK).
1	Locks the file region (LK_LOCK).
2	Locks the file region; nonblocking (LK_NBLCK).
3	Locks for writing (LK_RLCK).
4	Locks for writing; nonblocking (LK_NBRLCK).

Attempts to acquire a lock that take more than approximately 10 seconds result in an error.

open_osfhandle(handle, flags)

Creates a C runtime file descriptor from the file handle handle. flags is the bitwise-or of os.O_APPEND, os.O_RDONLY, and os.O_TEXT. Returns an integer file descriptor that can be used as a parameter to os.fdopen() to create a file object.

putch(char)

Print the character char to the console without buffering.

setmode(fd, flags)

Sets the line-end translation mode for the file descriptor fd. flags is os.O_TEXT for text mode and os.O_BINARY for binary mode.

ungetch(char)

Causes the character char to be "pushed back" into the console buffer. It will be the next character read by getch() or getche().

Note

A wide variety of Win32 extensions are available that provide access to the Microsoft Foundation Classes, COM components, graphical user interfaces, and so forth. These topics are far beyond the scope of this book, but detailed information about many of these topics is available in *Python Programming on Win32* by Mark Hammond and Andy Robinson (O'Reilly & Associates, 1999, ISBN 1-56592-621-8). http://www.python.org also maintains an extensive list of contributed modules for use under Windows.

os

Availability: A

The os module provides a portable interface to common operating system services. It does this by searching for an OS-dependent built-in module such as mac or posix and exporting the functions and data as found there. Unless otherwise noted, functions are available on Windows, Macintosh, and Unix.

The following general-purpose variables are defined:

environ

A mapping object representing the current environment variables. Changes to the mapping are reflected in the current environment.

linesep

The string used to separate lines on the current platform. May be a single character such as '\n' for POSIX or '\r' for MacOS, or multiple characters such as '\r\n' for Windows.

name

The name of the OS-dependent module imported: 'posix', 'nt', 'dos', 'mac', or 'os2'.

path

The OS-dependent standard module for pathname operations. This module can also be loaded using import os.path.

Process Environment

The following functions are used to access and modify various parameters related to the environment in which a process runs. Process, group, process group, and session IDs are integers unless otherwise noted.

chdir(*path*)

Changes the current working directory to *path*.

getcwd()

Returns a string with the current working directory.

getegid()

Returns the effective group ID. Unix.

geteuid()

Returns the effective user ID. Unix.

getgid()

Returns the real group ID of the process. Unix.

getpgrp()

Returns the ID of the current process group. Process groups are typically used in conjunction with job control. The process group is not the same as the group ID of the process. Unix.

getpid()

Returns the real process ID of the current process. Unix and Windows.

getppid()

Returns the process ID of the parent process. Unix.

getuid()

Returns the real user ID of the current process. Unix.

putenv(*varname, value*)

Sets environment variable *varname* to *value*. Changes affect subprocesses started with os.system(), popen(), fork(), and execv(). Assignments to items in os.environ automatically call putenv(). However, calls to putenv() don't update os.environ. Unix and Windows.

setgid(*gid*)

Sets the group ID of the current process. Unix.

setpgrp()

Creates a new process group by calling the system call setpgrp() or setpgrp(0, 0) depending on which version is implemented (if any). Returns the ID of the new process group. Unix.

setpgid(*pid, pgrp*)

Assigns process *pid* to process group *pgrp*. Unix.

setsid()

Creates a new session and returns the newly created session ID. Sessions are typically associated with terminal devices and the job control of processes that are started within them. Unix.

setuid(*uid*)

Sets the real user ID of the current process. This function is privileged and often can be performed only by processes running as root. Unix.

strerror(*code*)

Returns the error message corresponding to the integer error *code*. Unix and Windows. See the module errno.

umask(*mask*)

Sets the current numeric umask and returns the previous umask. The umask is used to clear permissions bits on files created by the process. See the os.open() function. Unix and Windows.

uname()

Returns a tuple of strings (*sysname, nodename, release, version, machine*) identifying the system type. Unix.

File Creation and File Descriptors

The following functions provide a low-level interface for manipulating files and pipes. In these functions, files are manipulated in terms of an integer file descriptor fd. The file descriptor can be extracted from a file object by invoking its fileno() method.

close(fd)

Closes file descriptor fd previously returned by open() or pipe().

dup(fd)

Duplicates the file descriptor fd. Returns a new file descriptor that's the lowest-numbered unused file descriptor for the process. The new and old file descriptors can be used interchangeably. Furthermore, they share states such as the file pointer and locks. Unix and Windows.

dup2(oldfd, newfd)

Duplicates file descriptor oldfd to newfd. If newfd already corresponds to a valid file descriptor, it's closed first. Unix and Windows.

fdopen(fd [, mode [, bufsize]])

Creates an open file object connected to the file descriptor fd. The mode and bufsize arguments have the same meaning as in the built-in open() function.

fstat(fd)

Returns the status for file descriptor fd. Returns the same values as the os.stat() function. Unix and Windows.

fstatvfs(fd)

Returns information about the file system containing the file associated with file descriptor fd. Returns the same values as the os.statvfs() function. Unix.

ftruncate(fd, length)

Truncates the file corresponding to file descriptor fd, so that it's at most length bytes in size. Unix.

lseek(fd, pos, how)

Sets the current position of file descriptor fd to position pos. Values of how are as follows: 0 sets the position relative to the beginning of the file, 1 sets it relative to the current position, and 2 sets it relative to the end of the file.

open(file [, flags [, mode]])

Opens the file file. flags is the bitwise-or of the following constant values:

Value	Description
O_RDONLY	Opens the file for reading.
O_WRONLY	Opens the file for writing.
O_RDWR	Opens for reading and writing (updates).
O_APPEND	Appends bytes to the end of the file.
O_CREAT	Creates the file if it doesn't exist.
O_NONBLOCK	Don't block on open, read, or write (Unix).
O_NDELAY	Same as O_NONBLOCK (Unix).
O_DSYNC	Synchronous writes (Unix).

continues >>

>>continued

Value	Description
O_NOCTTY	When opening a device, don't set controlling terminal (Unix).
O_TRUNC	If the file exists, truncates to zero length.
O_RSYNC	Synchronous reads (Unix).
O_SYNC	Synchronous writes (Unix).
O_EXCL	Error if O_CREAT and the file already exists.
O_TEXT	Text mode (Windows).
O_BINARY	Binary mode (Windows).

Synchronous I/O modes (O_SYNC, O_DSYNC, O_RSYNC) force I/O operations to block until they've been completed at the hardware level (for example, a write will block until the bytes have been physically written to disk). The mode parameter contains the file permissions represented as the bitwise-or of the following octal values:

Mode	Meaning
0100	User has execute permission.
0200	User has write permission.
0400	User has read permission.
0010	Group has execute permission.
0020	Group has write permission.
0040	Group has read permission.
0001	Others have execute permission.
0002	Others have write permission.
0004	Others have read permission.

The default mode of a file is (0777 & ~umask) where the umask setting is used to remove selected permissions. For example, a umask of 0022 removes write permission for groups and others. The umask can be changed using the os.umask() function. The umask setting has no effect on Windows and Macintosh.

pipe()

Creates a pipe that can be used to establish unidirectional communication with another process. Returns a pair of file descriptors (r, w) usable for reading and writing, respectively. This function is usually called prior to executing a fork() function. After the fork(), the sending process closes the read end of the pipe and the receiving process closes the write end of the pipe. At this point, the pipe is activated and data can be sent from one process to another using read() and write() functions. Unix.

popen(command [, mode [, bufsize]])

Opens a pipe to or from a command. The return value is an open file object connected to the pipe, which can be read or written depending on whether mode is 'r' (the default) or 'w'. bufsize has the same meaning as in the built-in open() function. The exit status of the command is returned by the close() method of the returned file object, except that when the exit status is zero, None is returned. Unix.

read(*fd*, *n*)

Reads at most *n* bytes from file descriptor *fd*. Returns a string containing the bytes read.

tcgetpgrp(*fd*)

Returns the process group associated with the control terminal given by *fd*. Unix.

tcsetpgrp(*fd*, *pg*)

Sets the process group associated with the control terminal given by *fd*. Unix.

ttyname(*fd*)

Returns a string that specifies the terminal device associated with the file descriptor *fd*. If *fd* isn't associated with a terminal device, an exception is raised. Unix.

write(*fd*, *str*)

Writes the string *str* to the file descriptor *fd*. Returns the number of bytes actually written.

Files and Directories

The following functions and variables are used to manipulate files and directories on the file system. To handle variances in file-naming schemes, the following variables contain information about the construction of pathnames.

Variable	Description
altsep	An alternative character used by the OS to separate pathname components, or None if only one separator character exists. This is set to '/' on DOS and Windows systems, where *sep* is a backslash.
curdir	The string used to refer to the current working directory: '.' for Unix and Windows and ':' for the Macintosh.
pardir	The string used to refer to the parent directory: '..' for Unix and Windows and ':::' for the Macintosh.
pathsep	The character used to separate search path components (as contained in the $PATH environment variable): ':' for Unix and ';' for DOS and Windows.
sep	The character used to separate pathname components: '/' for Unix and Windows and ':' for the Macintosh.

The following functions are used to manipulate files:

access(*path*, *accessmode*)

Checks read/write/execute permissions for this process or file path. *accessmode* is R_OK, W_OK, X_OK, or F_OK for read, write, execute, or existence, respectively. Returns 1 if access is granted, 0 if not. Unix.

chmod(*path*, *mode*)

Changes the mode of *path*. *mode* has the same values as described for the open() function. Unix and Windows.

chown(*path*, *uid*, *gid*)

Changes the owner and group ID of *path* to the numeric *uid* and *gid*. Unix.

getbootvol()

Returns the name of the boot disk. Macintosh.

`link(src, dst)`

Creates a hard link named *dst* that points to *src*. Unix.

`listdir(path)`

Returns a list containing the names of the entries in the directory *path*. The list is returned in arbitrary order and doesn't include the special entries of '.' and '..'.

`lstat(path)`

Like `stat()`, but doesn't follow symbolic links. Unix.

`mkfifo(path [, mode])`

Creates a FIFO (a named pipe) named *path* with numeric mode *mode*. The default mode is `0666`. Unix.

`mkdir(path [, mode])`

Creates a directory named *path* with numeric mode *mode*. The default mode is `0777`, although it may be ignored on some systems.

`makedirs(path [, mode])`

Recursive directory-creation function. Like `mkdir()`, but makes all the intermediate-level directories needed to contain the leaf directory. Raises an `OSError` exception if the leaf directory already exists or can't be created.

`readlink(path)`

Returns a string representing the path to which a symbolic link *path* points. Unix.

`remove(path)`

Removes the file *path*. This is identical to the `unlink()` function.

`removedirs(path)`

Recursive directory-removal function. Works like `rmdir()` except that, if the leaf directory is successfully removed, directories corresponding to the rightmost path segments will be pruned away until either the whole path is consumed or an error is raised (which is ignored, because it generally means that a parent directory isn't empty). Raises an `OSError` exception if the leaf directory couldn't be removed successfully.

`rename(src, dst)`

Renames the file or directory *src* to *dst*.

`renames(old, new)`

Recursive directory- or file-renaming function. Works like `rename()` except first attempting to create any intermediate directories needed to make the new pathname. After the rename, directories corresponding to the rightmost path segments of the old name will be pruned away using `removedirs()`.

`rmdir(path)`

Removes the directory *path*.

`stat(path)`

Performs a `stat()` system call on the given *path* to extract information about a file. The return value is a tuple of at least 10 integers in the order `st_mode`, `st_ino`, `st_dev`, `st_nlink`, `st_uid`, `st_gid`, `st_size`, `st_atime`, `st_mtime`, `st_ctime`. More items may be added at the end by some implementations, and on non–Unix platforms some items are filled with dummy values. The standard module `stat` defines functions and constants that are useful for extracting information from a `stat` tuple.

statvfs(path)

Performs a statvfs() system call on the given *path* to get information about the file system. The return value is a tuple of 10 integers in the order f_bsize, f_frsize, f_blocks, f_bfree, f_bavail, f_files, f_ffree, f_favail, f_flag, f_namemax. The standard module statvfs defines constants that can be used to extract information from the returned statvfs data. Unix.

symlink(src, dst)

Creates a symbolic link named *dst* that points to *src*.

sync()

Syncs the file system. Macintosh.

unlink(path)

Removes the file *path*. This is the same as remove().

utime(path, (atime, mtime))

Sets the access and modified time of the file to the given values. (The second argument is a tuple of two items.) The time arguments are specified in terms of the numbers returned by the time.time() function.

xstat(path)

The same as stat(), but the returned tuple includes three additional fields containing the size of the resource fork and the four-character creator and type codes. Macintosh.

Process Management

The following functions and variables are used to create, destroy, and manage processes.

defpath

This variable contains the default search path used by the exec*p*() functions if the environment doesn't have a 'PATH' variable.

execl(path, arg0, arg1, ...)

Equivalent to execv(path, (arg0, arg1, ...)). Unix and Windows.

execle(path, arg0, arg1, ..., env)

Equivalent to execve(path, (arg0, arg1, ...), env). Unix and Windows.

execlp(path, arg0, arg1, ...)

Equivalent to execvp(path, (arg0, arg1, ...)). Unix and Windows.

execv(path, args)

Executes the executable program path with argument list *args*, replacing the current process (that is, the Python interpreter). The argument list may be a tuple or list of strings. Unix and Windows.

execve(path, args, env)

Executes a new program like execv(), but additionally accepts a dictionary *env* that defines the environment in which the program runs. *env* must be a dictionary mapping strings to strings. Unix and Windows.

execvp(path, args)

This is like execv(path, args) but duplicates the shell's actions in searching for an executable file in a list of directories. The directory list is obtained from environ['PATH']. Unix and Windows.

execvpe(*path*, *args*, *env*)

The same as execvp(), but with an additional environment variable as in the execve() function. Unix and Windows.

_exit(*n*)

Exits immediately to the system with status *n*, without performing any cleanup actions. *Note:* The standard way to exit is sys.exit(*n*). Unix and Windows.

fork()

Creates a child process. Returns 0 in the newly created child process and the child's process ID in the original process. The child process is a clone of the original process and shares many resources such as open files. Unix.

kill(*pid*, *sig*)

Sends the process *pid* the signal *sig*. A list of signal names can be found in the signal module. Unix.

nice(*increment*)

Adds an increment to the process's scheduling priority (the "niceness"). Returns the new niceness. Typically, users can only decrease the priority of a process, since increasing the priority requires root access. Unix.

plock(*op*)

Locks program segments into memory. The value of *op* (defined in <sys/lock.h>) determines which segments are locked. This function isn't available on all platforms and often can be performed only by a process with an effective user ID of root. Unix.

spawnv(*mode*, *path*, *args*)

Executes the program path in a new process, passing the arguments specified in *args* as command-line parameters. *args* can be a list or a tuple. *mode* is one of the following constants:

Constant	Description
P_WAIT	Executes the program and waits for it to terminate. Returns the program's exit code.
P_NOWAIT	Executes the program and returns the process handle.
P_NOWAITO	Same as P_NOWAIT.
P_OVERLAY	Executes the program and destroys calling process (same as the **exec** functions).
P_DETACH	Executes the program and detaches from it. The calling program continues to run, but can't wait for the spawned process.

spawnv() is available only on Windows.

spawnve(*mode*, *path*, *args*, *env*)

Executes the program path in a new process, passing the arguments specified in *args* as command-line parameters and the contents of the mapping *env* as the environment. *args* can be a list or a tuple. *mode* has the same meaning as described for spawn(). Windows.

system(*command*)

Executes the command (a string) in a subshell. On Unix, the return value is the exit status of the process as returned by wait(). On Windows, the exit code is always 0. Unix and Windows.

`times()`

Returns a 5-tuple of floating-point numbers indicating accumulated times in seconds. On Unix, the tuple contains the user time, system time, children's user time, children's system time, and elapsed real time. On Windows, the tuple contains the user time, system time, and zeros for the other three values. Unix and Windows. Not supported on Windows 95/98.

`wait([pid])`

Waits for completion of a child process and returns a tuple containing its pid and exit status. The exit status is a 16-bit number whose low byte is the signal number that killed the process, and whose high byte is the exit status (if the signal number is zero). The high bit of the low byte is set if a core file was produced. *pid*, if given, specifies the process to wait for. If omitted, `wait()` returns when any child process exits. Unix.

`waitpid(pid, options)`

Waits for a change in the state of a child process given by process ID *pid*, and returns a tuple containing its process ID and exit status indication (encoded as for `wait()`). *options* should be `0` for normal operation or `WNOHANG` to avoid hanging if no child process status is available immediately. This function can also be used to gather information about child processes that have only stopped executing for some reason (refer to the Unix man pages for `waitpid` for details). Unix.

The following functions take a process status code as returned by `waitpid()` and are used to examine the state of the process (Unix only).

`WIFSTOPPED(status)`

Returns true if the process has been stopped.

`WIFSIGNALED(status)`

Returns true if the process exited due to a signal.

`WIFEXITED(status)`

Returns true if the process exited using the `exit()` system call.

`WEXITSTATUS(status)`

If `WIFEXITED(status)` is true, returns the integer parameter to the `exit()` system call. Otherwise, the return value is meaningless.

`WSTOPSIG(status)`

Returns the signal that caused the process to stop.

`WTERMSIG(status)`

Returns the signal that caused the process to exit.

Exception

`error`

Exception raised when a function returns a system-related error. This is the same as the built-in exception `OSError`. The exception carries two values: `errno` and `strerr`. The first contains the integer error value as described for the `errno` module. The latter contains a string error message. For exceptions involving the file system, the exception also contains a third attribute, *filename*, which is the filename passed to the function.

Example

The following example uses the os module to implement a minimalistic Unix shell that can run programs and perform I/O redirection:

```python
import os, sys, string
print "Welcome to the Python Shell!"
while 1:
    cmd = string.split(raw_input('pysh % '))
    if not cmd: continue
    progname = cmd[0]
    outfile = None
    infile = None
    args = [progname]
    for c in cmd[1:]:
        if c[0] == '>':
            outfile = c[1:]
        elif c[0] == '<':
            infile = c[1:]
        else:
            args.append(c)
    # Check for a change in working directory
    if progname == 'cd':
        if len(args) > 1:
            try:
                os.chdir(args[1])
            except OSError,e:
                print e
        continue
    # Exit from the shell
    if progname == 'exit':
        sys.exit(0)
    # Spawn a process to run the command
    pid = os.fork()
    if not pid:
        # Open input file (redirection)
        if infile:
            ifd = os.open(infile,os.O_RDONLY)
            os.dup2(ifd,sys.stdin.fileno())
        # Open output file (redirection)
        if outfile:
            ofd = os.open(outfile,os.O_WRONLY | os.O_CREAT | os.O_TRUNC)
            os.dup2(ofd,sys.stdout.fileno())
        # Run the command
        os.execvp(progname, args)
    else:
        childpid,ec = os.wait(pid)
        if ec:
            print "Exit code ",ec
```

▶ **See Also** os.path (p. 154), stat (p. 164), statvfs (p. 165), time (p. 170), popen2 (p. 156), signal (p. 161), fcntl (p. 132).

os.path

Availability: A

The os.path module is used to manipulate pathnames in a portable manner. It's imported by the os module.

abspath(*path*)

Returns an absolute version of the pathname *path*, taking the current working directory into account. For example, abspath('../Python/foo') might return '/home/beazley/Python/foo'.

basename(*path*)

Returns the base name of pathname *path*. For example, basename('/usr/local/python') returns 'python'.

commonprefix(*list*)

Returns the longest string that's a prefix of all strings in *list*. If *list* is empty, returns the empty string.

dirname(*path*)

Returns the directory name of pathname *path*. For example, dirname('/usr/local/python') returns '/usr/local'.

exists(*path*)

Returns true if *path* refers to an existing path.

expanduser(*path*)

Replaces pathnames of the form '~*user*' with a user's home directory. If the expansion fails or *path* doesn't begin with '~', the path is returned unmodified.

expandvars(*path*)

Expands environment variables of the form '$*name*' or '${*name*}' in *path*. Malformed or nonexistent variable names are left unchanged.

getatime(*path*)

Returns the time of last access as the number of seconds since the epoch (see the time module).

getmtime(*path*)

Returns the time of last modification as the number of seconds since the epoch (see the time module).

getsize(*path*)

Returns the file size in bytes.

isabs(*path*)

Returns true if *path* is an absolute pathname (begins with a slash).

isfile(*path*)

Returns true if *path* is a regular file. This function follows symbolic links, so both islink() and isfile() can be true for the same path.

isdir(*path*)

Returns true if *path* is a directory. Follows symbolic links.

islink(*path*)

Returns true if *path* refers to a symbolic link. Returns false if symbolic links are unsupported.

ismount(*path*)

Returns true if *path* is a mount point.

join(path1 [, path2 [, ...]])

Intelligently joins one or more path components into a pathname. For example, join('/home', 'beazley', 'Python') returns '/home/beazley/Python'.

normcase(path)

Normalizes the case of a pathname. On non–case-sensitive file systems, this converts path to lowercase. On Windows, forward slashes are also converted to backslashes.

normpath(path)

Normalizes a pathname. This collapses redundant separators and up-level references so that 'A//B', 'A/./B', and 'A/foo/../B' all become 'A/B'. On Windows, forward slashes are converted to backslashes.

samefile(path1, path2)

Returns true if path1 and path2 refer to the same file or directory. Macintosh and Unix.

sameopenfile(fp1, fp2)

Returns true if the open file objects fp1 and fp2 refer to the same file. Macintosh and Unix.

samestat(stat1, stat2)

Returns true if the stat tuples stat1 and stat2 as returned by fstat(), lstat(), or stat() refer to the same file. Macintosh and Unix.

split(path)

Splits path into a pair (head, tail), where tail is the last pathname component and head is everything leading up to that. For example, '/home/user/foo' gets split into ('/home/user', 'foo'). This tuple is the same as would be returned by (dirname(), basename()).

splitdrive(path)

Splits path into a pair (drive, filename) where drive is either a drive specification or the empty string. drive is always the empty string on machines without drive specifications.

splitext(path)

Splits a pathname into a base filename and suffix. For example, splitext('foo.txt') returns ('foo', '.txt').

walk(path, visitfunc, arg)

This function recursively walks all the directories rooted at path and calls the function visitfunc(arg, dirname, names) for each directory. dirname specifies the visited directory and names is a list of the files in the directory as retrieved using os.listdir(dirname). The visitfunc function can modify the contents of names to alter the search process if necessary.

▶ **See Also** fnmatch (p. 135), glob (p. 137), os (p. 145).

popen2

Availability: U

The popen2 module is used to spawn processes and connect to their input/output/error streams using pipes.

popen2(*cmd* [, *bufsize*])

Executes *cmd* as a subprocess and returns a pair of file objects (*child_stdout*, *child_stdin*) corresponding to the input and output streams of the subprocess. *bufsize* specifies the buffer size for the I/O pipes.

popen3(*cmd* [, *bufsize*])

Executes *cmd* as a subprocess like popen2(), but returns a triple (*child_stdout*, *child_stdin*, *child_stderr*) that includes the standard error stream.

In addition to the functions just described, the following class can be used to control processes:

Popen3(*cmd* [, *capturestderr* [, *bufsize*]])

This class represents a child process. *cmd* is the shell command to execute in a subprocess. The *capturestderr* flag, if true, specifies that the object should capture standard error output of the child process. *bufsize* is the size of the I/O buffers.

An instance *p* of the Popen3 class has the following methods and attributes:

p.poll()

Returns the exit code of the child or -1 if the child process hasn't finished yet.

p.wait()

Waits for the child process to terminate and return its exit code.

p.fromchild

A file object that captures the output of the child process.

p.tochild

A file object that sends input to the child process.

p.childerr

A file object that captures the standard error stream of the child process. May be None.

Note

The order of file objects returned by popen2() and popen3() differs from the standard Unix ordering of *stdin*, *stdout*, and *stderr*.

▶ **See Also** commands (p. 126), os.popen (p. 148).

pwd

Availability: U

The pwd module provides access to the Unix password database.

getpwuid(*uid*)

Returns the password database entry for a numeric user ID *uid*. Returns a 7-tuple (*pw_name*, *pw_passwd*, *pw_uid*, *pw_gid*, *pw_gecos*, *pw_dir*, *pw_shell*). The *pw_uid* and *pw_gid* items are integers; all others are strings. KeyError is raised if the entry can't be found.

getpwnam(*name*)

Returns the password database entry for a username.

getpwall()

Returns a list of all available password database entries. Each entry is a tuple as returned by getpwduid().

Example

```
>>> import pwd
>>> pwd.getpwnam('beazley')
('beazley', 'x', 100, 1, 'David M. Beazley', '/home/beazley',
'/usr/local/bin/tcsh')
>>>
```

▶ **See Also** grp (p. 137), getpass (p. 136), crypt (p. 126).

readline

Availability: Optional, U

The readline module enables and provides an interface to the GNU readline library. This library extends Python's interactive mode with command history, command completion, and advanced editing capabilities. These features are also extended to functions such as raw_input() and input().

The readline module enables the following key bindings when running interactively:

Key(s)	Description
Ctrl+a	Moves to the start of the line.
Ctrl+b	Moves back one character.
Esc b	Moves back one word.
Esc c	Capitalizes the current word.
Ctrl+d	Deletes the character under the cursor.
Esc d	Kills to the end of the current word.
Del	Deletes the character to the left of the cursor.
Esc Del	Kills to the start of the previous word.
Ctrl+e	Moves to the end of the line.
Ctrl+f	Moves forward one character.
Esc f	Moves forward one word.
Ctrl+k	Kills the text to the end of the line.
Ctrl+l	Clears the screen.
Esc l	Converts the current word to lowercase.
Ctrl+n	Moves down through the history list.
Ctrl+p	Moves up through the history list.
Ctrl+r	Reverses incremental search through the history.
Ctrl+t	Transposes characters.
Esc t	Transposes words.
Esc u	Converts the current word to uppercase.
Ctrl+w	Kills from the cursor to the previous whitespace.
Ctrl+y	Yanks back the most recently killed text.

Key(s)	Description
Esc y	Rotates the kill-ring and yanks the new top.
Esc <	Goes to the first line in history.
Esc >	Goes to the last line in history.

Notes

- Key sequences involving Esc are sometimes available using the Meta key.
- Many commands accept a numeric argument that's entered by first typing Esc *nnn*. For example, typing Esc 5 0 Ctrl+f moves forward 50 characters.

> ▶ **See Also** rlcompleter
> (http://www.python.org/doc/lib/module-rlcompleter.html).

resource

Availability: Optional, U

The resource module is used to measure and control the system resources used by a program. Resource usage is limited using the setrlimit() function. Each resource is controlled by a soft limit and a hard limit. The *soft limit* is the current limit, and may be lowered or raised by a process over time. The *hard limit* can be lowered to any value greater than the soft limit, but never raised (except by the superuser).

getrlimit(*resource*)

Returns a tuple (*soft*, *hard*) with the current soft and hard limits of a resource. *resource* is one of the following symbolic constants:

Constant	Description
RLIMIT_CORE	The maximum core file size (in bytes).
RLIMIT_CPU	The maximum CPU time (in seconds). If exceeded, a SIGXCPU signal is sent to the process.
RLIMIT_FSIZE	The maximum file size that can be created.
RLIMIT_DATA	The maximum size (in bytes) of the process heap.
RLIMIT_STACK	The maximum size (in bytes) of the process stack.
RLIMIT_RSS	The maximum resident set size.
RLIMIT_NPROC	The maximum number of processes that can be created.
RLIMIT_NOFILE	The maximum number of open file descriptors.
RLIMIT_OFILE	The BSD name for RLIMIT_NOFILE.
RLIMIT_MEMLOC	The maximum memory size that can be locked in memory.
RLIMIT_VMEM	The largest area of mapped memory that can be used.
RLIMIT_AS	The maximum area (in bytes) of address space that can be used.

setrlimit(*resource*, *limits*)

Sets new limits for a resource. *limits* is a tuple (*soft*, *hard*) of two integers describing the new limits. A value of -1 can be used to specify the maximum possible upper limit.

getrusage(*who*)

This function returns a large tuple that describes the resources consumed by either the current process or its children. *who* is one of the following values:

Value	Description
RUSAGE_SELF	Information about the current process.
RUSAGE_CHILDREN	Information about child processes.
RUSAGE_BOTH	Information about both current and child processes.

The returned tuple contains system resource usage data in the following order:

Offset	Resource
0	Time in user mode (float).
1	Time in system mode (float).
2	Maximum resident set size (pages).
3	Shared memory size (pages).
4	Unshared memory size (pages).
5	Unshared stack size (pages).
6	Page faults not requiring I/O.
7	Page faults requiring I/O.
8	Number of swapouts.
9	Block input operations.
10	Block output operations.
11	Messages sent.
12	Messages received.
13	Signals received.
14	Voluntary context switches.
15	Involuntary context switches.

getpagesize()

Returns the number of bytes in a system page.

Exception

error

Exception raised for unexpected failures of the getrlimit() and setrlimit() system calls.

Note

Not all resource names are available on all systems.

▶ **See Also** Unix man pages for getrlimit(2).

shutil

Availability: A

The shutil module is used to perform high-level file operations such as copying, removing, and renaming.

copyfile(src, dst)

Copies the contents of src to dst.

copymode(src, dst)

Copies the permission bits from src to dst.

copystat(src, dst)

Copies the permission bits, last access time, and last modification time from src to dst. The contents, owner, and group of dst are unchanged.

copy(src, dst)

Copies the file src to the file or directory dst, retaining file permissions.

copy2(src, dst)

Similar to copy(); copies the last access and modification times as well.

copytree(src, dst [, symlinks])

Recursively copies an entire directory tree rooted at src. The destination directory dst will be created (and shouldn't already exist). Individual files are copied using copy2(). If symlinks is true, symbolic links in the source tree are represented as symbolic links in the new tree. If symlinks is false or omitted, the contents of linked files are copied to the new directory tree. Errors are reported to standard output.

rmtree(path [, ignore_errors [, onerror]])

Deletes an entire directory tree. If ignore_errors is true, errors will be ignored. Otherwise, errors are handled by the onerror function (if supplied). This function must accept three parameters (func, path, excinfo) where func is the function that caused the error (os.remove() or os.rmdir()), path is the pathname passed to the function, and excinfo is the exception information returned by sys.exc_info(). If an error occurs and onerror is omitted, an exception is raised.

Note

On MacOS, the resource fork is ignored on file copies.

▶ **See Also** os.path (p. 154), macostools (p. 143).

signal

Availability: U, W, M

The signal module is used to write signal handlers in Python. Signals usually correspond to asychronous events that are sent to a program due to the expiration of a timer, arrival of incoming data, or some action performed by a user. The signal interface emulates that of Unix, although the module is supported on other platforms.

alarm(*time*)

If *time* is nonzero, schedules a `SIGALRM` signal to be sent to the program in *time* seconds. Any previously scheduled alarm is canceled. If time is zero, no alarm is scheduled and any previously set alarm is canceled. Returns the number of seconds remaining before any previously scheduled alarm, or zero if no alarm was scheduled. Unix.

getsignal(*signalnum*)

Returns the signal handler for signal *signalnum*. The returned object is a callable Python object. The function may also return `signal.SIG_IGN` for an ignored signal, `signal.SIG_DFL` for the default signal handler, or `None` if the signal handler wasn't installed from the Python interpreter.

pause()

Goes to sleep until the next signal is received. Unix.

signal(*signalnum*, *handler*)

Sets a signal handler for signal *signalnum* to the function *handler*. *handler* must be a callable Python object taking two arguments: the signal number and frame object. `signal.SIG_IGN` or `signal.SIG_DFL` can also be given to ignore a signal or use the default signal handler, respectively. The return value is the previous signal handler, `signal.SIG_IGN`, or `signal.SIG_DFL`. When threads are enabled, this function can only be called from the main thread. Otherwise, a `ValueError` exception is raised.

Individual signals are identified using symbolic constants of the form `SIG*`. These names correspond to integer values that are machine specific. Typical values are as follows:

Signal Name	Description
SIGABRT	Abnormal termination.
SIGALRM	Alarm.
SIGBUS	Bus error.
SIGCHLD	Change in child status.
SIGCLD	Change in child status.
SIGCONT	Continue.
SIGFPE	Floating-point error.
SIGHUP	Hangup.
SIGILL	Illegal instruction.
SIGINT	Terminal interrupt character.
SIGIO	Asynchronous I/O.
SIGIOT	Hardware fault.
SIGKILL	Terminate.
SIGPIPE	Write to pipe, no readers.
SIGPOLL	Pollable event.
SIGPROF	Profiling alarm.
SIGPWR	Power failure.
SIGQUIT	Terminal quit character.
SIGSEGV	Segmentation fault.
SIGSTOP	Stop.

Signal Name	Description
SIGTERM	Termination.
SIGTRAP	Hardware fault.
SIGTSTP	Terminal stop character.
SIGTTIN	Control TTY.
SIGTTOU	Control TTY.
SIGURG	Urgent condition.
SIGUSR1	User defined.
SIGUSR2	User defined.
SIGVTALRM	Virtual time alarm.
SIGWINCH	Window size change.
SIGXCPU	CPU limit exceeded.
SIGXFSZ	File size limit exceeded.

In addition, the module defines the following variables:

Variable	Description
SIG_DFL	Signal handler that invokes the default signal handler.
SIG_IGN	Signal handler that ignores a signal.
NSIG	One more than the highest signal number.

Example

The following example illustrates a timeout on establishing a network connection:

```
import signal, socket
def handler(signum, frame):
    print 'Timeout!'
    raise IOError, "Host not responding."
sock = socket.socket(socket.AF_INET, socket.SOCK_STREAM)
signal.signal(signal.SIGALRM, handler)
signal.alarm(5)                      # 5-second alarm
sock.connect("www.python.org", 80)   # Connect
signal.alarm(0)                      # Clear alarm
```

Notes

- Signal handlers remain installed until explicitly reset, with the exception of SIGCHLD (whose behavior is implementation specific).

- It's not possible to temporarily disable signals.

- Signals are only handled between the atomic instructions of the Python interpreter. The delivery of a signal can be delayed by long-running calculations written in C (as might be performed in an extension module).

- If a signal occurs during an I/O operation, the I/O operation may fail with an exception. In this case, the errno value is set to errno.EINTR to indicate an interrupted system call.

- Certain signals such as SIGSEGV can't be handled from Python.

- Python installs a small number of signal handlers by default. SIGPIPE is ignored, SIGINT is translated into a KeyboardInterrupt exception, and SIGTERM is caught in order to perform cleanup and invoke sys.exitfunc.

- Extreme care is needed if signals and threads are used in the same program. Currently, only the main thread of execution can set new signal handlers or receive signals.

- Signal handling on Windows and Macintosh is of only limited functionality. The number of supported signals is extremely limited on these platforms.

▶ **See Also** thread (p. 175), errno (p. 127).

stat

Availability: U, W

The stat module defines constants and functions for interpreting the results of os.stat(), os.fstat() and os.lstat(). These functions return a 10-tuple containing file information. The following variables define the indices within the tuple for certain items:

Variable	Description
ST_MODE	Inode protection mode.
ST_INO	Inode number.
ST_DEV	Device the inode resides on.
ST_NLINK	Number of links to the inode.
ST_UID	User ID of the owner.
ST_GID	Group ID of the owner.
ST_SIZE	File size in bytes.
ST_ATIME	Time of last access.
ST_MTIME	Time of last modification.
ST_CTIME	Time of last status change.

The following functions can be used to test file properties given the mode value returned using os.stat(path)[stat.ST_MODE]:

Function	Description
S_ISDIR(mode)	Returns nonzero if mode is from a directory.
S_ISCHR(mode)	Returns nonzero if mode is from a character special device file.
S_ISBLK(mode)	Returns nonzero if mode is from a block special device file.
S_ISREG(mode)	Returns nonzero if mode is from a regular file.
S_ISFIFO(mode)	Returns nonzero if mode is from a FIFO (named pipe).
S_ISLNK(mode)	Returns nonzero if mode is from a symbolic link.
S_ISSOCK(mode)	Returns nonzero if mode is from a socket.

Function	Description
S_IMODE(*mode*)	Returns the portion of the file's mode that can be set by os.chmod(). This is the file's permission bits, sticky bit, set-group-ID, and set-user-ID bits.
S_IFMT(*mode*)	Returns the portion of the file's mode that describes the file type (used by the S_IS*() functions above).

Note

Much of the functionality in this module is also provided in a more portable form by the os.path module.

▶ **See Also** os (p. 145), os.path (p. 154), statvfs (p. 165).

statvfs

Availability: U

The statvfs module defines constants used to interpret the result of the os.statvfs() function. The constants defined in this module define the indices into the tuple returned by os.statvfs() for specific information.

Constant	Description
F_BSIZE	Preferred file system block size.
F_FRSIZE	Fundamental file system block size.
F_BFREE	Total number of free blocks.
F_BAVAIL	Free blocks available to a non-superuser.
F_FILES	Total number of file nodes.
F_FFREE	Total number of free file nodes.
F_FAVAIL	Free nodes available to a non-superuser.
F_FLAG	Flags; system-dependent.
F_NAMEMAX	Maximum filename length.

▶ **See Also** os (p. 145), stat (p. 164).

tempfile

Availability: A

The tempfile module is used to generate temporary filenames and files:

mktemp([*suffix*])

Returns a unique temporary filename. *suffix* is an optional file suffix to append to the filename. This function only generates a unique filename and doesn't actually create or open a temporary file.

TemporaryFile([*mode* [, *bufsize* [, *suffix*]]])

Creates a temporary file and returns a file-like object that supports the same methods as an ordinary file object. *mode* is the file mode and defaults to 'w+b'. *bufsize* specifies the buffering behavior and has the same meaning as for the open() function.

suffix is the suffix to append to the filename (if any). The object returned by this function is only a wrapper around a built-in file object that's accessible in the file attribute. The file created by this function is automatically destroyed when the temporary file object is destroyed.

Two global variables are used to construct temporary names. They can be assigned to new values if desired. Their default values are system dependent.

Variable	Description
tempdir	The directory in which filenames returned by mktemp() reside.
template	The prefix of filenames generated by mktemp(). A string of decimal digits is added to template to generate unique filenames.

termios

Availability: Optional, U

The termios module provides a POSIX-style interface for controlling the behavior of TTYs and other serial communication devices. All the functions operate on integer file descriptors such as those returned by the os.open() function or the fileno() method of a file object. In addition, the module relies on a large collection of constants that are defined in the TERMIOS module, which should also be loaded.

tcgetattr(fd)

Returns a list [*iflag, oflag, cflag, lflag, ispeed, ospeed, cc*] of TTY attributes for a file descriptor *fd*. The meaning of these fields is as follows:

Field	Description
iflag	Input modes (integer).
oflag	Output modes (integer).
cflag	Control modes (integer).
lflag	Local modes (integer).
ispeed	Input speed (integer).
ospeed	Output speed (integer).
cc	A list of control characters (as strings).

The mode fields *iflag*, *oflag*, *cflag*, and *lflag* are bit fields that are interpreted using constants in TERMIOS.

Input Modes

Mode	Description
TERMIOS.IGNBRK	Ignores break condition on input.
TERMIOS.BRKINT	Generates SIGINT signal on break if IGNBRK isn't set.
TERMIOS.IGNPAR	Ignores framing and parity errors.
TERMIOS.PARMRK	Marks characters with a parity error.
TERMIOS.INPCK	Enables input parity checking.

Mode	Description
TERMIOS.ISTRIP	Strips off the eighth bit.
TERMIOS.INLCR	Translates newlines to carriage returns.
TERMIOS.IGNCR	Ignores carriage returns.
TERMIOS.ICRNL	Translates carriage returns to newlines.
TERMIOS.IUCLC	Maps uppercase characters to lowercase.
TERMIOS.IXON	Enables XON/XOFF flow control on output.
TERMIOS.IXANY	Enables any character to restart output.
TERMIOS.IXOFF	Enables XON/XOFF flow control on input.
TERMIOS.IXMAXBEL	Rings bell when the input queue is full.

Output Modes

Mode	Description
TERMIOS.OPOST	Implementation-defined output processing.
TERMIOS.OLCUC	Maps lowercase to uppercase on output.
TERMIOS.ONLCR	Maps newlines to carriage returns.
TERMIOS.OCRNL	Maps carriage returns to newlines.
TERMIOS.ONLRET	Don't output carriage returns.
TERMIOS.OFILL	Sends fill characters for delay.
TERMIOS.OFDEL	Sets the fill character to ASCII DEL.
TERMIOS.NLDLY	Newline delay mask. Values are NL0 and NL1.
TERMIOS.CRDLY	Carriage return delay mask. Values are CR0, CR1, CR2, or CR3.
TERMIOS.TABDLY	Horizontal tab delay mask: TAB0, TAB1, TAB2, TAB3, or XTABS.
TERMIOS.BSDLY	Backspace delay mask: BS0 or BS1.
TERMIOS.VTDLY	Vertical tab delay mask: VT0 or VT1.
TERMIOS.FFDLY	Formfeed delay mask: FF0 or FF1.

Control Modes

Mode	Description
TERMIOS.CSIZE	Character size mask: CS5, CS6, CS7, or CS8.
TERMIOS.CSTOPB	Sets two stop bits.
TERMIOS.CREAD	Enables receiver.
TERMIOS.PARENB	Enables parity generation and checking.
TERMIOS.PARODD	Uses odd parity.
TERMIOS.HUPCL	Lowers modem control lines when device is closed.
TERMIOS.CLOCAL	Ignores modem control lines.
TERMIOS.CRTSCTS	Flow control.

Local Modes

Mode	Description
`TERMIOS.ISIG`	Generates corresponding signals when `INTR`, `QUIT`, `SUSP`, or `DSUSP` characters are received.
`TERMIOS.ICANON`	Enables canonical mode.
`TERMIOS.XCASE`	Performs case conversion if `ICANON` is set.
`TERMIOS.ECHO`	Echoes input characters.
`TERMIOS.ECHOE`	If `ICANON` is set, the `ERASE` character erases the preceding input character. `WERASE` erases the preceding word.
`TERMIOS.ECHOK`	If `ICANON` is set, the `KILL` character erases the current line.
`TERMIOS.ECHONL`	If `ICANON` is set, echoes newline (`NL`) characters.
`TERMIOS.ECHOCTL`	If `ECHO` is set, echoes control characters as `^X`.
`TERMIOS.ECHOPRT`	Prints characters as they're erased.
`TERMIOS.ECHOKE`	Echoes `KILL` by erasing each character one at a time.
`TERMIOS.FLUSHO`	Output is being flushed.
`TERMIOS.NOFLSH`	Disables flushing the input/output queues when generating the `SIGINT` and `SIGQUIT` signals.
`TERMIOS.TOSTOP`	Sends the `SIGTTOU` signal to the process group of a background process that writes its controlling terminal.
`TERMIOS.PENDIN`	Reprints all characters in the input queue when the next character is typed.
`TERMIOS.IEXTEN`	Enables implementation-defined input processing.

Speeds

Speeds are defined by constants such as `TERMIOS.B0`, `TERMIOS.B50`, `TERMIOS.B75`, and `TERMIOS.B230400` indicating a baud rate. The available values are implementation specific and defined in `TERMIOS`.

Control Characters

The following symbols in `TERMIOS` are indices into the `cc` list. This can be used to changed various key bindings.

Character	Description
`TERMIOS.VINTR`	Interrupt character (typically Ctrl+C).
`TERMIOS.VQUIT`	Quit.
`TERMIOS.VERASE`	Erases the preceding character (typically Del).
`TERMIOS.VWERASE`	Erases the preceding word (Ctrl+w).
`TERMIOS.VKILL`	Deletes the entire line.
`TERMIOS.VREPRINT`	Reprints all characters that haven't been read yet.
`TERMIOS.VEOF`	End of file (Ctrl+D).
`TERMIOS.VNL`	Line delimiter (line feed).

Character	Description
TERMIOS.VSUSP	Suspends (Ctrl+Z).
TERMIOS.VSTOP	Stops output (Ctrl+S).
TERMIOS.VSTART	Starts output (Ctrl+Q).

tcsetattr(fd, when, attributes)

Sets the TTY attributes for a file descriptor fd. attributes is a list in the same form as returned by tcgetattr(). The when argument determines when the changes take effect:

Argument	Description
TERMIOS.TCSANOW	Changes take place immediately.
TERMIOS.TCSADRAIN	After transmitting queued output.
TERMIOS.TCSAFLUSH	After transmitting queued output and discarding queued input.

tcsendbreak(fd, duration)

Sends a break on file descriptor fd. A duration of zero sends a break for approximately 0.25–0.5 seconds. A nonzero duration is implementation-defined.

tcdrain(fd)

Waits until all output written to file descriptor fd has been transmitted.

tcflush(fd, queue)

Discards queued data on file descriptor fd. queue determines which data to discard:

Queue	Description
TERMIOS.TCIFLUSH	Input queue.
TERMIOS.TCOFLUSH	Output queue.
TERMIOS.TCIOFLUSH	Both queues.

tcflow(fd, action)

Suspends or resumes input or output on file descriptor fd. action is one of the following:

Action	Description
TERMIOS.TCOOFF	Suspends output.
TERMIOS.TCOON	Restarts output.
TERMIOS.TCIOFF	Suspends input.
TERMIOS.TCION	Restarts input.

Example

The following function prompts for a password with local echoing turned off:

```
def getpass():
    import termios, TERMIOS, sys
    fd = sys.stdin.fileno()
    tc = termios.tcgetattr(fd)
```

```
old = tc[3] & TERMIOS.ECHO
tc[3] = tc[3] & ~TERMIOS.ECHO        # Disable echo
try:
    termios.tcsetattr(fd, TERMIOS.TCSADRAIN, tc)
    passwd = raw_input("Password: ")
finally:
    tc[3] = tc[3] ¦ old              # Restore old echo setting
    termios.tcsetattr(fd, TERMIOS.TCSADRAIN, tc)
return passwd
```

▶ See Also tty (p. 172), curses (p. 243), getpass (p. 136), signal (p. 161).

time

Availability: A

The time module provides various time-related functions. In Python, time is measured as the number of seconds since the "epoch." The epoch is the beginning of time (the point at which time = 0 seconds). The epoch is January 1, 1970 on Unix and Windows, and January 1, 1900 on the Macintosh.

The following variables are defined:

accept2dyear

A Boolean value that indicates whether two-digit years are accepted. Normally this is true, but it's set to false if the environment variable $PYTHONY2K is set to a non-empty string. The value can be changed manually as well.

altzone

The timezone used during daylight savings time (DST), if applicable.

daylight

Sets to a nonzero value if a DST timezone has been defined.

timezone

The local (non-DST) timezone.

tzname

A tuple containing the name of the local timezone and the name of the local daylight saving timezone (if defined).

The following functions can be used:

asctime(*tuple*)

Converts a tuple representing a time as returned by gmtime() or localtime() to a string of the form 'Mon Jul 12 14:45:23 1999'.

clock()

Returns the current CPU time in seconds as a floating-point number.

ctime(*secs*)

Converts a time expressed in seconds since the epoch to a string representing local time. ctime(*secs*) is the same as asctime(*localtime(secs)*).

gmtime(*secs*)

Converts a time expressed in seconds since the epoch to a time tuple in Coordinated Univeral Time (Greenwich Mean Time). The returned tuple consists of nine integers of the form (*year, month, day, hour, minute, second, weekday, day, dst*). The following numerical ranges are used for tuple elements:

Element	Value
year	A four-digit value such as 1998.
month	1-12
day	1-31
hour	0-23
minute	0-59
second	0-59
weekday	0-6
day	1-366
dst	-1, 0, 1

The *dst* field is 1 if daylight saving time is in effect, 0 if not, and -1 if no information is available.

localtime(secs)

Returns a time tuple such as gmtime(), but corresponding to the local timezone.

mktime(tuple)

This function takes a time-tuple representing a time in the local timezone (in the same format as returned by localtime()) and returns a floating-point number representing the number of seconds since the epoch. An OverflowError exception is raised if the input value isn't a valid time.

sleep(secs)

Puts the current process to sleep for *secs* seconds. *secs* is a floating-point number.

strftime(format, tuple)

Converts a tuple representing a time as returned by gmtime() or localtime() to a string. *format* is a format string in which the following format codes can be embedded:

Directive	Meaning
%a	Locale's abbreviated weekday name.
%A	Locale's full weekday name.
%b	Locale's abbreviated month name.
%B	Locale's full month name.
%c	Locale's appropriate date and time representation.
%d	Day of the month as a decimal number [01-31].
%H	Hour (24-hour clock) as a decimal number [00-23].
%I	Hour (12-hour clock) as a decimal number [01-12].
%j	Day of the year as a decimal number [001-366].
%m	Month as a decimal number [01-12].
%M	Minute as a decimal number [00-59].
%p	Locale's equivalent of either AM or PM.
%S	Seconds as a decimal number [00-59].

continues >>

>>continued

Directive	Meaning
%U	Week number of the year [00-53] (Sunday as first day).
%w	Weekday as a decimal number [0(Sunday)-6].
%W	Week number of the year (Monday as first day).
%x	Locale's appropriate date representation.
%X	Locale's appropriate time representation.
%y	Year without century as a decimal number [00-99].
%Y	Year with century as a decimal number.
%Z	Timezone name (or by no characters if no timezone exists).
%%	The % character.

The format codes can optionally include a width and precision in the same manner as used with the % operator on strings.

strptime(*string* **[,** *format***])**

Parses a string representing a time and returns a time tuple of the same form as returned by localtime() or gmtime(). The format parameter uses the same specifiers as used by strftime() and defaults to "%a %b %d %H:%M:%S %Y". This is the same format as produced by the ctime() function. If the string can't be parsed, a ValueError exception is raised.

time()

Returns the current time as the number of seconds since the epoch in UTC (Coordinated Universal Time).

Notes

- When two-digit years are accepted, they're converted to four-digit years according to the POSIX X/Open standard, where the values 69–99 are mapped to 1969–1999 and the values 0–68 are mapped to 2000–2068.

- The functions in this module are not intended to handle dates and times far in the past or future. In particular, dates before the epoch are illegal, as are dates beyond the maximum time (2^{31} seconds since the epoch on many machines).

▶ See Also locale (p. 138).

tty

Availability: Optional, U

The tty module provides functions for putting a TTY into cbreak and raw modes. *Raw mode* forces a process to receive every character on a TTY with no interpretation by the system. *Cbreak mode* enables system processing for special keys such as the interrupt and quit keys (which generate signals).

setraw(*fd* **[,** *when***])**

Changes the mode of the file descriptor *fd* to raw mode. *when* specifies when the change occurs and is TERMIOS.TCSANOW, TERMIOS.TCSADRAIN, or TERMIOS.TCSAFLUSH (the default).

setcbreak(*fd* [, *when*])

Changes the mode of file descriptor *fd* to cbreak mode. *when* has the same meaning as in setraw().

Note

Requires the termios module.

▶ **See Also** termios (p. 166), curses (p. 243).

zlib

Availability: Optional, U, W, M

The zlib module supports data compression by providing access to the zlib library.

adler32(*string* [, *value*])

Computes the Adler-32 checksum of *string*. *value* is used as the starting value (which can be used to compute a checksum over the concatenation of several strings). Otherwise, a fixed default value is used.

compress(*string* [, *level*])

Compresses the data in *string* where *level* is an integer from 1 to 9 controlling the level of compression. 1 is the least (fastest) compression and 9 is the best (slowest) compression. The default value is 6. Returns a string containing the compressed data or raises error if an error occurs.

compressobj([*level*])

Returns a compression object. *level* has the same meaning as in the compress() function.

crc32(*string* [, *value*])

Computes a CRC checksum of *string*. If *value* is present, it's used as the starting value of the checksum. Otherwise, a fixed value is used.

decompress(*string* [, *wbits* [, *buffsize*]])

Decompresses the data in *string*. *wbits* controls the size of the window buffer and *buffsize* is the initial size of the output buffer. Raises error if an error occurs.

decompressobj([*wbits*])

Returns a compression object. The *wbits* parameter controls the size of the window buffer.

A compression object *c* has the following methods:

c.compress(*string*)

Compresses *string*. Returns a string containing compressed data for at least part of the data in *string*. This data should be concatenated to the output produced by earlier calls to c.compress() to create the output stream. Some input data may be stored in internal buffers for later processing.

c.flush([*mode*])

Compresses all pending input and returns a string containing the remaining compressed output. *mode* is Z_SYNC_FLUSH, Z_FULL_FLUSH, or Z_FINISH (the default). Z_SYNC_FLUSH and Z_FULL_FLUSH allow further compression and are used to allow partial error recovery on decompression. Z_FINISH terminates the compression stream.

A decompression object *d* has the following methods:

d.decompress(*string*)

Decompresses *string* and returns a string containing uncompressed data for at least part of the data in *string*. This data should be concatenated with data produced by earlier calls to decompress() to form the output stream. Some input data may be stored in internal buffers for later processing.

d.flush()

All pending input is processed, and a string containing the remaining uncompressed output is returned. The decompression object can't be used again after this call.

Exception

error

Exception raised on compression and decompression errors.

Note

The zlib library is available at http://www.cdrom.com/pub/infozip/zlib.

▶ **See Also** gzip (p. 138).

Threads

This section describes modules that can be used to develop multithreaded applications. First, a little terminology and background.

Thread Basics

A running program is called a *process*. Associated with each process is a system state including memory, lists of open files, a program counter that keeps track of the instruction being executed, and a call stack used to hold the local variables of functions. Normally, a process executes statements in a single sequence of control flow. This sequence is sometimes called a *thread* (or *main thread*).

When a program creates new processes using the os.system(), os.fork(), os.spawn(), and similar system calls, these processes run as independent programs—each with its own set of system resources and main thread of execution. However, it's also possible for a program to create additional threads of execution that exist inside the calling process and share data and system resources with the original thread of execution. Threads are particularly useful when an application wants to perform tasks concurrently without spawning child processes, or when subtasks need to read and write shared data.

A multithreaded program executes by dividing its processing time between all active threads. For example, a program with 10 active threads of execution would allocate approximately 1/10 of its CPU time to each thread and cycle between threads in rapid succession.

Since threads share the same data, an extreme degree of caution is required whenever shared data structures are updated by one of the threads. In particular, attempts to update a data structure by multiple threads at approximately the same time can lead to a corrupted and inconsistent program state (a problem formally known as a *race condition*). To fix these problems, threaded programs need to lock critical sections of code using mutual-exclusion locks and other similar synchronization primitives.

More information regarding the theory and implementation of threads and locks can be found in most operating system textbooks.

Python Threads

Python supports threads on Windows, Solaris, and systems that support the POSIX threads library (pthreads). However, threads are often disabled by default, so it may be necessary to rebuild the interpreter with thread support before using any of the modules in this section.

The scheduling of threads and thread switching is tightly controlled by a global interpreter lock that allows only a single thread of execution to be running in the interpreter at once. Furthermore, thread switching can only occur between the execution of individual byte codes in the interpreter. The frequency with which the interpreter checks for thread switching is set by the sys.setcheckinterval() function. By default, the interpreter checks for thread switching after every 10 bytecode instructions.

When working with extension modules, the interpreter may invoke functions written in C or C++. Unless specifically written to interact with a threaded Python interpreter, these functions will block the execution of all other threads until they complete execution. Thus, a long-running calculation in an extension module may limit the effectiveness of using threads. However, most of the I/O functions in the standard library have been written to work in a threaded environment.

Finally, programmers need to be aware that threads can interact strangely with signals and interrupts. For instance, the KeyboardInterrupt exception can be received by an arbitrary thread, while signals used in conjunction with the signal module are only received by the main thread. In addition, many of Python's most popular extensions such as Tkinter may not work properly in a threaded environment.

thread

Availability: Optional, U, W

The thread module provides low-level functions for working with threads.

allocate_lock()

Creates a new lock object of type LockType. Locks are initially unlocked.

exit()

Raises the SystemExit exception. Forces a thread to exit.

get_ident()

Returns the integer "thread identifier" of the current thread.

start_new_thread(*func*, *args* [, *kwargs*])

Executes the function *func* in a new thread. *func* is called using apply(*func*, *args*, *kwargs*). On success, control is immediately returned to the caller. When the function *func* returns, the thread exits silently. If the function terminates with an unhandled exception, a stack trace is printed and the thread exits (other threads continue to run, however).

A lock object *lck* returned by `allocate_lock()` has the following methods:

lck.**acquire([*waitflag*])**

Acquires the lock, waiting until the lock is released by another thread if necessary. If *waitflag* is omitted, the function returns None when the lock is acquired. If *waitflag* is set to 0, the lock is only acquired if it can be acquired immediately without waiting. If *waitflag* is nonzero, the method blocks until the lock is released. When *waitflag* is supplied, the function returns 1 if the lock was acquired successfully, 0 if not.

lck.**release()**

Releases the lock.

lck.**locked()**

Returns the lock status: 1 if locked, 0 if not.

Example

The following example shows a simple thread that prints the current time every five seconds:

```
import thread
import time
def print_time(delay):
    while 1:
        time.sleep(delay)
        print time.ctime(time.time())

# Start the new thread
thread.start_new_thread(print_time,(5,))
# Now go do something else while the thread runs
while 1:
    pass
```

Exception

error

Exception raised on thread-specific errors.

Notes

- Calling sys.exit() or raising the SystemExit exception is equivalent to calling thread.exit().

- The acquire() method on a lock can't be interrupted.

- When the main thread exits, whether the other threads survive depends on the system. On most systems, they're killed immediately without executing any cleanup. Furthermore, the cleanup actions of the main thread are somewhat limited. In particular, standard I/O files are not flushed, nor are object destructors invoked.

▶ **See Also** threading (p. 177).

threading

Availability: Optional, U, W

The threading module provides high-level thread support with a Thread class and classes for various synchronization primitives. It's built using the lower-level thread module.

The following utility functions are available:

activeCount()

Returns the number of currently active Thread objects.

currentThread()

Returns the Thread object corresponding to the caller's thread of control.

enumerate()

Returns a list of all currently active Thread objects.

Thread Objects

The Thread class is used to represent a separate thread of control. A new thread can be created as follows:

Thread(group=None, target=None, name=None, args=(), kwargs={})

Creates a new Thread instance. *group* is None and is reserved for future extensions. *target* is a callable object invoked by the run() method when the thread starts. By default, it's None, meaning that nothing is called. *name* is the thread name. By default, a unique name of the form "Thread-*N*" is created. *args* is a tuple of arguments that are passed to the *target* function. *kwargs* is a dictionary of keyword arguments that are passed to *target*.

A Thread object *t* supports the following methods:

t.start()

Starts the thread by invoking the run() method in a separate thread of control. This method can be invoked only once.

t.run()

This method is called when the thread starts. By default, it calls the target function passed in the constructor. This method can also be redefined in subclasses of Thread.

t.join([timeout])

Waits until the thread terminates or a timeout occurs. *timeout* is a floating-point number specifying a timeout in seconds. A thread can't join itself and it's an error to join a thread before it has been started.

t.getName()

Returns the thread name.

t.setName(name)

Sets the thread name.

t.isAlive()

Returns 1 if the thread is alive, 0 otherwise. A thread is alive from the moment the start() method returns until its run() method terminates.

t.isDaemon()

Returns the thread's daemon flag.

t.setDaemon(*daemonic*)

Sets the thread's daemon flag to the Boolean value daemonic. This must be called before start() is called. The initial value is inherited from the creating thread. The entire Python program exits when no active non-daemon threads are left.

A thread can be flagged as a "daemon thread" using the setDaemon() method. If only daemon threads remain, a program will exit. All programs have a main thread that represents the initial thread of control. It's not a daemon thread.

In some cases, dummy thread objects are created. These are threads of control started outside the threading module such as from a C extension module. Dummy threads are always considered alive, active, and daemonic, and can't be joined. Furthermore, they're never deleted, so it's impossible to detect the termination of such threads.

As an alternative to explicitly creating a Thread object, the Thread class can also be subclassed. If this approach is used, the run() method can be overridden to perform the activity of the thread. The constructor can also be overridden, but it's very important to invoke the base class constructor Thread.__init__() in this case. It's an error to override any other methods of the Thread class.

Lock Objects

A *primitive lock* (or *mutual exclusion lock*) is a synchronization primitive that's in either a "locked" or "unlocked" state. Two methods, acquire() and release(), are used to change the state of the lock. If the state is locked, attempts to acquire the lock are blocked until the lock is released. If more than one thread is waiting to acquire the lock, only one is allowed to proceed when the lock is released. The order in which waiting threads proceed is undefined.

A new Lock instance is created using the following constructor:

Lock()

Creates a new lock object, initially unlocked.

A Lock object *lck* supports the following methods:

lck.acquire([*blocking* = 1])

Acquires the lock, blocking until the lock is released if necessary. If blocking is supplied and set to zero, the function returns immediately with a value of 0 if the lock couldn't be acquired, or 1 if locking was successful.

lck.release()

Releases a lock. It's an error to call this method when the lock is in an unlocked state.

RLock

A *reentrant lock* is a synchronization primitive that's similar to a Lock, but that can be acquired multiple times by the same thread. This allows the thread owning the lock to perform nested acquire() and release() operations. In this case, only the outermost release() operation resets the lock to its unlocked state.

A new RLock object is created using the following constructor:

`RLock()`

> Creates a new reentrant lock object.

An RLock object `rlck` supports the following methods:

`rlck.acquire([blocking = 1])`

> Acquires the lock, blocking until the lock is released if necessary. If no thread owns the lock, it's locked and the recursion level set to 1. If this thread already owns the lock, the recursion level of the lock is increased by one and the function returns immediately.

`rlck.release()`

> Releases a lock by decrementing its recursion level. If the recursion level is zero after the decrement, the lock is reset to the unlocked state. Otherwise, the lock remains locked. This function should only be called by the thread that currently owns the lock.

Condition Variables

A *condition variable* is a synchronization primitive, built on top of another lock, that's used when a thread is interested in a particular change of state or event to occur. A typical use is a producer-consumer problem where one thread is producing data to be consumed by another thread. A new Condition instance is created using the following constructor:

`Condition([lock])`

> Creates a new condition variable. *lock* is an optional Lock or RLock instance. If not supplied, a new RLock instance is created for use with the condition variable.

A condition variable *cv* supports the following methods:

`cv.acquire(*args)`

> Acquires the underlying lock. This method calls the corresponding acquire(*args*) method on the underlying lock and returns its return value.

`cv.release()`

> Releases the underlying lock. This method calls the corresponding release() method on the underlying lock.

`cv.wait([timeout])`

> Waits until notified or until a timeout occurs. This method is called after the calling thread has already acquired the lock. When called, the underlying lock is released, and the thread goes to sleep until it's awakened by a notify() or notifyAll() call performed on the condition variable by another thread. Once awakened, the thread reacquires the lock and the method returns. *timeout* is a floating-point number in seconds. If this time expires, the thread is awakened, the lock reacquired, and control returned.

`cv.notify()`

> Wakes up a thread waiting on this condition variable. This method is called only after the calling thread has acquired the lock, and does nothing if no threads are waiting. Currently, this function only wakes up one waiting thread. Furthermore, the awakened thread doesn't return from its wait() call until it can reacquire the lock.

cv.notifyAll()

Wakes up all threads waiting on this condition.

Examples

The following examples show a producer-consumer problem using condition variables:

```
# Consume one item          # Produce one item
cv.acquire()                cv.acquire()
while not an_item_is_available():   make_an_item_available()
    cv.wait()  # Wait for item      cv.notify()  # Notify the consumer
cv.release()                cv.release()
```

Semaphore

A *semaphore* is a synchronization primitive based on a counter that's decremented by each acquire() call and incremented by each release() call. If the counter ever reaches zero, the acquire() method blocks until some other thread calls release().

Semaphore([value])

Creates a new semaphore. *value* is the initial value for the counter. If omitted, the counter is set to a value of 1.

A Semaphore instance *s* supports the following methods:

s.acquire([blocking])

Acquires the semaphore. If the internal counter is larger than zero on entry, decrements it by one and returns immediately. If it's zero, blocks until another thread calls release(). The blocking argument has the same behavior as described for Lock and RLock objects.

s.release()

Releases a semaphore by incrementing the internal counter by one. If the counter is zero and another thread is waiting, that thread is awakened. If multiple threads are waiting, only one will be returned from its acquire() call. The order in which threads are released is not deterministic.

Events

Events are used to communicate between threads. One thread signals an "event" and one or more other threads wait for it. An Event instance manages an internal flag that can be set to true with the set() method and reset to false with the clear() method. The wait() method blocks until the flag is true.

Event()

Creates a new Event instance with the internal flag set to false.

An Event instance *e* supports the following methods:

e.isSet()

Returns true if and only if the internal flag is true.

e.set()

Sets the internal flag to true. All threads waiting for it to become true are awakened.

e.clear()

Resets the internal flag to false.

e.wait([*timeout*])

Blocks until the internal flag is true. If the internal flag is true on entry, returns immediately. Otherwise, blocks until another thread calls set() to set the flag to true, or until the optional timeout occurs. *timeout* is a floating-point number specifying a timeout period in seconds.

Example

The following example illustrates the use of the threading module by fetching a collection of URLs in separate threads. In this example, threads are defined by subclassing the Thread class.

```python
import threading
import urllib
class FetchUrlThread(threading.Thread):
    def __init__(self, url,filename):
        threading.Thread.__init__(self)
        self.url = url
        self.filename = filename
    def run(self):
        print self.getName(), "Fetching ", self.url
        urllib.urlretrieve(self.url,self.filename)
        print self.getName(), "Saved in ", self.filename
urls = [ ('http://www.python.org','/tmp/index.html'),
         ('ftp://ftp.python.org/pub/python/src/py152.tgz','/tmp/py152.tgz'),
         ('ftp://ftp.swig.org/pub/swig1.1p5.tar.gz','/tmp/swig1.1p5.tar.gz'),
         ('http://www.jarjarmustdie.com','/tmp/jarjar.html')
       ]
# Go fetch a bunch of URLs in separate threads
for url,file in urls:
    t = FetchUrlThread(url,file)
    t.start()
```

▶ **See Also** thread (p. 175), Queue (p. 181).

Queue

Availability: Optional, U, W

The Queue module implements a multi-producer, multi-consumer FIFO queue that can be used to safely exchange information between multiple threads of execution. It's available only if thread support has been enabled.

The Queue module defines the following class:

Queue(*maxsize*)

Creates a new queue where *maxsize* is the maximum number of items that can be placed in the queue. If *maxsize* is less than or equal to zero, the queue size is infinite.

A Queue object *q* has the following methods:

q.qsize()

Returns the approximate size of the queue. Because other threads may be updating the queue, this number is not entirely reliable.

q.empty()

Returns 1 if the queue is empty, 0 otherwise.

q.full()

Returns 1 if the queue is full, 0 otherwise.

q.put(*item* [, *block*])

Puts *item* into the queue. If optional argument *block* is 1 (the default), the caller blocks until a free slot is available. Otherwise (*block* is 0), the Full exception is raised if the queue is full.

q.put_nowait(*item*)

Equivalent to *q*.put(*item*, 0).

q.get([*block*])

Removes and returns an item from the queue. If optional argument *block* is 1 (the default), the caller blocks until an item is available. Otherwise (*block* is 0), the Empty exception is raised if the queue is empty.

q.get_nowait()

Equivalent to get(0).

Exceptions

Exception	Description
Empty	Exception raised when nonblocking get() (or get_nowait()) is called on a Queue object that's empty or locked.
Full	Exception raised when nonblocking put() (or put_nowait()) is called on a Queue object that's full or locked.

▶ **See Also** thread (p. 175), threading (p. 177).

Network Programming

This section describes the modules used to implement network servers and clients. Python provides extensive network support ranging from access to low-level network interfaces to high-level clients and frameworks for writing network applications. Before beginning, a very brief (and admittedly terse) introduction to network programming is presented. Readers are advised to consult a book such as *Unix Network Programming, Volume 1: Networking APIs - Sockets and XTI* by W. Richard Stevens (Prentice Hall, 1997, ISBN 0-13-490012-X) for many of the advanced details.

Python's network programming modules primarily support two Internet protocols: TCP and UDP. The *TCP* protocol is a reliable connection-oriented protocol used to establish a two-way communications stream between machines. *UDP* is a lower-level packet-based protocol (connectionless) in which machines send and receive discrete packets of information without formally establishing a connection. Unlike TCP, UDP communication is unreliable and thus inherently more complicated to manage in applications that require reliable communications. Consequently, most Internet protocols utilize TCP connections.

Both network protocols are handled through a programming abstraction known as a *socket*. A socket is an object similar to a file that allows a program to accept incoming connections, make outgoing connections, and send and receive data. Before two machines can establish a connection, both must create a socket object.

Furthermore, the machine receiving the connection (the server) must bind its socket object to a port. A port is a 16-bit number in the range 0–65535 that's managed by the operating system and used by clients to uniquely identify servers. Ports 0–1023 are reserved by the system and used by common network protocols. The following table shows the port assignments for a number of common protocols:

Service	Port Number
FTP-Data	20
FTP-Control	21
Telnet	23
SMTP (Mail)	25
Finger	79
HTTP (WWW)	80
NNTP (News)	119

The process of establishing a TCP connection involves a precise sequence of system calls on both the server and client, as shown in the following figure.

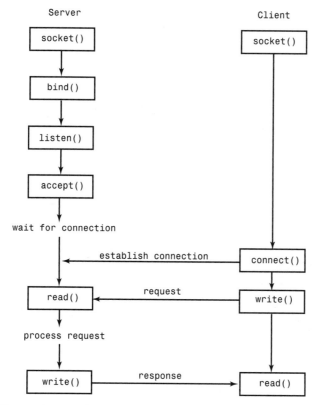

TCP connection protocol.

For TCP servers, the socket object used to receive connections is not the same socket used to perform subsequent communication with the client. In particular, the accept() system call returns a new socket object that's actually used for the connection. This allows a server to manage connections from a large number of clients simultaneously.

UDP communication is performed in a similar manner except that clients and servers don't establish a "connection" with each other, as shown in the following figure.

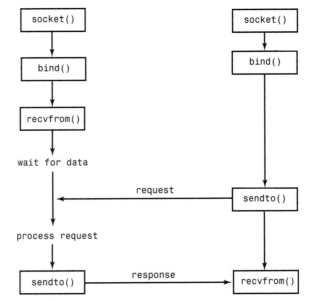

UDP connection protocol.

The following example illustrates the TCP protocol with a client and server written using the socket module. In this case, the server simply returns the current time to the client as a string.

```
# Time server program
from socket import *
import time

s = socket(AF_INET, SOCK_STREAM)    # Create a TCP socket
s.bind("",8888)                      # Bind to port 8888
s.listen(5)                          # Listen, but allow no more than
                                     # 5 pending connections.
while 1:
    client,addr = s.accept()     # Get a connection
    print "Got a connection from ",addr
    client.send(time.ctime(time.time()))   # Send back to client
    client.close()
```

Here's the client program:

```
# Time client program
from socket import *
s = socket(AF_INET,SOCK_STREAM)      # Create a TCP socket
s.connect("foo.bar.com", 8888)       # Connect to the server
```

```
tm = s.recv(1024)              # Receive no more than 1024 bytes
s.close()
print "The time is ", tm
```

The remainder of this section describes modules of two different flavors. First are modules and frameworks related to socket programming. Second are a variety of modules that implement the client-side interface to common Internet protocols. With the exception of HTTP, the details of these protocols are not presented. However, details can be found in the online documentation and in relevant Internet Request for Comments (RFCs) available at http://www.ietf.org. Where applicable, RFC numbers and sources for additional information are stated.

asyncore

Availability: U, W, M

The asyncore module is used to build network applications in which network activity is handled asynchronously as a series of events dispatched by an event loop (built using the select() system call). Such an approach is useful in network programs that wish to provide concurrency, but without the use of threads or processes. This method can also provide the best performance for short transactions. All the functionality of this module is provided by the dispatcher class, which is a thin wrapper around an ordinary socket object.

dispatcher([sock])

Base class defining an event-driven nonblocking socket object. sock is an existing socket object. If omitted, a socket must be created using the create_socket() method (described shortly). Once created, network events are handled by special handler methods (described later). In addition, all open dispatcher objects are saved in an internal list that's used by a number of polling functions.

The following methods of the dispatcher class are called to handle network events. They should be defined in classes derived from dispatcher.

d.handle_read()

Called when new data is available to be read from a socket.

d.handle_write()

Called when an attempt to write data is made.

d.handle_expt()

Called when out of band (OOB) data for a socket is received.

d.handle_connect()

Called when a connection is made.

d.handle_close()

Called when the socket is closed.

d.handle_accept()

Called on listening sockets when a new connection arrives.

d.readable()

This function is used by the select() loop to see whether the object is willing to read data. Returns 1 if so, 0 if not. This method is called to see if the handle_read() method should be called with new data.

d.writable()

Called by the select() loop to see if the object wants to write data. Returns 1 if so, 0 otherwise. This method is always called to see whether the handle_write() method should be called to produce output.

In addition to the preceding methods, the following methods are used to perform low-level socket operations. They're similar to those available on a socket object.

d.create_socket(*family*, *type*)

Creates a new socket. Arguments are the same as for socket.socket().

d.connect(*address*)

Makes a connection. *address* is a tuple (*host*, *port*).

d.send(*data*)

Sends data.

d.recv(*size*)

Receives at most *size* bytes.

d.listen([*backlog*])

Listens for incoming connections.

d.bind(*address*)

Binds the socket to *address*. *address* is typically a tuple (*host*, *port*).

d.accept()

Accepts a connection. Returns a pair (*client*, *addr*) where *client* is a socket object used to send and receive data on the connection and *addr* is the address of the client.

d.close()

Closes the socket.

The following functions are used to handle events:

poll([*timeout* [, *ignore_exception*]])

Polls all the open dispatcher objects for network events using select() and calls the appropriate handler functions if necessary. *timeout* is an optional timeout that's 0.0 by default. *ignore_exception*, if set, causes all exceptions generated in event handlers to be ignored (the default).

loop([*timeout*])

Polls for events indefinitely. Does nothing but repeatedly call poll(). *timeout* is the timeout period and is set to 30 seconds by default.

Example

The following example implements a minimalistic Web server using asyncore. It implements two classes—asynhttp for accepting connections and asynclient for processing client requests.

```
# A minimal HTTP server with no error checking.
import asyncore, socket,
import string, os, stat, mimetypes
# Class that does nothing but accept connections
class asynhttp(asyncore.dispatcher):
    def __init__(self, port):
```

```
        asyncore.dispatcher.__init__(self)
        self.create_socket(socket.AF_INET,socket.SOCK_STREAM)
        self.bind(("",port))
        self.listen(5)
    # Accept an incoming connection and create a client
    def handle_accept(self):
        client,addr = self.accept()
        print "Connection from ", addr
        return asynclient(client)
# Handle clients
class asynclient(asyncore.dispatcher):
    def __init__(self, sock = None):
        asyncore.dispatcher.__init__(self,sock)
        self.got_request = 0        # Read HTTP request?
        self.request_data = []
        self.responsef = None       # Response file
        self.sent_headers = 0       # Send HTTP headers?
        self.clientf = sock.makefile("r+",0)  # Request file
    # Only readable if request header not read
    def readable(self):
        if not self.got_request: return 1
    # Read request header (until blank line)
    def handle_read(self):
        data = string.strip(self.clientf.readline())
        if data:
            self.request_data.append(data)
            return
        self.got_request = 1
        request = string.split(self.request_data[0])
        if request[0] == 'GET':
            filename = request[1][1:]
            self.responsef = open(filename)
            self.content_type,enc = mimetypes.guess_type(filename)
            self.content_length = os.stat(filename)[stat.ST_SIZE]
        else:
            self.close()
    # Only writable if a response is ready
    def writable(self):
        if self.responsef: return 1
        return 0
    # Write response data
    def handle_write(self):
        # Send HTTP headers if not sent yet
        if not self.sent_headers:
            self.send("HTTP/1.0 200 OK\n")
            if not self.content_type:
                self.content_type = "text/plain"
            self.send("Content-type: %s\n" % (self.content_type,))
            self.send("Content-length: %d\n\n" % (self.content_length,))
            self.sent_headers = 1
        # Read some data and send it
        data = self.responsef.read(8192)
        if data:
            sent = self.send(data)
            self.response.seek(sent-len(data),1)  # Adjust for unsent data
        else:
            self.response.close()
            self.close()
# Create the server
a = asynhttp(80)
# Poll forever
asyncore.loop()
```

Note

This module requires the select module.

> ▶ **See Also** socket (p. 202), select (p. 199), httplib (p. 195), SocketServer (p. 207).

BaseHTTPServer

Availability: A

The BaseHTTPServer module defines two base classes used to implement HTTP servers.

HTTPServer(*server_address, request_handler*)

Creates a new HTTPServer object. *server_address* is a tuple of the form (*host, port*) on which the server will listen. *request_handler* is a class object used to handle requests (described shortly).

The HTTPServer class is derived from SocketServer.TCPServer and supports the same methods. In particular, the following functions are most relevant:

Function	Description
h.handle_request()	Processes a single request.
h.serve_forever()	Handles an infinite number of requests.

Requests are handled by defining a handler derived from the following class:

BaseHTTPRequestHandler(*request, client_address, server*)

This class is used to handle HTTP requests. When a connection is received, the request and HTTP headers are parsed. An attempt is then made to execute a method of the form do_REQUEST based on the request type. For example, a 'GET' method invokes do_GET() and a 'POST' method invokes do_POST. By default, this class does nothing, so these methods must be defined in subclasses.

The following class variables are defined for BaseHTTPRequestHandler:

BaseHTTPRequestHandler.server_version

Specifies the server software version string—for example, 'ServerName/1.2'.

BaseHTTPRequestHandler.sys_version

Python system version, such as 'Python/1.5'.

BaseHTTPRequestHandler.error_message_format

Format string used to build error messages sent to the client. The format string is applied to a dictionary containing the attributes code, message, and explain. For example:

```
"""<head>
    <title>Error response</title>
    </head>
    <body>
    <h1>Error response</h1>
    <p>Error code %(code)d.
    <p>Message: %(message)s.
    <p>Error code explanation: %(code)s = %(explain)s.
    </body>"""
```

BaseHTTPRequestHandler.protocol_version

HTTP protocol version used in responses. The default is 'HTTP/1.0'.

BaseHTTPRequestHandler.MessageClass

Class used to parse HTTP headers. The default is mimetools.Message.

BaseHTTPRequestHandler.responses

Mapping of integer error codes to two-element tuples (*message, explain*) that describe the problem.

An instance *b* of the BaseHTTPRequestHandler has the following attributes:

Attribute	Description
b.client_address	Client address as a tuple (*host, port*).
b.command	Request type such as 'GET', 'POST', 'HEAD', and so on.
b.path	Contains the request path.
b.request_version	HTTP version string from the request, such as 'HTTP/1.0'.
b.headers	HTTP headers, typically represented as mimetools.Message object.
b.rfile	Input stream for optional input data.
b.wfile	Output stream for writing a response back to the client.

The following methods are used:

b.handle()

Request dispatcher. Parses the request and calls a method of the form do_*().

b.send_error(*code* [, *message*])

Sends an error reply to the client. *code* is the numeric HTTP error code. *message* is an optional error message.

b.send_response(*code* [, *message*])

Sends a response header. The HTTP response line is sent, followed by Server and Date headers.

b.send_header(*keyword, value*)

Writes a MIME header entry to the output stream. *keyword* is the header keyword, *value* is its value.

b.end_headers()

Sends a blank line to signal the end of the MIME headers.

b.log_request([*code* [, *size*]])

Logs a successful request. *code* is the HTTP code and *size* is the size of the response in bytes (if available).

b.log_error(*format*, ...)

Logs an error message. By default, log_message() is called.

b.log_message(*format*, ...)

Logs an arbitrary message to sys.stderr. *format* is a format string applied to any additional arguments passed. The client address and current time are prefixed to every message.

b.version_string()

Returns the server software's version string—a combination of the server_version and sys_version variables.

b.date_time_string()

Returns the current date and time, formatted for a header.

b.log_date_time_string()

Returns the current date and time, formatted for logging.

b.address_string()

Performs a name lookup on the client's IP address and returns a hostname formatted for logging.

Example

The following example handles GET methods and simply echoes the request back to the client on a Web page.

```
import BaseHTTPServer
class EchoHandler(BaseHTTPServer.BaseHTTPRequestHandler):
    # Echo the request information back on a web page
    def do_GET(self):
        self.send_response(200)
        self.send_header("Content-type","text/html")
        self.end_headers()
        self.wfile.write("""
<html><head><title>Your Request</title></head>
<body>
<pre>
You requested the following : %s
The request headers were :
%s
</pre></body></html>
""" % (self.path, self.headers))

server = BaseHTTPServer.HTTPServer(('',80),EchoHandler)
server.serve_forever()
```

Note

The contents of this module are rarely used directly. See the SimpleHTTPServer and CGIHTTPServer modules.

> **See Also** SimpleHTTPServer (p. 200), CGIHTTPServer (p. 194), SocketServer (p. 207), httplib (p. 195), mimetools (p. 214).

cgi

Availability: A

The cgi module is used to implement CGI scripts in Web applications. CGI scripts are programs executed by a Web server when it wants to process user input submitted through an HTML form such as the following:

```
<FORM ACTION="/cgi-bin/foo.cgi" METHOD="GET">
Your name : <INPUT type="Text" name="name" size="30">
Your email address: <INPUT type="Text" name="email" size="30">
<INPUT type="Submit" name="submit-button" value="Subscribe">
</FORM>
```

When the form is submitted, the Web server executes the CGI program foo.cgi. CGI programs receive input from two sources: sys.stdin and environment variables set by the server. The following table lists common environment variables set by Web servers:

Variable	Description
AUTH_TYPE	Authentication method.
CONTENT_LENGTH	Length of data passed in sys.stdin.
CONTENT_TYPE	Type of query data.
DOCUMENT_ROOT	Document root directory.
GATEWAY_INTERFACE	CGI revision string.
HTTP_ACCEPT	MIME types accepted by the client.
HTTP_COOKIE	Netscape persistent cookie value.
HTTP_FROM	Email address of client (often disabled).
HTTP_REFERER	Referring URL.
HTTP_USER_AGENT	Client browser.
PATH_INFO	Extra path information passed.
PATH_TRANSLATED	Translated version of PATH_INFO.
QUERY_STRING	Query string.
REMOTE_ADDR	Remote IP address of the client.
REMOTE_HOST	Remote hostname of the client.
REMOTE_IDENT	User making the request.
REMOTE_USER	Authenticated username.
REQUEST_METHOD	Method ('GET' or 'POST').
SCRIPT_NAME	Name of the program.
SERVER_NAME	Server hostname.
SERVER_PORT	Server port number.
SERVER_PROTOCOL	Server protocol.
SERVER_SOFTWARE	Name and version of the server software.

As output, a CGI program writes to standard output sys.stdout. The gory details of CGI programming can be found in a book such as *CGI Programming with Perl, 2nd Edition* by Shishir Gundavaram (O'Reilly & Associates, 1999, ISBN 1-56592-419-3). For our purposes, there are really only two things to know. First, the contents of an HTML form are passed to a CGI program in a sequence of text known as a *query string*. In Python, the contents of the query string are accessed using the FieldStorage class. For example:

```
import cgi
form = cgi.FieldStorage()
name = form["name"].value      # Get 'name' field from a form
email = form["email"].value    # Get 'email' field from a form
```

Second, the output of a CGI program consists of two parts: an HTTP header and the raw data (which is typically HTML). A simple HTTP header looks like this:

```
print "Content-type: text/html"    # HTML Output
print                              # Blank line (required!)
```

The rest of the output is the raw output. For example:

```
print "<TITLE>My CGI Script</TITLE>"
print "<H1>Hello World!</H1>"
print "You are %s (%s)" % (name, email)
```

Most of the work in the cgi module is performed by creating an instance of the FieldStorage class. This class reads the contents of a form by reading and parsing the query string passed in an environment variable or standard input. Because input can be read from standard input, only one instance should be created. An instance f of FieldStorage has the following attributes:

Attribute	Description
f.name	The field name, if specified.
f.filename	Client-side filename used in uploads.
f.value	Value as a string.
f.file	File-like object from which data can be read.
f.type	Content type.
f.type_options	Dictionary of options specified on the content-type line of the HTTP request.
f.disposition	The 'content-disposition' field; None if not specified.
f.disposition_options	Dictionary of disposition options.
f.headers	A dictionary-like object containing all the HTTP header contents.

In addition, the cgi module defines a class MiniFieldStorage that contains only the attribute's name and value. This class is used to represent individual fields of a form passed in the query string, whereas FieldStorage is used to contain multiple fields and multipart data.

Instances of FieldStorage are accessed like a Python dictionary where the keys are the field names on the form. When accessed in this manner, the objects returned are themselves an instance of FieldStorage for multipart data or file uploads, an instance of MiniFieldStorage for simple fields, or a list of such instances in cases where a form contains multiple fields with the same name.

If a field represents an uploaded file, accessing the value attribute reads the entire file into memory as a string. Because this may consume a large amount of memory on the server, it may be preferable to read uploaded data in smaller pieces by reading from the file attribute directly. For instance, the following example reads uploaded data line by line:

```
fileitem = form["userfile"]
if fileitem.file:
    # It's an uploaded file; count lines
    linecount = 0
    while 1:
        line = fileitem.file.readline()
        if not line: break
        linecount = linecount + 1
```

The following functions provide a more low-level CGI interface:

escape(s [, quote])

Converts the characters '&', '<', and '>' in string s to HTML–safe sequences such as '>', '<', and '>'. If the optional flag *quote* is true, the double–quote character (") is also translated.

parse([fp [, environ [, keep_blank_values [, strict_parsing]]]])

Parses a form into a dictionary. *fp* is a file object from which data is read (defaults to stdin). *environ* is a dictionary containing environment variables (defaults to os.environ). *keep_blank_values*, if set, instructs the parser to map blank entries into empty strings. Otherwise, blank entries are ignored (the default). The *strict_parsing* option specifies what to do with parsing errors. By default, errors are ignored. If set, parsing errors result in a ValueError exception. Returns a dictionary mapping field names to lists of values.

parse_header(string)

Parses the data supplied after an HTTP header field such as 'content-type'. The data is split into a primary value and a dictionary of secondary parameters that are returned in a tuple. For example, this command:

```
parse_header('text/html'; a=hello; b="world")
```

returns this result:

```
('text/html', {'a':'hello', 'b':'world'}).
```

parse_multipart(fp, pdict)

Parses input of type 'multipart/form-data' as is commonly used with file uploads. *fp* is the input file and *pdict* is a dictionary containing parameters of the content-type header. Returns a dictionary mapping field names to lists of values. This function doesn't work with nested multipart data. The FieldStorage class should be used instead.

parse_qs(qs [, keep_blank_values [, strict_parsing]]):

Parses a query string *qs*. *keep_blank_values* and *strict_parsing* have the same meaning as in parse(). Returns a dictionary mapping field names to lists of values.

print_directory()

Formats the contents of the current working directory in HTML. Used for debugging.

print_environ()

Formats the shell environment in HTML. Used for debugging.

print_environ_usage()

Prints a list of useful environment variables in HTML. Used for debugging.

print_form(form)

Formats the data supplied on a form in HTML. *form* must be an instance of FieldStorage. Used for debugging.

test()

Writes a minimal HTTP header and prints all the information provided to the script in HTML format. Primarily used for debugging.

Notes

- The process of installing a CGI program varies widely according to the type of Web server being used. Typically programs are placed in a special "cgi-bin" directory. A server may also require additional configuration.

- On Unix, Python CGI programs may require a line such as the following as the first line of the program:

```
#!/usr/local/bin/python
import cgi
...
```

- To simplify debugging, it's sometimes useful to set sys.stderr to sys.stdout. This will force Python error messages to be sent to the output stream (which will then appear in the text sent to the browser).

- If you invoke an external program (for example, via the os.system() or os.popen() functions), be careful not to pass arbitrary strings received from the client to the shell. This is a well-known security hole that hackers can use to execute arbitrary shell commands on the server. In particular, never pass any part of a URL or form data to a shell command unless it has first been thoroughly checked by making sure that the string contains only alphanumeric characters, dashes, underscores, and periods.

- On Unix, don't give a CGI program setuid mode. This is a security liability and not supported on all machines.

- Don't use 'from cgi import *' with this module.

> ▶ **See Also** CGIHTTPServer (p. 194).

CGIHTTPServer

Availability: A

The CGIHTTPServer module provides a simple HTTP server handler that can run CGI scripts. The server is defined by the following request handler class, intended for use with the BaseHTTPServer module:

CGIHTTPRequestHandler(*request, client_address, server*)

Serves files from the current directory and all its subdirectories. In addition, the handler will run a file as a CGI script if it's located in a special CGI directory. The handler supports both GET and POST methods.

The list of valid CGI directories is contained in the following attribute:

CGIHTTPRequestHandler.cgi_directories

List of CGI directories. Defaults to ['/cgi-bin', '/htbin'].

Example

```
from BaseHTTPServer import HTTPServer
from CGIHTTPServer import CGIHTTPRequestHandler
import os
# Change to the document root
os.chdir("/home/httpd/html")
# Start the CGI server
serv = HTTPServer(("",80),CGIHTTPRequestHandler)
serv.serve_forever()
```

Notes

- For security, CGI scripts are executed with a UID of user nobody.

- Problems with the CGI script will be translated to error 403.

- Requests are handled using the do_GET and do_POST methods, both of which can be redefined in subclasses.

  ▶ **See Also** BaseHTTPServer (p. 188), SimpleHTTPServer (p. 200),
  cgi (p. 190), httplib (p. 195).

ftplib

Availability: A

The ftplib module is used to implement the client side of the FTP protocol. It's rarely necessary to use this module directly, as the urllib module provides a higher-level interface. The following example illustrates the use of this module:

```
>>> import ftplib
>>> ftp = ftplib.FTP('ftp.python.org')
>>> ftp.login()
>>> ftp.retrlines('LIST')
total 40
drwxrwxr-x  12 root      4127       512 Apr  6 19:57 .
drwxrwxr-x  12 root      4127       512 Apr  6 19:57 ..
drwxrwxr-x   2 root      4127       512 Aug 25  1998 RCS
lrwxrwxrwx   1 root      bin         11 Jun 29 18:34 README -> welcome.msg
drwxr-xr-x   3 root      wheel      512 May 19  1998 bin
...
>>> ftp.retrbinary('RETR README', open('README', 'wb').write)
'226 Transfer complete.'
>>> ftp.quit()
```

Consult the online documentation for a complete description of the functionality contained in this module.

  ▶ **See Also** urllib (p. 209), http://www.python.org/doc/lib/module-ftplib.html,
  Internet RFC 959.

httplib

Availability : A

This module implements the client side of the Hypertext Transfer Protocol (HTTP) used in World Wide Web applications. The HTTP protocol is a simple text-based protocol that works as follows:

1. A client makes a connection to a Web server and sends a request header of the following form:

```
GET /document.html HTTP/1.0
Connection: Keep-Alive
User-Agent: Mozilla/4.61 [en] (X11; U; SunOS 5.6 sun4u)
Host: rustler.cs.uchicago.edu:8000
Accept: image/gif, image/x-xbitmap, image/jpeg, image/pjpeg, image/png, */*
Accept-Encoding: gzip
Accept-Language: en
Accept-Charset: iso-8859-1,*,utf-8

Data (optional)
...
```

The first line defines the request type, document (the selector), and protocol version. Following the request line are a series of header lines containing various information about the client, such as passwords, cookies, cache preferences, and client software. Following the header lines, a single blank line appears to indicate the end of the headers. After the header, data may appear in the event that the request is sending from a form or uploading a file. Each of the lines in the header should be terminated by a carriage return and a newline ('\r\n').

2. The server sends a response of the following form:

```
HTTP/1.0  200  OK
Content-type: text/html
Content-length:  72883 bytes
...
Header: data

Data
...
```

The first line of the server response indicates the HTTP protocol version, a success code, and return message. Following the response line are a series of header fields that contain information about the type of the returned document, the document size, Web server software, cookies, and so forth. The header is terminated by a single blank line followed by the raw data of the requested document.

The following request methods are the most common:

Method	Description
GET	Get a document.
POST	Post data to a form.
HEAD	Return header information only.
PUT	Upload data to the server.

The following response codes are returned by servers:

Code	Description
Success Codes (2xx)	
200	OK.
201	Created.
202	Accepted.
204	No content.
Redirection (3xx)	
300	Multiple choices.
301	Moved permanently.
302	Moved temporarily.
303	Not modified.
Client Error (4xx)	
400	Bad request.
401	Unauthorized.

Code	Description
403	Forbidden.
404	Not found.
Server Error (5xx)	
500	Internal server error.
501	Not implemented.
502	Bad gateway.
503	Service unavailable.

A wide range of optional header fields can appear in both the request and response headers. These headers are specified in a format known as RFC 822, in which headers are specified in the form *Header*: *data*. For example:

```
Date: Fri, 16 Jul 1999 17:09:33 GMT
Server: Apache/1.3.6 (Unix)
Last-Modified: Mon, 12 Jul 1999 19:08:14 GMT
ETag: "741d3-44ec-378a3d1e"
Accept-Ranges: bytes
Content-Length: 17644
Connection: close
Content-Type: text/html
```

The following function creates an instance of an HTTP class that's used to create a connection:

HTTP([*host* [, *port*]])

Establishes a connection with an HTTP server. *host* is the hostname and *port* is an optional port number. If no port number is given, the port is extracted from the hostname if it's of the form '*host:port*'. Otherwise, port 80 is used. If no host is passed, no connection is made and the connect() method should be used to make the connection manually.

An instance *h* of the HTTP class has the following methods:

h.connect(*host* [, *port*])

Connects to the server given by *host* and *port*. This should be called only if the instance was created without a host.

h.send(*data*)

Sends data to the server. This should only be used after the endheaders() method.

h.putrequest(*request, selector*)

Sends a line to the server containing the request string, selector string, and the HTTP version (HTTP/1.0).

h.putheader(*header, argument* [, ...])

Sends an RFC 822 style header to the server. It sends a line to the server consisting of the header, a colon and a space, and the first argument. If more arguments are given, continuation lines are sent, each consisting of a tab and an argument.

h.endheaders()

Sends a blank line to the server, indicating the end of the headers.

h.getreply()

Closes the sending end of the connection, reads the reply from the server, and returns a triple (*replycode, message, headers*). *replycode* is the integer reply code from the request, such as 200 on success. *message* is the message string corresponding to the reply code. *headers* is an instance of the class mimetools.Message, containing the HTTP headers received from the server.

h.getfile()

Returns a file object from which the data returned by the server can be read, using the read(), readline(), or readlines() method.

Example

```
import httplib
h = httplib.HTTP('www.python.org')
h.putrequest('GET', '/index.html')
h.putheader('Accept', 'text/html')
h.putheader('Accept', 'text/plain')
h.endheaders()
errcode, errmsg, headers = h.getreply()
print errcode # Should be 200
f = h.getfile()
data = f.read() # Get the raw HTML
f.close()
```

Notes

- This module is used by the urllib module.

- Only HTTP 0.9 and HTTP 1.0 are supported at this time.

    ▶ **See Also** urllib (p. 209), mimetools (p. 214), asyncore (p. 185), BaseHTTPServer (p. 188), SimpleHTTPServer (p. 200), CGIHTTPServer (p. 194).

imaplib

Availability: A

The imaplib module provides a low-level client-side interface for connecting to an IMAP4 mail server using the IMAP4rev1 protocol. Documents describing the protocol, as well as sources and binaries for servers implementing it, can be found at the University of Washington's IMAP Information Center.

The following example shows how the module is used by opening a mailbox and printing all messages:

```
import getpass, imaplib, string
m = imaplib.IMAP4()
m.login(getpass.getuser(), getpass.getpass())
m.select()
typ, data = m.search(None, 'ALL')
for num in string.split(data[0]):
    typ, data = m.fetch(num, '(RFC822)')
    print 'Message %s\n%s\n' % (num, data[0][1])
m.logout()
```

    ▶ **See Also** poplib (p. 199), http://www.python.org/doc/lib/module-imaplib.html, http://www.cac.washington.edu/imap, Internet RFC 1730, RFC 2060.

nntplib

Availability: A

The nntplib module provides a low-level interface to the client side of the NNTP (Network News Transfer Protocol) protocol. For details about using this module, see the online documentation. The following example shows how the module can be used to post a news message from a file containing valid news headers:

```
s = NNTP('news.foo.com')
f = open('article')
s.post(f)
s.quit()
```

▶ **See Also** http://www.python.org/doc/lib/module-nntplib.html, Internet RFC 977.

poplib

Availability: A

The poplib module provides a low-level client-side connection to a POP3 mail server. Consult the online reference for specific details. The following example opens a mailbox and retrieves all messages:

```
import getpass, poplib
M = poplib.POP3('localhost')
M.user(getpass.getuser())
M.pass_(getpass.getpass())
numMessages = len(M.list()[1])
for i in range(numMessages):
    for j in M.retr(i+1)[1]:
        print j
```

▶ **See Also** http://www.python.org/doc/lib/module-poplib.html, Internet RFC 1725.

select

Availability: U, W, M

The select module provides access to the select() system call. select() is typically used to implement polling or to multiplex processing across multiple input/output streams without using threads or subprocesses. On Unix and Macintosh, it works for files, sockets, pipes, and most other file types. On Windows, it only works for sockets.

select(*iwtd, owtd, ewtd* [, *timeout*])

Queries the input, output, and exceptional status of a group of file descriptors. The first three arguments are lists containing either integer file descriptors or objects with a method fileno() that can be used to return a file descriptor. The *iwtd* parameter specifies objects waiting for input, *owtd* specifies objects waiting for output, and *ewtd* specifies objects waiting for an exceptional condition. Each list may be empty. *timeout* is a floating-point number specifying a timeout period in seconds. If omitted, the function waits until at least one file descriptor is ready. If 0, the function merely performs a poll and returns immediately. The return value is a triple of lists containing the objects that are ready. These are subsets of the first three arguments. If none of the objects is ready before the timeout occurs, three empty lists are returned.

Exception

error

Exception raised when an error occurs. Its value is the same as returned by IOError and OSError.

Example

The following code shows how select() could be used in an event loop that wants to periodically query a collection of sockets for an incoming connection:

```
import socket, select
# Create a few sockets
s1 = socket.socket(socket.AF_INET, socket.SOCK_STREAM)
s1.bind("",8888)
s1.listen(5)
s2 = socket.socket(socket.AF_INET, socket.SOCK_STREAM)
s2.bind("",8889)
s2.listen(5)
# Event loop
while 1:
        ... processing ...
        # Poll the sockets for activity
        input,output,exc = select.select([s1,s2],[],[],0)
        # Loop over all of the sockets that have pending input
        for sock in input:
                # Accept an incoming connection
                client = sock.accept()
                ... handle client ...
                client.close()
        # Done. Carry on.
        ... more processing ...
```

Note

There's an upper limit on the number of file selectors that can be given to select(). It's often 64 for Windows and 256 for Unix.

▶ **See Also** asyncore (p. 185), socket (p. 202), os (p. 145).

SimpleHTTPServer

Availability: A

The SimpleHTTPServer module provides a simple HTTP server handler that can serve files from the current directory. The module defines the following handler class, intended for use with the BaseHTTPServer module:

SimpleHTTPRequestHandler(*request, client_address, server*)

Serves files from the current directory and all its subdirectories. The class implements the do_HEAD() and do_GET() methods to support HEAD and GET requests, respectively. All IOError exceptions result in a 404 File not found error. Attempts to access a directory result in a 403 Directory listing not supported error.

The following class attributes are available:

SimpleHTTPRequestHandler.server_version

Server version string.

SimpleHTTPRequestHandler.extensions_map

A dictionary mapping suffixes into MIME types. Unrecognized file types are considered to be of type 'text/plain'.

Example

```
from BaseHTTPServer import HTTPServer
from SimpleHTTPServer import SimpleHTTPRequestHandler
import os
# Change to the document root
os.chdir("/home/httpd/html")
# Start the SimpleHTTP server
serv = HTTPServer(("",80),SimpleHTTPRequestHandler)
serv.serve_forever()
```

▶ **See Also** BaseHTTPServer (p. 188), CGIHTTPServer (p. 194), httplib (p. 195).

smtplib

Availability: A

The smtplib module provides a low-level SMTP client interface that can be used to send mail. For specific details about the module, see the online reference. The following example shows how the module might be used by prompting the user for an address and sending a message:

```
import string, sys
import smtplib
def prompt(prompt):
    sys.stdout.write(prompt + ": ")
    return string.strip(sys.stdin.readline())
fromaddr = prompt("From")
toaddrs  = string.splitfields(prompt("To"), ',')
print "Enter message, end with ^D:"
msg = ""
while 1:
    line = sys.stdin.readline()
    if not line:
        break
    msg = msg + line
print "Message length is " + `len(msg)`
server = smtplib.SMTP('localhost')
server.sendmail(fromaddr, toaddrs, msg)
server.quit()
```

▶ **See Also** poplib (p. 199), imaplib (p. 198),
http://www.python.org/doc/lib/module-smtplib.html,
Internet RFC 821 (Simple Mail Transfer Protocol),
Internet RFC 1869 (SMTP Service Extensions).

socket

Availability: A

The `socket` module provides access to the BSD socket interface. Although it's based on Unix, this module is available on all platforms.

gethostbyname(*hostname*)

Translates a hostname such as `'www.python.org'` to an IP address. The IP address is returned as a string such as `'132.151.1.90'`.

gethostbyname_ex(*hostname*)

Translates a hostname to an IP address, but returns a triple (*hostname*, *aliaslist*, *ipaddrlist*) where *hostname* is the primary hostname, *aliaslist* is a list of alternative hostnames for the same address, and *ipaddrlist* is a list of IP addresses for the same interface on the same host. For example, gethostbyname_ex(`"www.python.org"`) returns (`'parrot.python.org'`, [`'www.python.org'`], [`'132.151.1.90'`]).

gethostname()

Returns the hostname of the local machine.

gethostbyaddr(*ip_address*)

Returns the same information as gethostbyname_ex() given an IP address such as `'132.151.1.90'`.

getprotobyname(*protocolname*)

Translate an Internet protocol name such as `'icmp'` to a constant such as IPPROTO_CMP that can be passed to the third argument of the socket() function.

getservbyname(*servicename*, *protocolname*)

Translates an Internet service name and protocol name to a port number for that service. For example, getservbyname(`'ftp'`, `'tcp'`) returns 21. The protocol name should be `'tcp'` or `'udp'`.

socket(*family*, *type* [, *proto*])

Creates a new socket using the given address family, socket type, and protocol number. *family* is one of the following constants:

Constant	Description
AF_INET	IPv4 protocols (TCP, UDP).
AF_UNIX	Unix domain protocols.

The socket type is one of the following constants:

Constant	Description
SOCK_STREAM	Stream socket (TCP).
SOCK_DGRAM	Datagram socket (UDP).
SOCK_RAW	Raw socket (available with AF_INET only).
SOCK_SEQPACKET	Sequenced connection-mode transfer of records.

The protocol number is usually omitted (and defaults to 0). It's usually used only in conjunction with raw sockets (SOCK_RAW) and is set to one of the following constants when used: IPPROTO_ICMP, PPROTO_IP, IPPROTO_RAW, IPPROTO_TCP, IPPROTO_UDP.

To open a TCP connection, use socket(AF_INET, SOCK_STREAM). To open a UDP connection, use socket(AF_INET, SOCK_DGRAM). The function returns an instance of SocketType (described shortly).

fromfd(fd, family, type [, proto])

Creates a socket object from an integer file descriptor fd. The address family, socket type, and protocol number are the same as for socket(). The file descriptor must refer to a previously created socket. Returns an instance of SocketType.

ntohl(x)

Converts 32-bit integers from network (big-endian) to host byte order.

ntohs(x)

Converts 16-bit integers from network to host byte order.

htonl(x)

Converts 32-bit integers from host to network byte order.

htons(x)

Converts 16-bit integers from host to network byte order.

Sockets are represented by an instance of type SocketType. The following methods are available on a socket s:

s.accept()

Accepts a connection and returns a pair (conn, address) where conn is a new socket object that can be used to send and receive data on the connection, and address is the address of the socket on the other end of the connection.

s.bind(address)

Binds the socket to an address. The format of address depends on the address family. In most cases, it's a tuple of the form (hostname, port). For IP addresses, the empty string represents INADDR_ANY, and the string '<broadcast>' represents INADDR_BROADCAST. The INADDR_ANY hostname (the empty string) is used to indicate that the server allows connections on any Internet interface on the system. This is often used when a server is multihomed. The INADDR_BROADCAST hostname ('<broadcast>') is used when a socket is being used to send a broadcast message.

s.close()

Closes the socket. Sockets are also closed when they're garbage collected.

s.connect(address)

Connects to a remote socket at address. The format of address depends on the address family, but it's normally a pair (hostname, port). Raises error if an error occurs.

If you're connecting to a server on the same computer, you can use the name "localhost" as the first argument to s.connect.

s.connect_ex(address)

The same as connect(address), but returns 0 on success or the value of errno on failure.

s.fileno()

Returns the socket's file descriptor.

s.getpeername()

Returns the remote address to which the socket is connected as a pair (*ipaddr*, *port*). Not supported on all systems.

s.getsockname()

Return the socket's own address as a pair (*ipaddr*, *port*).

s.getsockopt(*level*, *optname* [, *buflen*])

Returns the value of a socket option. *level* defines the level of the option and is `SOL_SOCKET` for socket-level options or a protocol number such as `IPPROTO_IP` for protocol-related options. *optname* selects a specific option. If *buflen* is omitted, an integer option is assumed and its integer value is returned. If *buflen* is given, it specifies the maximum length of the buffer used to receive the option. This buffer is returned as a string, where it's up to the caller to decode its contents using the `struct` module or other means. The following list shows commonly used option names for level `SOL_SOCKET`:

Option Name	Value	Description
SO_KEEPALIVE	0, 1	Periodically probes the other end of the connection and terminates if it's half-open.
SO_RCVBUF	int	Size of receive buffer (in bytes).
SO_SNDBUF	int	Size of send buffer (in bytes).
SO_REUSEADDR	0, 1	Allows local address reuse.
SO_RCVLOWAT	int	Number of bytes read before select() returns the socket as readable.
SO_SNDLOWAT	int	Number of bytes available in send buffer before select() returns the socket as writable.
SO_RCVTIMEO	*tvalue*	Timeout on receive calls in seconds.
SO_SNDTIMEO	*tvalue*	Timeout on send calls in seconds.
SO_OOBINLINE	0, 1	Places out-of-band data into the input queue.
SO_LINGER	*linger*	Lingers on close() if the send buffer contains data.
SO_DONTROUTE	0, 1	Bypasses routing table lookups.
SO_ERROR	int	Gets error status.
SO_BROADCAST	0, 1	Allows sending of broadcast datagrams.
SO_TYPE	int	Gets socket type.
SO_USELOOPBACK	0, 1	Routing socket gets copy of what it sends.

tvalue is a binary structure that's decoded as (*second*, *microsec*) = `struct.unpack("ll", tvalue)`.

linger is a binary structure that's decoded as (*linger_onoff*, *linger_sec*) = `struct.unpack("ii", linger)`.

The following options are available for level `IPPROTO_IP`:

Option Name	Value	Description
IP_ADD_MEMBERSHIP	*ipmreg*	Join multicast group (set only).
IP_DROP_MEMBERSHIP	*ipmreg*	Leave a multicast group (set only).
IP_HDRINCL	*int*	IP header included with data.
IP_MULTICAST_IF	*inaddr*	Outgoing interface.
IP_MULTICAST_LOOP	*uchar*	Loopback.
IP_MULTICAST_TTL	*uchar*	Time to live.
IP_OPTIONS	*char[44]*	IP header options.
IP_TOS	*int*	Type of service.
IP_TTL	*int*	Time to live.

inaddr is a 32-bit binary structure containing an IP address (struct.unpack('bbbb', *inaddr*)). *ipmreg* is a 64-bit binary structure containing two IP addresses in the same format as *inaddr*. *uchar* is a one-byte unsigned integer as created by struct.pack('b',*uvalue*). char[44] is a string containing at most 44 bytes.

Not all options are available on all machines. Refer to an advanced networking book for specific details about each option.

s.listen(*backlog*)

Starts listening for incoming connections. *backlog* specifies the maximum number of pending connections the operating system should queue before connections are refused. The value should be at least 1, with 5 being sufficient for most applications.

s.makefile([*mode* [, *bufsize*]])

Creates a file object associated with the socket. *mode* and *bufsize* have the same meaning as with the built-in open() function. The file object uses a duplicated version of the socket file descriptor (created using os.dup()), so the file object and socket object can be closed or garbage collected independently.

s.recv(*bufsize* [, *flags*])

Receives data from the socket. The data is returned as a string. The maximum amount of data to be received is specified by *bufsize*. *flags* provides additional information about the message and is usually omitted (in which case it defaults to zero). If used, it's usually set to one of the following constants (system dependent):

Constant	Description
MSG_PEEK	Look at data, but don't discard (receive only).
MSG_WAITALL	Don't return until the requested number of bytes have been read (receive only).
MSG_OOB	Receive/send out-of-band data.
MSG_DONTROUTE	Bypass routing table lookup (send only).

s.recvfrom(*bufsize* [, *flags*])

Similar to the recv() method except that the return value is a pair (*data*, *address*) where *data* is a string containing the data received and *address* is the address of the socket sending the data. The optional *flags* argument has the same meaning as for recv(). This function is primarily used in conjunction with the UDP protocol.

s.send(*string* [, *flags*])

Sends data in *string* to a connected socket. The optional *flags* argument has the same meaning as for recv(), described earlier. Returns the number of bytes sent.

s.sendto(*string* [, *flags*], *address*)

Sends data to the socket. *flags* has the same meaning as for recv(). *address* is a tuple of the form (*host*, *port*) that specifies the remote address. The socket should not already be connected. Returns the number of bytes sent. This function is primarily used in conjunction with the UDP protocol.

s.setblocking(*flag*)

If *flag* is zero, the socket is set to nonblocking mode. Otherwise, the socket is set to blocking mode (the default). In nonblocking mode, if a recv() call doesn't find any data or if a send() call can't immediately send the data, the error exception is raised. In blocking mode, these calls block until they can proceed.

s.setsockopt(*level*, *optname*, *value*)

Sets the value of the given socket option. *level* and *optname* have the same meaning as for *getsockopt*. The value can be an integer or a string representing the contents of a buffer. In the latter case, it's up to the caller to ensure that the string contains the proper data. See getsockopt() for socket option names, values, and descriptions.

s.shutdown(*how*)

Shuts down one or both halves of the connection. If *how* is 0, further receives are disallowed. If *how* is 1, further sends are disallowed. If *how* is 2, further sends and receives are disallowed.

Exception

error

This exception is raised for socket or address-related errors. It returns a pair (*errno*, *mesg*) with the error returned by the underlying system call.

Example

A simple example of a TCP connection is shown on page 184. The following example illustrates a simple UDP client and server:

```
# UDP message server
# Receive small packets from anywhere and print them out
import socket
s = socket.socket(socket.AF_INET, socket.SOCK_DGRAM)
s.bind("",10000)
while 1:
    data, address = s.recvfrom(256)
    print address[0], "said : ", data

# UDP message client
# Send a message packet to the server
import socket
s = socket.socket(socket.AF_INET, socket.SOCK_DGRAM)
while 1:
    msg = raw_input("Say something : ")
    if msg:
        s.sendto(msg, ("servername",10000))
    else:
        break
s.close()
```

Notes

- Not all constants and socket options are available on all platforms.

- The socket module currently doesn't support a number of other network protocols such as IPX and IPv6. However, a number of additions to the socket module are likely to appear in future Python releases.

  ▶ **See Also** SocketServer (p. 207), asyncore (p. 185), select (p. 199).

SocketServer

Availability: A

The SocketServer module is used to write TCP, UDP, and Unix domain socket servers. Rather than having to implement servers using the low-level socket module, this module provides four classes that implement the above protocols:

TCPServer(*address, handler*)

A server supporting the TCP protocol. *address* is a 2-tuple of the form (*host, port*), where *host* is the hostname and *port* is the port number. Typically, *host* is set to the empty string. *handler* is an instance of the **BaseRequestHandler** class described later.

UDPServer(*address, handler*)

A server supporting the Internet UDP protocol. *address* and *handler* are the same as for TCPServer().

UnixStreamServer(*address, handler*)

A server implementing a stream-oriented protocol using Unix domain sockets.

UnixDatagramServer(*address, handler*)

A server implementing a datagram protocol using Unix domain sockets.

Instances of all four server classes have the following methods and attributes:

s.fileno()

Returns the integer file descriptor for the server socket.

s.handle_request()

Waits for a request and handles it by creating an instance of the handler class (described shortly) and invoking its handle() method.

s.serve_forever()

Handles an infinite number of requests.

s.address_family

The protocol family of the server, either socket.AF_INET or socket.AF_UNIX.

s.RequestHandlerClass

The user-provided request handler class that was passed to the server constructor.

s.server_address

The address on which the server is listening, such as ('127.0.0.1', 80).

s.socket

The socket object being used for incoming requests.

In addition, the server classes define the following class attributes (<*ServerClass*> should be filled in with the name of one of the four available classes):

<ServerClass>.request_queue_size

The size of the request queue that's passed to the socket's listen() method. The default value is 5.

<ServerClass>.socket_type

The socket type used by the server, such as socket.SOCK_STREAM or socket.SOCK_DGRAM.

Requests are handled by defining a subclass of the class BaseRequestHandler. When the server receives a connection, it creates an instance *h* of the handler class and invokes the following methods:

h.finish()

Called to perform cleanup actions after the handler() method has completed. By default, it does nothing. It's not called if either the setup() or handle() method generates an exception.

h.handle()

This method is called to perform the actual work of a request. It's called with no arguments, but several instance variables are set to useful values. *h*.request contains the request, *h*.client_address contains the client address, and *h*.server contains an instance of the server that called the handler. For stream services such as TCP, the *h*.request attribute is a socket object. For datagram services, it's a string containing received data.

h.setup()

This method is called before the handle() method to perform initialization actions. By default, it does nothing.

The process of creating a server involves the following steps:

1. Define a request handler class by subclassing BaseRequestHandler.

2. Create an instance of one of the server classes by passing the server's address and the request handler class.

3. Call the handle_request() or serve_forever() method of the server to process connections.

The following code illustrates the process for a very simple HTTP server that simply echoes the HTTP request back in a Web page:

```
import SocketServer
import socket
import string
# Read an HTTP request from a client and bounce it back in a web-page
class EchoHandler(SocketServer.BaseRequestHandler):
    def handle(self):
        f = self.request.makefile()
        self.request.send("HTTP/1.0 200 OK\r\n")
        self.request.send("Content-type: text/plain\r\n\r\n")
        self.request.send("Received connection from %s\r\n\r\n" %
                          (self.client_address,))
        while 1:
            line = f.readline()
            self.request.send(line)
```

```
        if not string.strip(line):
            break
    f.close()
# Create the server and start serving
serv = SocketServer.TCPServer(("",80),EchoHandler)
serv.serve_forever()
```

By default, the server classes process requests one at a time in a synchronous manner. The servers can alternatively handle requests in a subprocess (using os.fork()) or as a separate thread by instantiating one of the following server classes instead of the four classes listed earlier:

- ForkingUDPServer(*address, handler*)

- ForkingTCPServer(*address, handler*)

- ThreadingUDPServer(*address, handler*)

- ThreadingTCPServer(*address, handler*)

Finally, two additional classes can be used as base classes for handlers: StreamRequestHandler and DatagramRequestHandler. When used, these classes override the setup() and finish() methods of the handle to provide two file attributes self.rfile and self.wfile that can be used to read and write data to and from the client, respectively. For example:

```
# Read an HTTP request from a client and bounce it back
class EchoHandler(SocketServer.StreamRequestHandler):
    def handle(self):
        self.wfile.write("HTTP/1.0 200 OK\r\n")
        self.wfile.write("Content-type: text/plain\r\n\r\n")
        self.wfile.write("Received connection from %s\r\n\r\n" %
                         (self.client_address,))
        while 1:
            line = self.rfile.readline()
            self.wfile.write(line)
            if not string.strip(line):
                break
```

Note

All the server classes can be specialized by subclassing. The online documentation contains more information about this topic.

   ▶ **See Also** socket (p. 202), BaseHTTPServer (p. 188), SimpleHTTPServer (p. 200), CGIHTTPServer (p. 194), thread (p. 175), os (p. 145).

urllib

Availability: A

The urllib module is used to fetch data from the World Wide Web.

urlopen(*url* [, *data*])

   Given a uniform resource locator (URL) such as http://www.python.org or ftp://foo.com/pub/foo.tar, this function opens a network connection and returns a file-like object. If the URL doesn't have a scheme identifier such as ftp: or http:, or if it's file:, a local file is opened. If a connection can't be made or an error occurs, an IOError exception is raised. If the URL is an HTTP request, the optional *data* argument specifies that the request should be made using a POST method, in which case the data is uploaded to the server. In this case, the data must be encoded in an 'application/x-www-form-urlencoded' format as produced by the urlencode() function.

urlretrieve(*url* [, *filename* [, *hook*]])

Opens a URL and copies its data to a local file, if necessary. If *url* is a local file or a cached copy of the data exists, no copying is performed. *filename* specifies the name of the local file where data will be saved. If omitted, a temporary filename will be generated. *hook* is a function called after a connection has been made and after each block of data has been read. It's called with three arguments: the number of blocks transferred so far, the block size in bytes, and the total size of the file in bytes. The function returns a tuple (*filename*, *headers*) where *filename* is the name of the local file where the data was saved and *headers* is the information returned by the info() method as described for urlopen(). If the URL corresponds to a local file or if a cached copy was used, *headers* will be None. Raises an IOError if an error occurs.

urlcleanup()

Clears the local cache created by urlretrieve().

quote(*string* [, *safe*])

Replaces special characters in *string* with escape sequences suitable for including in a URL. Letters, digits, and the underscore (_), comma (,) period (.), and hyphen (-) characters are unchanged. All other characters are converted into escape sequences of the form '%xx'. *safe* provides additional characters that should not be quoted and is '/' by default.

quote_plus(*string* [, *safe*])

Calls quote() and additionally replaces all spaces with plus signs.

unquote(*string*)

Replaces escape sequences of the form '%xx' with their single-character equivalent.

unquote_plus(*string*)

Like unquote(), but additionally replaces plus signs with spaces.

urlencode(*dict*)

Converts a dictionary to a URL-encoded string suitable for use as the data argument of the urlopen() function. The resulting string is a series of 'key=value' pairs separated by '&' characters, where both *key* and *value* are quoted using quote_plus().

The file-like object returned by urlopen() supports the following methods:

Method	Description
u.read([*nbytes*])	Reads *nbytes* of data.
u.readline()	Reads a single line of text.
u.readlines()	Reads all input lines and returns a list.
u.fileno()	Returns the integer file descriptor.
u.close()	Closes the connection.

Method	Description
u.info()	Returns the mimetools.Message object containing meta-information associated with the URL. For HTTP, the HTTP headers included the server response are returned. For FTP, the headers include the 'content-length'. For local files, the headers include a date, 'content-length', and 'content-type' field.
u.geturl()	Returns the real URL of the returned data, taking into account any redirection that may have occurred.

Notes

- The only supported protocols are HTTP (versions 0.9 and 1.0), FTP, Gopher, and local files.
- Caching is currently not implemented.
- If a URL points to a local file but the file can't be opened, the URL is opened using the FTP protocol.

    ▶ **See Also** httplib (p. 195), ftplib (p. 195), urlparse (p. 211), mimetools (p. 214).

urlparse

Availability: A

The urlparse module is used to manipulate URL strings such as
"http://www.python.org".The general form of a URL is as follows:

"*scheme:/netloc/path;parameters?query#fragment*"

urlparse(*urlstring* [, *default_scheme* [, *allow_fragments*]])

Parses the URL in *urlstring* and returns a tuple (*scheme, netloc, path, parameters, query, fragment*). *default_scheme* specifies the scheme ("http","ftp", and so on) to be used if none is present in the URL. If *allow_fragments* is zero, fragment identifiers are not allowed.

urlunparse(*tuple*)

Constructs a URL string from a tuple as returned by urlparse().

urljoin(*base, url* [, *allow_fragments*])

Constructs an absolute URL by combining a base URL *base* with a relative URL *url. allow_fragments* has the same meaning as for urlparse().If the last component of the base URL is not a directory, it's stripped.

Examples

```
>>> urlparse("http://www.python.org/index.html")
('http', 'www.python.org', '/index.html', '', '', '')

>>> urlunparse(('http', 'www.python.org', '/index.html', '', '', ''))
'http://www.python.org/index.html'

>>> urljoin("http://www.python.org/index.html","Help.html")
'http://www.python.org/Help.html'
```

    ▶ **See Also** urllib (p. 209), Internet RFC 1738, Internet RFC 1808.

Internet Data Handling and Encoding

The modules in this section are used to encode and decode data formats that are widely used in Internet applications.

base64

Availability: A

The base64 module is used to encode and decode data using base64 encoding. base64 is commonly used to encode binary data in mail attachments.

decode(*input*, *output*)

Decodes base64-encoded data. *input* is a filename or a file object open for reading. *output* is a filename or a file object open for writing.

decodestring(*s*)

Decodes a base64-encoded string *s*. Returns a string containing the decoded binary data.

encode(*input*, *output*)

Encodes data using base64. *input* is a filename or a file object open for reading. *output* is a filename or a file object open for writing.

encodestring(*s*)

Encodes a string *s* using base64.

▶ **See Also** binascii (p. 212), Internet RFC 1421 (http://www.ietf.org).

binascii

Availability: A

The binascii module is used to convert data between binary and a variety of ASCII encodings such as base64, binhex, and UU encoding.

a2b_uu(*string*)

Converts a line of uuencoded data to binary. Lines normally contain 45 (binary) bytes, except for the last line. Line data may be followed by whitespace.

b2a_uu(*data*)

Converts a string of binary data to a line of uuencoded ASCII characters. The length of *data* should not be more than 45 bytes.

a2b_base64(*string*)

Converts a string of base64-encoded data to binary.

b2a_base64(*data*)

Converts a string of binary data to a line of base64-encoded ASCII characters. The length of *data* should not be more than 57 bytes.

a2b_hqx(*string*)

Converts a string of binhex4-encoded data to binary without performing RLE decompression.

rledecode_hqx(*data*)

Performs an RLE (Run-Length Encoding) decompression of the binary data in *data*. Returns the decompressed data unless the data input is incomplete, in which case the Incomplete exception is raised.

rlecode_hqx(*data*)

Performs a binhex4 RLE compression of *data*.

b2a_hqx(*data*)

Converts the binary data to a string of binhex4-encoded ASCII characters. *data* should already be RLE coded and have a length divisible by three.

crc_hqx(*data*, *crc*)

Computes the binhex4 CRC checksum of the data. *crc* is a starting value of the checksum.

Exceptions

Exception	Description
Error	Exception raised on errors.
Incomplete	Exception raised on incomplete data.

▶ **See Also** base64 (p. 212), binhex (p. 213), uu (p. 225).

binhex

Availability: A

The binhex module is used to encode and decode files in binhex4, a format commonly used to represent files on the Macintosh.

binhex(*input*, *output*)

Converts a binary file with name *input* to a binhex file. *output* is a filename or an open file-like object supporting write() and close() methods.

hexbin(*input* [, *output*])

Decodes a binhex file. *input* is either a filename or a file-like object with read() and close() methods. *output* is the name of the output file. If omitted, the output name is taken from the binhex file.

Notes

- Both the data and resource forks are handled on the Macintosh.
- Only the data fork is handled on other platforms.

▶ **See Also** binascii (p. 212), macostools (p. 143).

mailcap

Availability: U

The mailcap module is used to read mailcap files. Mailcap files are used to tell mail readers and Web browsers how to process files with different MIME types. The contents of a mailcap file typically look something like this:

```
video/mpeg; xmpeg %s
application/pdf; acroread %s
```

When data of a given MIME type is encountered, the mailcap file is consulted to find an application for handling that data.

getcaps()

Reads all available mailcap files and returns a dictionary mapping MIME types to a mailcap entry. mailcap files are read from $HOME/.mailcap, /etc/mailcap, /usr/etc/mailcap, and /usr/local/etc/mailcap.

findmatch(*caps*, *mimetype* [, *key* [, *filename* [, *plist*]]])

Searches the dictionary *caps* for a mailcap entry matching *mimetype*. *key* is a string indicating an action and is typically 'view', 'compose', or 'edit'. *filename* is the name of the file that's substituted for the %s keyword in the mailcap entry. *plist* is a list of named parameters and is described further in the online documentation. Returns a tuple (*cmd*, *mailcap*) containing the command from the mailcap file and the raw mailcap entry.

Example

```
import mailcap
caps = mailcap.getgaps()
cmd, mc = mailcap.findmatch(caps,'application/pdf',filename='/tmp/tmp1234')
if cmd:
    os.system(cmd + " &")
else:
    print "No application for type application/pdf"
```

▶ **See Also** mimetypes (p. 216), http://www.python.org/doc/lib/module-mailcap.html, RFC 1524.

mimetools

Availability: A

The mimetools module provides a number of functions for manipulating MIME-encoded messages. MIME (Multipurpose Internet Mail Extensions) is a standard for sending multipart multimedia data through Internet mail. Parts of the standard are also used in other settings, such as the HTTP protocol. A MIME-encoded message looks similar to the following:

```
Content-Type: multipart/mixed; boundary="====_931526447=="
Date: Fri, 09 Jul 1999 03:20:47 -0500
From: John Doe <johndoe@foo.com>
To: Jane Doe (janedoe@foo.com>
Subject: Important Message From John Doe

--====_931526447==
Content-Type: text/plain; charset="us-ascii"

Here is that document you asked for ... don't show anyone else ;-)

--====_931526447==
Content-Type: application/msword; name="list.doc"
Content-Transfer-Encoding: base64
Content-Disposition: attachment; filename="list.doc"

SXQgd2FzIGEgbG9uZyBob3QgZGF5IGluIHRoZSBtb250aCBvaCBvaBKdWx5LCB3aGVuIExhaGcnJ5IHN0
```

YXJ0ZWQgdGFsa2luZwphYm91dCBzb2Npby1wb2xpdGljYWwgc2NhbGFibGUgaW1tZXJzaXZlIHZp
cnRiYWwgdGVtcG9yYWwkY29sbGFib3JhdGl2ZSBwYXJhbGxlbCBoaWdoIHBlcmZvcm1hbmNlIHdl
Yi1iYXN1ZCBtb2JpbGUKb2JqZWN0LW9yaWVudGVkIHNjaWVudGlmaWMgY29tcHV0aW5GVudm1y
b25tZW50cy4gIEZ2cnR1bmF0ZWx5LCBQZXRhQZXR1CmhhZCByZW1lbWJlcmVkIHRvIGJyaW5ghcyAu
NDUuLi4KCg==

`--====_931526447==--`

MIME messages are broken into parts delimited by a line separator such as
`"--====_931526447=="` above. The final separator has a trailing `"--"` appended to
indicate the end of the message. Immediately following each separator is a set of RFC
822 headers describing the content-type and encoding. Data is separated from the
headers by a single blank line.

The `mimetools` module defines the following functions to parse headers and decode
data.

Message(*file* [, *seekable*])

Parses MIME headers and returns a `Message` object derived from the
`rfc822.Message` class. *file* and *seekable* have the same meaning as for `rfc822.Message`.

choose_boundary()

Creates a unique string of the form `'hostipaddr.uid.pid.timestamp.random'` that
can be used as a part-boundary when generating a message.

decode(*input*, *output*, *encoding*)

Reads encoded data from the open file object *input* and writes the decoded data
to the open file object *output*. *encoding* specifies the encoding method: `'base64'`,
`'quoted-printable'`, or `'uuencode'`.

encode(*input*, *output*, *encoding*)

Reads data from the open file object *input*, encodes it, and writes it to the open
file object *output*. Encoding types are the same as for `decode()`.

copyliteral(*input*, *output*)

Read lines of text from the open file *input* until EOF and writes them to the open
file *output*.

copybinary(*input*, *output*)

Read blocks of binary data from the open file *input* until EOF and writes them to
the open file *output*.

Instances of the `Message` class support all of the methods described in the `rfc822`
module. In addition, the following methods are available:

***m*.getplist()**

Returns the parameters for the content-type header as a list of strings. For example,
if the message contains the header `'Content-type: text/html; charset=US-ASCII'` this
function returns `['charset=US-ASCII']`. For parameters of the form `'key=value'`, *key* is
converted to lowercase, while *value* is unchanged.

***m*.getparam(*name*)**

Returns the value of the first parameter of the form `'name=value'` from the
`'content-type'` header. If *value* is surrounded by quotes of the form `'<...>'` or `"..."`,
they're removed.

m.`getencoding()`

Returns the encoding specified in the `'content-transfer-encoding'` message header. If no such header exists, returns `'7bit'`.

m.`gettype()`

Returns the message type from the `'content-type'` header. Types are returned as a string of the form `'type/subtype'`. If no content-type header is available, `'text/plain'` is returned.

m.`getmaintype()`

Returns the primary type from the `'content-type'` header. If no such header exists, returns `'text'`.

m.`getsubtype()`

Returns the subtype from the `'content-type'` header. If no such header exists, returns `'plain'`.

▶ **See Also** `rfc822` (p. 223), `mimetypes` (p. 216), `MimeWriter` (p. 219), `multifile` (p. 220), `mailcap` (p. 213), Internet RFC 1521 (`http://www.ietf.org`).

mimetypes

Availability: A

The `mimetypes` module is used to guess the MIME type associated with a file, based on its filename extension. It also converts MIME types to their standard filename extensions. MIME types consist of a type/subtype pair. The following table shows the MIME types currently recognized by this module:

File Suffix	MIME Type
`.a`	`application/octet-stream`
`.ai`	`application/postscript`
`.aif`	`audio/x-aiff`
`.aifc`	`audio/x-aiff`
`.aiff`	`audio/x-aiff`
`.au`	`audio/basic`
`.avi`	`video/x-msvideo`
`.bcpio`	`application/x-bcpio`
`.bin`	`application/octet-stream`
`.cdf`	`application/x-netcdf`
`.cpio`	`application/x-cpio`
`.csh`	`application/x-csh`
`.dll`	`application/octet-stream`
`.dvi`	`application/x-dvi`
`.exe`	`application/octet-stream`
`.eps`	`application/postscript`
`.etx`	`text/x-setext`
`.gif`	`image/gif`

File Suffix	MIME Type
.gtar	application/x-gtar
.hdf	application/x-hdf
.htm	text/html
.html	text/html
.ief	image/ief
.jpe	image/jpeg
.jpeg	image/jpeg
.jpg	image/jpeg
.latex	application/x-latex
.man	application/x-troff-man
.me	application/x-troff-me
.mif	application/x-mif
.mov	video/quicktime
.movie	video/x-sgi-movie
.mpe	video/mpeg
.mpeg	video/mpeg
.mpg	video/mpeg
.ms	application/x-troff-ms
.nc	application/x-netcdf
.o	application/octet-stream
.obj	application/octet-stream
.oda	application/oda
.pbm	image/x-portable-bitmap
.pdf	application/pdf
.pgm	image/x-portable-graymap
.pnm	image/x-portable-anymap
.png	image/png
.ppm	image/x-portable-pixmap
.py	text/x-python
.pyc	application/x-python-code
.ps	application/postscript
.qt	video/quicktime
.ras	image/x-cmu-raster
.rgb	image/x-rgb
.rdf	application/xml
.roff	application/x-troff
.rtf	application/rtf
.rtx	text/richtext
.sgm	text/x-sgml

continues >>

>>continued

File Suffix	MIME Type
.sgml	text/x-sgml
.sh	application/x-sh
.shar	application/x-shar
.snd	audio/basic
.so	application/octet-stream
.src	application/x-wais-source
.sv4cpio	application/x-sv4cpio
.sv4crc	application/x-sv4crc
.t	application/x-troff
.tar	application/x-tar
.tcl	application/x-tcl
.tex	application/x-tex
.texi	application/x-texinfo
.texinfo	application/x-texinfo
.tif	image/tiff
.tiff	image/tiff
.tr	application/x-troff
.tsv	text/tab-separated-values
.txt	text/plain
.ustar	application/x-ustar
.wav	audio/x-wav
.xbm	image/x-xbitmap
.xml	text/xml
.xsl	application/xml
.xpm	image/x-xpixmap
.xwd	image/x-xwindowdump
.zip	application/zip

guess_type(*filename*)

Guesses the MIME type of a file based on its filename or URL. Returns a tuple (*type*, *encoding*) where *type* is a string of the form type/subtype and *encoding* is the program used to encode the data (for example, compress or gzip). Returns (None, None) if the type can't be guessed.

guess_extension(*type*)

Guesses the standard file extension for a file based on its MIME type. Returns a string with the filename extension including the leading dot (.). Returns None for unknown types.

init([*files*])

Initializes the module. *files* is a sequence of filenames that are read to extract type information. These files contain lines that map a MIME type to a list of acceptable file suffixes such as the following:

```
image/jpeg:            jpe jpeg jpg
text/html:             htm html
...
```

read_mime_types(filename)

Loads type mapping from a given filename. Returns a dictionary mapping filename extensions to MIME type strings. Returns None if filename doesn't exist or can't be read.

knownfiles

List of common names for mime.types files.

suffix_map

Dictionary mapping suffixes to suffixes. This is used to allow recognition of encoded files for which the encoding and the type are indicated by the same extension. For example, the .tgz extension is mapped to .tar.gz to allow the encoding and type to be recognized separately.

encodings_map

Dictionary mapping filename extensions to encoding types.

types_map

Dictionary mapping filename extensions to MIME types.

▶ **See Also** mimetools (p. 214).

MimeWriter

Availability: A

The MimeWriter module defines the class MimeWriter that's used to generate MIME-encoded multipart files.

MimeWriter(fp)

Creates a new instance of the MimeWriter class. fp is an open file object to be used for writing. A StringIO object can also be used.

An instance m of the MimeWriter class has the following methods:

m.addheader(key, value [, prefix])

Adds a header line of the form "key: value" to the MIME message. prefix determines where the header is inserted; 0 appends to the end (the default) and 1 inserts at the start.

m.flushheaders()

Write all the headers accumulated so far.

m.startbody(ctype [, plist [, prefix]])

Returns a file-like object that's used to write to the body of the message. ctype specifies the content type and plist is a list of tuples of the form (name, value) containing additional parameters for the content-type declaration. prefix has the same meaning as for the addheader() method except that its default value is set to insert at the start.

m.startmultipartbody(subtype [, boundary [, plist [, prefix]]])

Returns a file-like object that's used to write the body of a multipart message. subtype specifies the multipart subtype such as 'mixed' and boundary can be used to provide a user-defined boundary specifier. *plist* is a list containing optional parameters for the subtype, and *prefix* is the same as in the `startbody()` method. Subparts are created using `nextpart()`.

m.`nextpart()`

Returns a new instance of `MimeWriter` that represents an individual part in a multipart message. `startmultipartbody()` must be called prior to calling this method.

m.`lastpart()`

This is used to indicated the last part of a multipart message. It should always be called to terminate a multipart message.

Example

The following example takes a list of files passed on the command line and produces a multipart MIME document in which each file is encoded using base64 encoding:

```
import sys
import mimetools, mimetypes, MimeWriter
# Open the output file and create a MimeWriter
out = open("output.txt","w")
writer = MimeWriter.MimeWriter(out)
# Start a multipart message
writer.startmultipartbody("mixed")
writer.flushheaders()
# Iterate over files passed on the command line
for file in sys.argv[1:]:
    subpart = writer.nextpart()  # Create a new subpart
    # Attempt to guess the file's MIME type and encoding
    type,encoding = mimetypes.guess_type(file)
    if encoding:
            subpart.addheader("Content-encoding",encoding)
            subpart.addheader("Content-transfer-encoding","base64")
    if type:
        pout = subpart.startbody(type, [("name",file)])
    else:
        pout = subpart.startbody("text/plain",[("name",file)])
    infile = open(file,"rb")
    # Encode the raw data using base64
    mimetools.encode(infile,pout,'base64')
    infile.close()

# Clean up
writer.lastpart()
out.close()
```

▶ **See Also** `mimetypes` (p. 216), `mimetools` (p. 214), `rfc822` (p. 223), `multifile` (p. 220).

`multifile`

Availability: A

The `multifile` module defines an object that can be used to read multipart text files as found in MIME-encoded messages. The `multifile` object works by splitting a file into a series of logical file-like objects that are delimited by a unique boundary string such as the following:

```
--128.135.11.144.100.4397.932677969.082.3036
Part 1
...
--128.135.11.144.100.4397.932677969.082.3036
Part 2
...
--128.135.11.144.100.4397.932677969.082.3036--
```

In this case, the boundary string is of the form returned by the mimetools.choose_boundary() function. The last boundary string (with a trailing --) marks the end of the multipart data.

MultiFile(*fp* [, seekable])

Create a multi-file object. *fp* is a file-like object containing input data. The input object's readline() method is used to read data. If the seekable option is set, the multi-file object allows random access using the seek() and tell() methods.

A MultiFile object *m* supports the following methods:

m.push(*str*)

Pushes a boundary string into the reader. When this string is encountered in the input, it signals an end of section or end of message. More than one boundary marker can be pushed to handle nested multipart data. However, encountering any other boundary than the most recently pushed value raises an error.

m.readline()

Reads a line of text. If the line matches the most recently pushed boundary, ' ' is returned to indicate the end of the part. Furthermore, if the boundary corresponds to an end marker, the *m*.last attribute is set to 1. Raises Error if an EOF is encountered before all boundary strings have been popped.

m.readlines()

Returns all lines remaining in the current part as a list of strings.

m.read()

Reads all lines remaining in the current part and returns as a single string.

m.next()

Skips to the next section. Returns true if a next section exists, false if an end marker is encountered.

m.pop()

Pops a section boundary. This boundary will no longer be interpreted as EOF.

m.seek(*pos* [, whence])

Seeks to a new position within the current section. The *pos* and *whence* arguments are interpreted as for a file seek.

m.tell()

Returns the file position relative to the start of the current section.

Finally, MultiFile instances have two public-instance variables:

Variable	Description
m.level	Nesting depth of the current part.
m.last	True if the last end-of-file was an end-of-message marker.

Example

```
# Unpack a MIME encoded mail message into parts
import mimetools, multifile, sys
def unpack_part(file,partno):
    headers = mimetools.Message(file)    # Get headers
    type = headers.getmaintype()         # Get main content type
    if type == 'multipart':              # Multipart?
        boundary = headers.getparam("boundary")
        file.push(boundary)
        file.readlines()
        while not mf.last:
            file.next()
            partno = partno + 1
            unpack_part(mf,partno)
        file.pop()
        return
    name = headers.getparam("name")      # Get filename
    if not name: name = "part%d" % (partno,)
    encoding = headers.getencoding()
    print "Unpacking '%s'. Encoding = %s" % (name, encoding)
    if encoding == '7bit':
        outfile = open(name,"w")
        mimetools.copyliteral(file,outfile)
    else:
        outfile = open(name,"wb")
        mimetools.decode(file,outfile,encoding)
    outfile.close()
# Read a filename from options and unpack it
f = open(sys.argv[1])
mf = multifile.MultiFile(f,0)
unpack_part(mf)
```

Note

The `MultiFile` class defines a number of methods that can be specialized in a subclass. Please refer to the online library reference.

▶ **See Also** `mimetools` (p. 214), `MimeWriter` (p. 219), `http://www.python.org/doc/lib/module-multifile.html`.

quopri

Availability: A

The `quopri` module performs quoted-printable transport encoding and decoding. This format is primarily used to encode text files.

decode(*input*, *output*)

Decodes. *input* and *output* are file objects.

encode(*input*, *output*, *quotetabs*)

Encodes. *input* and *output* are file objects. *quotetabs*, if set to true, forces tab characters to be quoted in addition to the normal quoting rules.

▶ **See Also** `binascii` (p. 212), Internet RFC 1521 (`http://www.ietf.org`).

rfc822

Availability: A

The rfc822 module is used to parse email headers presented in a format defined by the Internet standard RFC 822. Headers of this form are used in a number of contexts including mail handling and in the HTTP protocol. A collection of RFC 822 headers looks like this:

```
Return-Path: <beazley@cs.uchicago.edu>
Date: Sat, 17 Jul 1999 10:18:21 -0500 (CDT)
Message-Id: <199907171518.KAA24322@gargoyle.cs.uchicago.edu>
References: <s78caef3.037@mail.conservation.state.mo.us>
        <Pine.WNT.4.04.9907150938330.210-100000@rigoletto.ski.org>
        <199907170324.WAA21001@gargoyle.cs.uchicago.edu>
        <37909181.892EF733@callware.com>
Reply-To: beazley@cs.uchicago.edu
Mime-Version: 1.0 (generated by tm-edit 7.78)
Content-Type: text/plain; charset=US-ASCII
From: David Beazley <beazley@cs.uchicago.edu>
To: psa-members@python.org
Subject: Re: [PSA MEMBERS] Python Conferences

Hi, this is just a reminder...
```

Each header line is of the form 'headername: values' and may span multiple lines provided that additional lines are indented with whitespace. Header names are not case-sensitive, so a field name of 'Content-Type' is the same as 'content-type'. A list of headers is terminated by a single blank line.

RFC 822 headers are parsed by creating an instance of the Message class.

Message(file [, seekable])

Reads RFC 822 headers from the file-like object *file* and returns a Message object. Headers are read using file.readline() until a blank line is encountered. *seekable* is a flag that's set to zero if *file* is unseekable (such as a file created from a socket).

A Message object *m* behaves almost exactly like a dictionary except that its key values aren't case-sensitive and it doesn't support certain dictionary operations, including update() and clear().

Method	Description
m[name]	Returns the value for header *name*.
m[name]=value	Adds a header.
m.keys()	Returns a list of header names.
m.values()	Returns a list of header values.
m.items()	Returns a list of header (name, value) pairs.
m.has_key(name)	Tests for the existence of a header name.
m.get(name [, default])	Gets a header value. Returns *default* if not found.
len(m)	Returns the number of headers.
str(m)	Converts headers to an RFC 822-formatted string.

In addition, the following methods are available:

`m.getallmatchingheaders(`*name*`)`

Returns a list of all lines with headers that match *name*, including continuation lines (if any).

`m.getfirstmatchingheader(`*name*`)`

Returns the list of lines for the first header matching *name*, including any continuation lines. Returns None if *name* doesn't match any headers.

`m.getrawheader(`*name*`)`

Returns a string containing the raw text after the colon for the first header matching *name*. Returns None if no match is found.

`m.getheader(`*name* `[, ` *default*`])`

Like getrawheader(*name*), but strips all leading and trailing whitespace. *default* specifies a default value to return if no matching header is found.

`m.getaddr(`*name*`)`

Returns a pair (*full name, email address*) for a header containing an email address. If no header matches *name*, (None, None) is returned.

`m.getaddrlist(`*name*`)`

Parses a header containing a list of email addresses and returns a list of tuples as returned by the getaddr() method. If multiple headers match the named header, all are parsed for addresses (for example, multiple 'cc' headers).

`m.getdate(`*name*`)`

Parses a header containing a date and returns a 9-tuple compatible with time.mktime(). Returns None if no match is found or the date can't be parsed.

`m.getdate_tz(`*name*`)`

Parses a header containing a date and returns a 10-tuple where the first nine elements are the same as returned by getdate() and the tenth is a number with the offset of the date's timezone from UTC (Greenwich Mean Time). Returns None if no match is found or the date is unparsable.

Finally, messages have two instance attributes:

Variable	Description
`m.headers`	A list containing the entire set of header lines.
`m.fp`	The file-like object passed when the Message was created.

In addition to Message, the `rfc822` module defines the following utility functions:

`parsedate(`*date*`)`

Parses an RFC 822-formatted date such as 'Mon, 19 Jul 1999 17:30:08 -0600' and returns a 9-tuple that's compatible with the time.mktime() function. Returns None if *date* can't be parsed.

`parsedate_tz(`*date*`)`

Parses a date, but returns a 10-tuple where the first nine elements are the same as returned by parsedate() and the tenth item is the offset of the date's timezone from UTC. Returns None if *date* can't be parsed.

`mktime_tz(`*`tuple`*`)`

Turns a 10-tuple as returned by `parsedate_tz()` into a UTC timestamp. If the timezone item is `None`, assumes local time.

`AddressList(`*`addrlist`*`)`

Converts a string containing a list of email addresses into an `AddressList` object. The following operations can be performed on `AddressList` objects:

Operation	Description
`len(a)`	Number of addresses in a list.
`str(a)`	Converts *a* back into a string of email addresses.
`a + b`	Combines two lists of addresses, removing duplicates.
`a - b`	Removes all addresses in list *b* from list *a*.

Example

```
import rfc822
# Open a mail message
f = open("mailmessage")
# Read the headers
m = rfc822.Message(f)
# Extract a few fields
m_from = m["From"]
m_to = m.getaddr("To")
m_subject = m["Subject"]
```

Note

The `Message` class defines a few additional methods that can be specialized in a subclass. Please refer to the online documentation for details.

▶ **See Also** mimetools (p. 214), MimeWriter (p. 219), mimetypes (p. 216), mailcap (p. 213), Internet RFC 822 (http://www.ietf.org), http://www.python.org/doc/lib/module-rfc822.html.

uu

Availability: A

The uu module is used to encode and decode files in uuencode format, transferring binary data over an ASCII-only connection.

`encode(`*`input, output`* `[,` *`name`* `[,` *`mode`*`]])`

Uuencodes a file. *input* is a file object opened for reading or a filename. *output* is a file object opened for writing or a filename. *name* specifies the name of the file that's encoded in the uuencoded file. *mode* specifies the mode of the file. By default, *name* and *mode* are taken from the input file.

`decode(`*`input`* `[,` *`output`* `[,` *`mode`*`]])`

Decodes a uuencoded file. *input* is a file object opened for reading or a filename. *output* is a file object opened for writing or a filename. *mode* is used to set permission bits and overrides the setting encoded in the input file.

▶ **See Also** binascii (p. 212).

xdrlib

Availability: A

xdrlib is used to encode and decode data in the Sun XDR (External Data Representation) format. XDR is often used as a portable way to encode binary data for use in networked applications. It's used extensively in applications involving remote procedure calls (RPC).

Encoding and decoding is controlled through the use of two classes:

Packer()

Creates an object for packing data into an XDR representation.

Unpacker(*data*)

Creates an object for unpacking XDR-encoded data. *data* is a string containing XDR-encoded data values.

An instance *p* of the Packer class supports the following methods:

p.get_buffer()

Returns the current pack buffer as a string.

p.reset()

Resets the pack buffer to the empty string.

p.pack_uint(*x*)

Packs a 32-bit unsigned integer *x*.

p.pack_int(*x*)

Packs a 32-bit signed integer *x*.

p.pack_enum(*x*)

Packs an enumeration *x* (an integer).

p.pack_bool(*x*)

Packs a Boolean value *x*.

p.pack_uhyper(*x*)

Packs a 64-bit unsigned integer *x*.

p.pack_hyper(*x*)

Packs a 64-bit signed integer *x*.

p.pack_float(*x*)

Packs a single-precision floating-point number.

p.pack_double(*x*)

Packs a double-precision floating-point number.

p.pack_fstring(*n*, *s*)

Packs a fixed-length string of length *n*.

p.pack_fopaque(*n*, *data*)

Packs a fixed-length opaque data stream. Similar to pack_fstring().

p.pack_string(*s*)

Packs a variable-length string *s*.

p.pack_opaque(*data*)

Packs a variable-length opaque data string *data*. Similar to pack_string().

p.pack_bytes(*bytes*)

Packs a variable-length byte stream *bytes*. Similar to pack_string().

p.pack_list(*list*, *pack_func*)

Packs a list of homogeneous items. *pack_func* is the function called to pack each data item (for example, *p*.pack_int). For each item in the list, an unsigned integer 1 is packed first, followed by the data item. An unsigned integer 0 is packed at the end of the list.

p.pack_farray(*n*, *array*, *pack_func*)

Packs a fixed-length list of homogeneous items. *n* is the list length, *array* is a list containing the data, and *pack_func* is the function called to pack each data item.

p.pack_array(*list*, *pack_func*)

Packs a variable-length list of homogeneous items by first packing its length and then calling the pack_farray() method.

An instance *u* of the Unpacker class supports the following methods:

u.reset(*data*)

Resets the string buffer with the given data.

u.get_position()

Returns the current unpack position in the data buffer.

u.set_position(*position*)

Sets the data buffer unpack position to *position*.

u.get_buffer()

Returns the current unpack data buffer as a string.

u.done()

Indicates unpack completion. Raises an Error exception if all of the data hasn't been unpacked.

In addition, every data type that can be packed with a Packer can be unpacked with an Unpacker. Unpacking methods are of the form unpack_type(), and take no arguments. They return the unpacked object.

u.unpack_int()

Unpacks a 32-bit signed integer.

u.unpack_uint()

Unpacks a 32-bit unsigned integer.

u.unpack_enum()

Unpacks an enumeration (an integer).

u.unpack_bool()

Unpacks a Boolean value.

u.unpack_hyper()

Unpacks a 64-bit signed integer.

u.`unpack_uhyper()`

Unpacks a 64-bit unsigned integer.

u.`unpack_float()`

Unpacks a single-precision floating-point number.

u.`unpack_double()`

Unpacks a double-precision floating-point number.

u.`unpack_fstring(n)`

Unpacks a fixed-length string. *n* is the number of characters expected.

u.`unpack_fopaque(n)`

Unpacks a fixed-length opaque data stream, similarly to `unpack_fstring()`.

u.`unpack_string()`

Unpacks a variable-length string.

u.`unpack_opaque()`

Unpacks and returns a variable-length opaque data string.

u.`unpack_bytes()`

Unpacks and returns a variable-length byte stream.

u.`unpack_list(unpack_func)`

Unpacks and returns a list of homogeneous items as packed by `pack_list()`. *unpack_func* is the function called to perform the unpacking for each item (for example, `unpack_int`).

u.`unpack_farray(n, unpack_func)`

Unpacks and returns (as a list) a fixed-length array of homogeneous items. *n* is the number of list elements to expect and *unpack_func* is the function used to unpack each item.

u.`unpack_array(unpack_func)`

Unpacks and returns a variable-length list of homogeneous items. *unpack_func* is the function used to unpack each item.

Exceptions

Exception	Description
`Error`	The base exception class. `Error` has a single public data member `msg` containing the description of the error.
`ConversionError`	Class derived from `Error`. Contains no additional instance variables.

Note

Objects created with `xdrlib` can be pickled using the `pickle` module.

▶ **See Also** `struct` (p. 118), `array` (p.106), Internet RFC 1014 (http://www.ietf.org).

Restricted Execution

Normally, a Python program has complete access to the machine on which it runs. In particular, it can open files and network connections, and perform other potentially sensitive operations. In certain applications, however, this is undesirable—especially in Internet applications, in which a program may be subject to attackers or when code from an untrusted source is executed.

To provide some measure of safety, Python provides support for restricted execution. Restricted execution is based on the notion of separating trusted and untrusted code. In particular, a program running in trusted mode (a *supervisor*) can create an execution environment (or *sandbox*) in which untrusted code can be executed with limited privileges. The capabilities of the untrusted code are tightly controlled by the supervisor, which can restrict the set of objects that can be accessed as well as the behavior of individual functions.

Python's restricted execution mode is implemented by playing a number of tricks with dictionaries, namespaces, and the environment in which untrusted code executes. As a result, untrusted code uses the same set of function names and modules that would be used in a normal program (as opposed to separate, secure API). The only difference is that certain modules and built-in functions may be unavailable (or redefined to secure versions).

Internally, the interpreter determines whether a piece of code is restricted by looking at the identity of the `__builtins__` object in its global namespace. If it's the same as the standard `__builtin__` module, the code is unrestricted. Otherwise, it's restricted. When running in restricted mode, the interpreter imposes a number of further restrictions that are designed to prevent untrusted code from becoming privileged:

- The `__dict__` attribute of classes and instances is not accessible.
- The `func_globals` attribute of functions is not accessible.

These restrictions are imposed to prevent untrusted code from altering its global namespace (which is used by the supervisor to restrict the set of objects that are accessible).

Finally, it should be noted that although the Python restricted execution environment prevents access to critical operations, it doesn't prevent denial of service attacks in which an untrusted program might try to exhaust memory or use an unlimited amount of CPU time.

Restricted execution is supported through the use of two modules: `rexec` and `Bastion`. `rexec` restricts the environment in which code runs. `Bastion` restricts the access untrusted code has to objects created by the supervisor.

rexec

Availability: A

The `rexec` module is used to run code in a restricted environment. The environment is encapsulated in a class `RExec` that contains attributes specifying the capabilities for the code to execute.

RExec([*hooks* [, *verbose*]])

Creates an instance of the `RExec` class that represents a restricted environment. *hooks* is an instance of a class used to implement nonstandard methods for importing modules and isn't described here. *verbose* is a flag that causes some debugging output to be printed to standard output.

The following class variables are used by the __init__() method when an instance of the RExec class is created. Changing them on an instance has no effect, so it's better to create a subclass of RExec that modifies their values.

RExec.nok_builtin_names

A tuple of strings containing the names of built-in functions not available to restricted programs. The default value is ('open', 'reload', '__import__').

RExec.ok_builtin_modules

A tuple of strings containing the names of built-in modules that can be safely imported. The default value is as follows:

```
('audioop', 'array', 'binascii', 'cmath', 'errno', 'imageop',
'marshal', 'math', 'md5', 'operator', 'parser', 'regex', 'rotor',
'select', 'strop', 'struct', 'time')
```

RExec.ok_path

The list of directories that are searched when an import is performed in the restricted environment. The default value is the same as sys.path.

RExec.ok_posix_names

A tuple of names for functions in the os module that are available to restricted programs. The default value is as follows:

```
('error', 'fstat', 'listdir', 'lstat', 'readlink',
'stat', 'times', 'uname', 'getpid', 'getppid',
'getcwd', 'getuid', 'getgid', 'geteuid', 'getegid').
```

RExec.ok_sys_names

A tuple of names for functions and variables in the sys module that are available to restricted programs. The default value is as follows:

```
('ps1', 'ps2', 'copyright', 'version', 'platform', 'exit', 'maxint')
```

An instance r of RExec uses the following methods to execute restricted code:

r.r_eval(code)

The same as eval() except that code is executed in the restricted environment. code is a string or a compiled code object. Returns the value of the resulting expression.

r.r_exec(code)

The same as the exec statement except that execution is performed in the restricted environment. code is a string or a compiled code object.

r.r_execfile(filename)

The same as execfile() except that code is executed in the restricted environment.

r.s_eval(code)

The same as r_eval() except that access to sys.stdin, sys.stdout, and sys.stderr is allowed.

r.s_exec(code)

The same as r_exec() except that access to sys.stdin, sys.stdout, and sys.stderr is allowed.

r.s_execfile(*code*)

The same as r_execfile() except that access to sys.stdin, sys.stdout, and sys.stderr is allowed.

The following methods are called implicitly by code executing in the restricted environment and can be redefined in subclasses of RExec:

r.r_import(*modulename* [, *globals* [, *locals* [, *fromlist*]]])

Imports a module *modulename*. An ImportError exception should be raised if the module is unsafe.

r.r_open(*filename* [, *mode* [, *bufsize*]])

Opens a file in the restricted environment. The arguments are the same as the built-in open() function. By default, files can be opened for reading, but not for writing.

r.r_reload(*module*)

Reloads the module object *module*.

r.r_unload(*module*)

Unloads the module object *module*.

r.s_import(*modulename* [, *globals* [, *locals* [, *fromlist*]]])

Same as r_import(), but with access to standard I/O streams.

r.s_reload(*module*)

Same as r_reload(), but with access to standard I/O streams.

r.s_unload(*module*)

Same as r_unload(), but with access to standard I/O streams.

Example

The following program executes Python code submitted through a CGI script in a restricted environment along with limits on CPU and memory usage.

```
#!/usr/local/bin/python
import rexec
import cgi, StringIO, sys, string, resource
form = cgi.FieldStorage()
code = form["code"].value        # Get some arbitrary code to execute
code = string.replace(code,"\015","")
sys.stderr = sys.stdout   # Make error messages appear

print "Content-type: text/plain\n\n"
print """The output of your program is : \n\n"""
class CGIExec(rexec.RExec):
    def r_open(*args):
        raise SystemError, "open not supported"
r = CGIExec()        # Create sandbox
# Restrict memory usage to 4 Mbytes
resource.setrlimit(resource.RLIMIT_DATA,(4000000,4000000))
# Set CPU time limit to 10 seconds
resource.setrlimit(resource.RLIMIT_CPU,(10,10))
# Go run the code
r.s_exec(code)       # Execute the untrusted code
```

▶ **See Also** Bastion (p. 232).

Bastion

Availability: A

The `Bastion` module is used to restrict access to attributes of objects. It's primarily used in conjunction with the `rexec` module when a privileged program wants to allow restricted programs to access attributes of unrestricted objects. The idea behind a `Bastion` is simple—a wrapper is placed around an object that causes every method access to be redirected through a filter function that's responsible for accepting or rejecting the access. Furthermore, all access to data attributes (non-methods) is prohibited.

Bastion(*object* [, *filter* [, *name* [, *class*]]])

Returns a bastion for the object *object*. *filter* is a function that accepts a string containing a method name and returns true or false if access to the method is permitted or denied, respectively. *name* is the name of the object that's printed by the bastion's `str()` method. *class* is the class object that implements Bastion objects and isn't described here (it's rarely necessary to supply this).

Example

In this example, you want to restrict access to a `StringIO` object so that only read operations are permitted (see the `StringIO` module):

```
import StringIO, Bastion

str = StringIO("")
...
strbast = Bastion.Bastion(str, lambda x: x in ['read','readline','readlines'])
strbast.readline()        # Okay
strbast.write("Ha ha")    # Fails. AttributeError : write
```

Notes

- If the *filter* function is omitted, a bastion limits access to all methods beginning with an underscore.

- Bastions can't be placed around built-in types such as files and sockets.

Miscellaneous Modules

The modules in this category are used for miscellaneous tasks that don't fit into any of the other categories.

bisect

Availability: A

The `bisect` module provides support for keeping lists in sorted order. It uses a bisection algorithm to do most of its work.

bisect(*list*, *item* [, *low* [, *high*]])

Returns the index of the proper insertion point for *item* to be placed in *list* in order to maintain *list* in sorted order. *low* and *high* are indices specifying a subset of the list to be considered.

insert(*list*, *item* [, *low* [, *high*]])

Inserts *item* in *list* in sorted order.

cmd

Availability: A

The cmd module provides a class Cmd that's used as a framework for building a line-oriented command interpreter. The Cmd class is never instantiated directly, but is used as a base class for a class that actually implements the interpreter. An instance *c* of the Cmd class provides the following methods:

c.cmdloop([*intro*])

Prints a banner message contained in *intro* and repeatedly issues a prompt, reads a line of input, and dispatches an appropriate action. For each line of text, the first word is stripped off and used as a command name. For a command name of 'foo', an attempt is made to invoke a method do_foo() with the remainder of the input line as a string argument. If a line contains only the character '?', a predefined method do_help() is dispatched. If the command name is '!', a method do_shell() is invoked (if defined). An end-of-file is converted into a string 'EOF' and dispatched to a command do_EOF. Subclasses of Cmd inherit a predefined method do_help(). When this method is invoked with an argument 'bar', it tries to invoke the method help_bar(). With no arguments, do_help() lists all of the available help topics by listing all commands with corresponding help_* methods, undocumented commands (commands without corresponding help_* methods), and miscellaneous topics (help methods without a corresponding command). Each of the command methods should return an integer code indicating success or failure. A negative value indicates an error and causes the interpreter to return. Otherwise, the interpreter continues to read input after each command. If the readline module has been loaded, the command interpreter will have line editing and history capabilities.

c.onecmd(*str*)

Interprets *str* as a single line of input.

c.emptyline()

This method is called when an empty line of input is typed. It should be defined by the user. If not overridden, it repeats the last nonempty command entered.

c.default(*line*)

Called when an unrecognized command is typed. By default, it prints an error message and exits.

c.precmd()

Method executed just before the input prompt is issued. It should be overridden by derived classes.

c.postcmd()

Method executed immediately after a command dispatch has finished.

c.preloop()

Method executed once when cmdloop() is executed.

c.postloop()

Method executed when cmdloop() is about to return.

The following instance variables should also be defined by subclass of Cmd.

Variable	Description
c.prompt	Prompt printed to solicit input.
c.identchars	String of characters accepted for the command prefix.
c.lastcmd	Last nonempty command seen.
c.intro	Intro text banner; overridden using the argument to cmdloop().
c.doc_header	Header to issue if the help section has a section for documented commands.
c.misc_header	Header to issue for miscellaneous help topics.
c.undoc_header	Header for undocumented commands.
c.ruler	Character used to draw separator lines under help message headers. If empty, no ruler line is drawn. The default is '='.

Example

The following example shows how this module can be used to implement an interpreter wrapper around the callable objects of a module. It also shows the interesting feature of code being executed in a class definition.

```
# cmdhelp.py
# Builds a command interpreter that allows arbitrary Python
# commands to be typed, but reads their doc strings to create
# a collection of help commands.  Just do an execfile(cmdhelp.py)
# in a module to utilize this.

import cmd, sys, traceback

# Define the interpreter class
class Interpreter(cmd.Cmd):
    symbols = globals()
    prompt = "?>> "
    intro  = "Interpreter for " + __name__

    # Find all of the callable objects and look for
    # their doc strings

    for n in symbols.keys():
        c = symbols[n]
        if callable(c):
            if c.__doc__:
                exec """
def help_%s(self):print %s.__doc__
""" % (n,n)

    # Execute an arbitrary statement
    def default(self,l):
    try:
        exec self.lastcmd in globals()
    except:
        traceback.print_exc()

    # Do nothing on empty line
    def emptyline(self):
        pass
```

```
        def do_EOF(self,arg):
            return -1

# Create an instance
interp = Interpreter()
```

The following code shows how this code might be used:

```
Python 1.5.2 (#1, Jun 23 1999, 07:54:16)  [GCC 2.7.2.3] on linux2
Copyright 1991-1995 Stichting Mathematisch Centrum, Amsterdam
>>> from socket import *
>>> execfile("cmdhelp.py")
>>> interp.cmdloop()
Interpreter for __main__
?>> help
Miscellaneous help topics:
=========================
getservbyname    gethostbyaddr    htons        socket
ntohs            gethostbyname    fromfd       getprotobyname
gethostname      htonl
Undocumented commands:
======================
EOF              help
?>> help socket
socket(family, type[, proto]) -> socket object
Open a socket of the given type.  The family argument
specifies the address family; it is normally AF_INET,
sometimes AF_UNIX.  The type argument specifies whether this
is a stream (SOCK_STREAM) or datagram (SOCK_DGRAM) socket.
The protocol argument defaults to 0, specifying the default
protocol.
?>> s = socket(AF_INET, SOCK_STREAM)
?>> s.connect("www.python.org",80)
...
```

▶ **See Also** shlex (p. 237).

md5

Availability: U, W, M

The md5 module implements RSA's MD5 message-digest algorithm. To use this module, you create an md5 object using the new() function. Data is then fed to this object to compute the 128-bit hash value of the message digest.

new([arg])

Returns a new md5 object. If *arg* is present, the method call update(*arg*) is also made.

An md5 object *m* has the following methods:

m.update(arg)

Updates the md5 object *m* with the string *arg*. Repeated calls are equivalent to a single call with the concatenation of all the arguments.

m.digest()

Returns the digest of all data passed to the object using the update() method so far. Returns a 16-byte string that may contain nonprintable characters, including null bytes.

m.copy()

Returns a copy of the md5 object.

Example

```
import md5
m = md5.new()            # Create a new MD5 object
m.update("Hello")
m.update("World")
d = m.digest()           # Get the digest
```

The following shortcut can also be used:

```
d = md5.new("Hello World").digest()
```

▶ **See Also** sha (p. 236), Internet RFC 1321.

sha

Availability: U

The sha module implements the secure hash algorithm (SHA). SHA takes a sequence of input text and produces a 160-bit hash value. To compute the hash value, create an sha object using the new() function and feed data to it.

new([string])

Returns a new sha object. If string is present, the method call update(string) is made.

blocksize

Size of the blocks fed into the hash function. This is always 1.

digestsize

The size of the resulting digest in bytes. This is always 20.

An instance s of an sha object has the following methods:

s.update(arg)

Updates the sha object with the string arg. Repeated calls are equivalent to a single call with the concatenation of all the arguments.

s.digest()

Returns the digest of all data passed to the object using the update() method so far. Returns a 20-byte string that may contain nonprintable characters, including null bytes.

s.copy()

Returns a copy of the sha object.

s.hexdigest()

Returns the digest value as a string of hexadecimal digits.

Note

The SHA algorithm is defined by NIST document *FIPS PUB 180-1: Secure Hash Standard*. It's available online at http://csrc.nist.gov/fips/fip180-1.ps.

▶ **See Also** md5 (p. 235).

shlex

Availability: U, W, M

The `shlex` module provides a class `shlex` that can be used to build lexical analyzers for simple syntaxes such as shells.

`shlex([stream])`

Creates an instance of the `shlex` class. *stream* specifies a file or stream-like object where characters will be read. This object must provide `read()` and `readline()` methods. If omitted, input is taken from `sys.stdin`.

An instance `s` of the `shlex` class supports the following methods:

`s.get_token()`

Returns a token (as a string). If tokens have been saved with `push_token()`, a token is popped off the stack. Otherwise, the token is read from the input stream. An end-of-file returns an empty string.

`s.push_token(str)`

Pushes a token onto the token stack.

In addition, the following instance variables can be set:

Variable	Description
`s.commenters`	String of characters recognized as starting a comment. Comments continue to the end of the line. Includes `'\#'` by default.
`s.wordchars`	String of characters that form multi-character tokens. Includes all ASCII alphanumeric characters and the underscore by default.
`s.whitespace`	String of whitespace characters that will be skipped.
`s.quotes`	Characters that will be considered to be string quotes. Includes single and double quotes by default.
`s.lineno`	Source line number.
`s.token`	The token buffer.

Note

Any character not declared to be a word character, whitespace, or a quote is returned as a single-character token. Also, words must be delimited by whitespace. Special symbols such as quotes and comments are not recognized within words. Thus, a word such as `isn't` is returned as a single token.

▶ **See Also** `cmd` (p. 233).

The Python Debugger

The Python debugger is loaded by importing the `pdb` module. The `pdb` module provides an interactive source code debugger that allows post-mortem debugging, inspection of stack frames, breakpoints, single stepping of source lines, and code evaluation.

The debugger is started by loading the pdb module and issuing one of the following functions:

run(statement [, globals [, locals]])

Executes the string *statement* under debugger control. The debugger prompt will appear immediately before any code executes. Typing 'continue' will force it to run. *globals* and *locals* define the global and local namespaces in which the code runs.

runeval(expression [, globals [, locals]])

Evaluates the *expression* string under debugger control. The debugger prompt will appear before any code executes, as with run(). On success, the value of the expression is returned.

runcall(function [, argument, ...])

Calls a function within the debugger. *function* is a callable object. The debugger prompt will appear before any code executes. The return value of the function is returned upon completion.

set_trace()

Starts the debugger at the point at which this function is called. This can be used to hard-code a debugger breakpoint into a specific code location.

post_mortem(traceback)

Starts post-mortem debugging of a traceback object.

pm()

Enters post-mortem debugging using the traceback in sys.last_traceback. When the debugger starts, it will present a prompt such as the following:

```
>>> import pdb
>>> import buggymodule
>>> pdb.run('buggymodule.start()')
> <string>(0)?()
(Pdb)
```

(Pdb) is the debugger prompt at which the following commands are recognized. *Note:* Some commands have a short and a long form. In this case, parentheses are used to indicate both forms. For example, h(elp) means that either "h" or "help" is acceptable.

h(elp) [command]

Shows the list of available commands. Specifying a command returns help for that command.

w(here)

Prints a stack trace.

d(own)

Moves the current frame one level down in the stack trace.

u(p)

Moves the current frame one level up in the stack trace.

b(reak) [loc [, condition]]

Sets a breakpoint at location *loc*. *loc* is one of the following:

Setting	Description
n	A line number in the current file.
filename:n	A line number in another file.
function	A function name in the current file.
filename:function	A function name in another file.

If *loc* is omitted, all the current breakpoints are printed. *condition* is an expression that must evaluate to true before the breakpoint is honored.

tbreak [*loc* [, *condition*]]

Sets a temporary breakpoint that's removed after its first hit.

cl(ear) [*bpnumber* [*bpnumber* ...]]

Clears a list of breakpoint numbers. If breakpoints are specified, all breaks are cleared.

disable [*bpnumber* [*bpnumber* ...]]

Disables the set of specified breakpoints. Unlike with clear, they can be reenabled later.

enable [*bpnumber* [*bpnumber* ...]]

Enables a specified set of breakpoints.

ignore *bpnumber* [*count*]

Ignores a breakpoint for *count* executions.

condition *bpnumber* [*condition*]

Places a condition on a breakpoint. *condition* is an expression that must evaluate to true before the breakpoint is recognized. Omitting the condition clears any previous condition.

s(tep)

Executes a single source line and stops inside called functions.

n(ext)

Executes until the next line of the current function. Skips the code contained in function calls.

r(eturn)

Runs until the current function returns.

c(ont(inue))

Continues execution until the next breakpoint is encountered.

l(ist) [*first* [, *last*]]

Lists source code. Without arguments, lists 11 lines around the current line. With one argument, lists 11 lines around that line. With two arguments, lists lines in a given range. If *last* is less than *first*, it's interpreted as a count.

a(rgs)

Prints the argument list of the current function.

p *expression*

Evaluates the expression in the current context and prints its value.

alias [*name* [*command*]]

Creates an alias called *name* that executes *command*. The substrings "%1","%2", and so forth are replaced by parameters when the alias is typed. "%*" is replaced by all parameters. If no command is given, the current alias list is shown. Aliases can be nested and can contain anything that can be legally typed at the pdb prompt. For example:

```
#Print instance variables (usage "pi classInst")
alias pi for k in %1.__dict__.keys(): print "%1.",k,"=",%1.__dict__[k]
#Print instance variables in self
alias ps pi self
```

unalias *name*

Deletes the specified alias.

[!]*statement*

Executes the (one-line) *statement* in the context of the current stack frame. The exclamation point can be omitted unless the first word of the statement resembles a debugger command. To set a global variable, you can prefix the assignment command with a "global" command on the same line:

```
(Pdb) global list_options; list_options = ['-l']
(Pdb)
```

q(uit)

Quits from the debugger.

Notes

- Entering a blank line repeats the last command entered.

- Commands that the debugger doesn't recognize are assumed to be Python statements and are executed in the context of the program being debugged.

- If a file .pdbrc exists in the user's home directory or in the current directory, it's read in and executed as if it had been typed at the debugger prompt.

The Python Profiler

This section describes the Python profiler—a tool that can be used to analyze the runtime performance of a program.

profile

Availability: A

The profile module is used to collect profiling information.

run(*command* [, *filename*])

Executes the contents of *command* using the exec statement under the profile. *filename* is the name of a file in which raw profiling data is saved. If omitted, a report such as the following is printed to standard output:

```
126 function calls (6 primitive calls) in 5.130 CPU seconds
Ordered by: standard name
ncalls  tottime  percall  cumtime  percall filename:lineno(function)
     1    0.030    0.030    5.070    5.070 <string>:1(?)
 121/1    5.020    0.041    5.020    5.020 book.py:11(process)
     1    0.020    0.020    5.040    5.040 book.py:5(?)
     2    0.000    0.000    0.000    0.000 exceptions.py:101(__init__)
     1    0.060    0.060    5.130    5.130 profile:0(execfile('book.py'))
     0    0.000             0.000           profile:0(profiler)
```

Different parts of the report generated by run() are interpreted as follows:

Section	Description
primitive calls	Number of non-recursive function calls.
ncalls	Total number of calls (including self-recursion).
tottime	Time spent in this function (not counting subfunctions).
percall	tottime/ncalls.
cumtime	Total time spent in the function.
percall	cumtime/(primitive calls).
filename:lineno(function)	Location and name of each function.

When there are two numbers in the first column (for example, "121/1"), the latter is the number of primitive calls, and the former is the actual number of calls.

Notes

- Analysis of saved profile data is performed by the pstats module.

- To obtain accurate information, it may be necessary to calibrate the profiler. Please refer to the online documentation for details.

pstats

Availability: A

The pstats module defines a class Stats that's used to analyze the data saved by the profile module.

Stats(*filename*)

Reads profiling data from *filename*—a file previously created by the profile.run() function. Returns a statistics object that can be used to print reports.

A statistics object *s* has the following methods:

s.strip_dirs()

Removes leading path information from filenames.

s.add(*filename* [, ...])

Accumulates additional profiling information into the current profile. *filename* is the name of a file containing data previously saved by profile.run().

s.sort_stats(*key* [, ...])

Sorts statistics according to a series of keys. Each key can be one of the following values:

Key Name	Description
`'calls'`	Call count.
`'cumulative'`	Cumulative time.
`'file'`	Filename.
`'module'`	Filename.
`'pcalls'`	Primitive call count.
`'line'`	Line number.
`'name'`	Function name.
`'nfl'`	Name/file/line.
`'stdname'`	Standard name.
`'time'`	Internal time.

Time values and call counts are sorted in descending order. Line numbers and filenames are sorted in ascending order.

s.print_stats(*restriction* [, ...])

Prints a profile report to standard output. The order is the same as produced by the last `sort_stats()` method. The arguments are used to eliminate entries in the report. Each restriction can be an integer to select a maximum line count, a decimal to select a percentage of the lines, or a regular expression to pattern-match against the names that are printed.

s.print_callers(*restrictions* [, ...])

Prints a list of all functions that called each function in the profile database. The ordering is identical to `print_stats()`. *restrictions* has the same meaning as for `print_stats()`.

s.print_callees (*restrictions* [, ...])

Prints a list of a functions that were called by each function. *restrictions* has the same meaning as for `print_stats()`.

Undocumented Modules

The modules listed in this section aren't covered in detail in this book, but have descriptions in the online library reference and elsewhere.

Python Services

Module	Description
`code`	Code object support.
`codeop`	Compiles Python code.
`compileall`	Byte-compiles Python files in a directory.
`dis`	Disassembler.
`imp`	Provides access to the implementation of the `import` statement.
`keyword`	Tests whether a string is a Python keyword.

Module	Description
linecache	Retrieves lines from files.
parser	Accesses parse-trees of Python source code.
pprint	Pretty printer for objects.
pyclbr	Extracts information for class browsers.
py_compile	Compiles Python source to bytecode files.
repr	Alternate implementation of the repr() function.
symbol	Constants used to represent internal nodes of parse trees.
token	Terminal nodes of the parse tree.
tokenize	Scanner for Python source code.
user	User configuration file parsing.

String Processing

Module	Description
fpformat	Floating-point number formatting.
regex	Regular expression matching (obsolete).
regsub	Regular expression substitution (obsolete).

Operating System Modules

Module	Description
curses	Curses library interface.
dl	Access to Unix shared libraries.
dircache	Directory cache.
mutex	Mutual exclusion locks.
pty	Pseudo terminal handling.
pipes	Interface to shell pipelines.
posixfile	File locking.
nis	Interface to Sun's NIS.
sched	Event scheduler.
statcache	Caching version of stat() function.
syslog	Interface to Unix syslog daemon.

Network

Module	Description
gopherlib	Gopher protocol.
telnetlib	Telnet protocol.

Internet Data Handling

Module	Description
formatter	Generic output formatting.
htmllib	HTML parsing.
mailbox	Reading various mailbox formats.
mhlib	Access to MH mailboxes.
mimify	MIME processing of mail messages.
netrc	netrc file processing.
sgmllib	Simple SGML parsing.
xmllib	Simple XML parsing.

Multimedia Services

Module	Description
audioop	Manipulates raw audio data.
imageop	Manipulates raw image data.
aifc	Reads and writes AIFF and AIFC files.
sunau	Reads and writes Sun AU files.
wave	Reads and writes WAV files.
chunk	Reads IFF chunked data.
colorsys	Conversions between color systems.
rgbimg	Reads and writes SGI RGB files.
imghdr	Determines the type of an image.
sndhdr	Determines the type of a sound file.

SGI Irix

Module	Description
al	Audio functions on SGI.
cd	CD-ROM access on SGI.
fl	FORMS library.
flp	FORMS design loader.
fm	Font manager interface.
gl	Graphics library interface.
imgfile	Support for SGI imglib files.
jpeg	Reads and writes JPEG files.

Sun-Specific Services

Module	Description
sunaudiodev	Access to Sun audio hardware.

Miscellaneous

Module	Description
ConfigParser	Configuration file parser.
calendar	Calendar-generation functions.
winsound	Playing sounds on Windows.

B
Extending and Embedding Python

This appendix covers the C API used to build extension modules and embed the Python interpreter into other applications. It's not intended to be a tutorial, so readers may want to consult the "Embedding and Extending the Python Interpreter" document available at http://www.python.org/doc/ext, as well as the "Python/C API Reference Manual" available at http://www.python.ord/doc/api. The functions described in this section are current as of Python 1.5 and are likely to be compatible with future releases of Python 1.x. No such claim is made for Python 2.0 or later releases.

Enabling Optional Modules

A number of modules in the standard library are disabled due to system differences and dependencies on third-party packages. To enable these modules, you must edit a configuration file and rebuild the interpreter (it should also be noted that this is primarily an issue for Unix systems).

The file `Python-1.5.2/Modules/Setup` in the Python source distribution contains configuration data for modules built into the Python interpreter. It contains entries of this form:

```
signal signalmodule.c          # signal(2)
...
#readline readline.c -lreadline -ltermcap
```

Each line indicates the name of a module, followed by source files, compiler options, and link libraries needed to compile that module. A line starting with # is a comment and denotes modules that have been disabled. Long lines can be broken into multiple lines by placing a backslash (\) at the end of lines to be continued. To enable an optional module, the `Setup` file should be edited to reflect the installation locations of required third-party libraries. For example, to enable the `readline` module, the `Setup` file might be modified as follows:

```
...
readline readline.c -I/usr/local/include -L/usr/local/lib -lreadline -ltermcap
```

The interpreter must be rebuilt and reinstalled by typing make and `make install` in the top-level directory of the source tree for the changes to `Setup` to take effect.

Extension Module Example

Extension modules are used to extend the interpreter with functions in C or C++. For example, suppose you wanted to access the following C functions in a Python module named spam:

```
/* Compute the greatest common divisor of positive
   integers x and y */
int gcd(int x, int y) {
    int g;
    g = y;
    while (x > 0) {
        g = x;
        x = y % x;
        y = g;
    }
    return g;
}
/* Print some data */
void print_data(char *name, char *email, char *phone) {
    printf("Name    : %s\n", name);
    printf("Email   : %s\n", email);
    printf("Phone   : %s\n", phone);
}
```

To access these functions from an extension module, you must write code such as that in Listing B.1:

Listing B.1   Accessing Functions from an Extension Module

```
/* "spam" module */

/* Include the Python C API */
#include "Python.h"

/* External declarations */
extern int gcd(int,int);
extern void print_data(char *, char *, char *);

/* Wrapper for the gcd() function */
PyObject *spam_gcd(PyObject *self, PyObject *args) {
    int x, y, g;
    /* Get Python arguments */
    if (!PyArg_ParseTuple(args,"ii",&x,&y)) {
        return NULL;
    }
    /* Call the C function */
    g = gcd(x,y);
    return Py_BuildValue("i",g);
}

/* Wrapper for the print_data() function */
PyObject *spam_print_data(PyObject *self, PyObject *args, PyObject *kwargs) {
    char *name = "None";
    char *email = "None";
    char *phone = "None";
    static char *argnames[] = {"name","email","phone",NULL};

    /* Get Python arguments */
    if (!PyArg_ParseTupleAndKeywords(args,kwargs,"|sss",argnames,
        &name,&email,&phone)) {
        return NULL;
```

```
    }
    /* Call the C function */
    print_data(name,email,phone);
    return Py_BuildValue("");          /* Return None */
}
/* Method table mapping names to wrappers */
static PyMethodDef spammethods[] = {
    {"gcd", spam_gcd, METH_VARARGS},
    {"print_data", spam_print_data, METH_VARARGS | METH_KEYWORDS },
    {NULL, NULL}
};
/* Module initialization function */
void initspam() {
    Py_InitModule("spam", spammethods);
}
```

Extension modules always need to include "Python.h". For each C function to be accessed, a wrapper function is written. These wrapper functions either accept two arguments (self and args, both of type PyObject *) or three arguments (self, args, and kwargs, all of type PyObject *). The self parameter is used when the wrapper function is implementing a built-in method to be applied to an instance of some object. In this case, the instance is placed in the self parameter. Otherwise, self is set to NULL. args is a tuple containing the function arguments passed by the interpreter. kwargs is a dictionary containing keywords arguments.

Arguments are converted from Python to C using the PyArg_ParseTuple() or PyArg_ParseTupleAndKeywords() function. Similarly, the Py_BuildValue() function is used to construct an acceptable return value. These functions are described in later sections.

Functions signal an error by returning NULL. If a function has no return value (that is, void), the None object must be returned. For example:

```
PyObject *wrap_foo(PyObject *self, PyObject *args) {
    ...
    /* Return None */
    return Py_BuildValue("");
}
```

None can also be returned as follows:

```
PyObject *wrap_foo(PyObject *self, PyObject *args) {
    ...
    /* Return None */
    Py_INCREF(Py_None);
    return Py_None;
}
```

The method table spammethods in Listing B.1 is used to associate Python names with the C wrapper functions. These are the names used to call the function from the interpreter. The METH_VARARGS flag indicates the calling conventions for a wrapper. In this case, only positional arguments in the form of a tuple are accepted. It can also be set to METH_VARARGS | METH_KEYWORDS to indicate a wrapper function accepting keyword arguments.

The module initialization function initspam is used to initialize the contents of the module. In this case, the Py_InitModule("spam",spammethods) function creates a module spam and populates it with built-in function objects corresponding to the functions listed in the method table.

Compilation of Extensions

Extension modules are usually compiled into shared libraries or DLLs that can be dynamically loaded by the interpreter. This process varies on every machine, but the Python distribution contains a file Makefile.pre.in that's configured to build such extensions without knowing many of the messy details. To build an extension, follow these steps:

1. Create a file called Setup such as the following:

   ```
   *shared*
   spam spam.c spamwrapper.c
   ```

2. Copy the file Makefile.pre.in from the Python installation. It's usually located in the directory *<python>*/lib/python1.5/config where *<python>* is the directory in which the Python library is installed.

3. Type the following:

   ```
   make -f Makefile.pre.in boot
   make
   ```

At this point, a shared library such as spammodule.so (or some variant of this name) will be created for use. In some instances, it may be necessary to build an extension module manually. This almost always requires advanced knowledge of various compiler and linker options. Following is an example on Linux:

```
linux % gcc -c -fpic -I/usr/local/include/python1.5 spam.c spamwrapper.c
linux % gcc -shared spam.o spamwrapper.o -o spammodule.so
```

When building a module, it's important to note that the name of the shared library must match the name of the module used in the wrapper code. For example, if the module is named spam, the initialization function must be named initspam and the shared library must be called spammodule.so (possibly with a different file extension, depending on your machine).

Once compiled, an extension module is used like any other module, by simply using the import statement:

```
linux % python
Python 1.5.2 (#1, Jul 11 1999, 13:56:14) [C] on linux
Copyright 1991-1995 Stichting Mathematisch Centrum, Amsterdam
>>> import spam
>>> spam.gcd(63,56)
7
>>> spam.gcd(71,89)
1
>>> spam.print_data(name="Dave",phone="555-1212")
Name   : Dave
Email  : None
Phone  : 555-1212
>>>
```

Converting Data from Python to C

The following functions are used to convert arguments passed from Python to C.

```
int PyArg_ParseTuple(PyObject *args, char *format, ...);
```

Parses a tuple of objects in args into a series of C variables. *format* is a format string that describes the expected contents of args as shown in Table B.1. All the remaining arguments contain the addresses of C variables into which the results will be placed. Zero is returned if the arguments could not be parsed.

```
int PyArg_ParseTupleAndKeywords(PyObject *args, PyObject *kwdict,
                                char *format, char **kwlist, ...);
```

Parses both a tuple of arguments and a dictionary containing keyword arguments contained in *kwdict*. *format* has the same meaning as for `PyArg_ParseTuple()`. The only difference is that *kwlist* is a null-terminated list of strings containing the names of all the arguments. Returns 1 on success, 0 on error.

Table B.1   Format Specifiers for `PyArg_Parse*`

Format	PyType	C Type	Description
`"s"`	String	`char *`	Null-terminated string.
`"s#"`	String	`char *, int`	String and length. May contain null bytes.
`"z"`	String or None	`char *`	Null-terminated string or NULL.
`"z#"`	String or None	`char *, int`	String and length, or NULL.
`"b"`	Integer	`char`	8-bit integer.
`"h"`	Integer	`short`	Short 16-bit integer.
`"i"`	Integer	`int`	Integer.
`"l"`	Integer	`long`	Long integer.
`"c"`	String	`char`	Single character. The Python string must have a length of 1.
`"f"`	Float	`float`	Single-precision floating point.
`"d"`	Float	`double`	Double-precision floating point.
`"D"`	Complex	`Py_complex`	Complex number.
`"O"`	Any	`PyObject *`	Any Python object.
`"O!"`	Any	`type, PyObject *`	Python object of a specific type.
`"O&"`	Any	`converter, any`	Python object processed through a converter function *converter*.
`"S"`	String	`PyStringObject *`	Python string object.
`"(items)"`	Tuple	`vars`	Tuple of items. *items* is a string of format specifiers from this table. *vars* is a list of C variable addresses corresponding to the items in *items*.
`"|"`	—	—	Start of optional arguments.
`":"`	—	—	End of arguments—function name.
`";"`	—	—	End of arguments—error message.

The "O!" conversion requires two C arguments—a pointer to a Python type object and a pointer to a PyObject * into which a pointer to the object is placed. A TypeError is raised if the type of the object doesn't match the type object. For example:

```
/* Parse a List Argument */
PyObject *listobj1;
PyArg_ParseTuple(args,"O!", &PyList_Type, &listobj1);
```

The "O&" conversion uses a function to convert a PyObject * to a C datatype. *converter* is a pointer to a function with the prototype int *converter*(PyObject *obj*, void *addr*) where *obj* is the passed Python object, and *addr* is the address supplied to *any*. *converter*() should return 1 on success, 0 on failure. On error, the converter should also raise an exception. For example:

```
struct Point {
    int x;
    int y;
;

int convert_point(PyObject *obj, void *addr) {
    Point *paddr = (Point *) addr;
    return PyArg_ParseTuple(obj,"ii", &p->x, &p->y);
}
...
PyObject *wrapper(PyObject *self, PyObject *args) {
    Point p;
    ...
    /* Get a point */
    if (!PyArg_ParseTuple(args,"O&",convert_point, &p))
        return NULL;
    ...
}
```

"¦" specifies that all remaining arguments are optional. This can appear only once in a format specifier and can't be nested.

":" indicates the end of the arguments. Any text that follows is used as the function name in any error messages.

";" signals the end of the arguments. Any following text is used as the error message.

Note: Only one of : and ; should be used.

Examples:

```
int        ival, ival2, len;
double     dval;
char       *sval;
PyObject *o1, *o2;

/* Parse an integer, double, and a string */
PyArg_ParseTuple(args,"ids", &ival, &dval, &sval);

/* Parse a string and length */
PyArg_ParseTuple(args,"s#", &sval, &len);

/* Parse optional arguments */
PyArg_ParseTuple(args,"id¦s", &ival, &dval, &sval);

/* Parse with an error message */
PyArg_ParseTuple(args,"ii; gcd requires 2 integers", &ival, &ival2);

/* Parse two tuples */
PyArg_ParseTuple(args,"(ii)(ds)", &ival, &ival2, &dval, &sval);
```

Converting Data from C to Python

The following function is used to convert the values contained in C variables to a Python object:

```
PyObject *Py_BuildValue(format, ...)
```

This constructs a Python object from a series of C variables. *format* is a string describing the desired conversion. The remaining arguments are the values of C variables to be converted.

The *format* specifier is similar to that used with the `PyArg_ParseTuple*` functions, as shown in Table B.2.

Table B.2   Format Specifiers for **Py_BuildValue()**

Format	PyType	C Type	Description
`"s"`	String	`char *`	Null-terminated string. If the C string pointer is NULL, None is returned.
`"s#"`	String	`char *, int`	String and length. May contain null bytes. If the C string pointer is NULL, None is returned.
`"z"`	String or None	`char *`	Same as `"s"`.
`"z#"`	String or None	`char *, int`	Same as `"s#"`.
`"b"`	Integer	`char`	8-bit integer.
`"h"`	Integer	`short`	Short 16-bit integer.
`"i"`	Integer	`int`	Integer.
`"l"`	Integer	`long`	Long integer.
`"c"`	String	`char`	Single character. Creates a Python string of length 1.
`"f"`	Float	`float`	Single-precision floating point.
`"d"`	Float	`double`	Double-precision floating point.
`"O"`	Any	`PyObject *`	Any Python object. The object is unchanged except for its reference count, which is incremented by 1. If a NULL pointer is given, a NULL pointer is returned.
`"O&"`	Any	`converter, any`	C data processed through a converter function.
`"S"`	String	`PyStringObject *`	Same as `"O"`.
`"N"`	Any	`PyObject *`	Same as `"O"` except that the reference count is not incremented.
`"(items)"`	Tuple	`vars`	Creates a tuple of items. *items* is a string of format specifiers from this table. *vars* is a list of C variables corresponding to the items in *items*.

continues >>

Table B.2   continued

Format	PyType	C Type	Description
"[items]"	List	vars	Creates a list of items. items is a string of format specifiers. vars is a list of C variables corresponding to the items in items.
"{items}"	Dictionary	vars	Create a dictionary of items.

Examples:

```
Py_BuildValue("")                              None
Py_BuildValue("i",37)                          37
Py_BuildValue("ids",37,3.4,"hello")            (37, 3.5, "hello")
Py_BuildValue("s#","hello",4)                  "hell"
Py_BuildValue("()")                            ()
Py_BuildValue("(i)",37)                        (37,)
Py_BuildValue("[ii]",1,2)                      [1,2]
Py_BuildValue("[i,i]",1,2)                     [1,2]
Py_BuildValue("{s:i,s:i}","x",1,"y",2)         {'x':1, 'y':2}
```

Error Handling

Errors are indicated by returning NULL to the interpreter. Prior to returning NULL, an exception should be raised or cleared using one of the following functions:

Function	Description
void PyErr_Clear()	Clears any previously raised exceptions.
PyObject *PyErr_Occurred()	Checks to see whether an error has been generated. If so, returns the current exception object. Otherwise, returns NULL.
void PyErr_NoMemory()	Raises a MemoryError exception.
void PyErr_SetFromErrno(PyObject *exc)	Raises an exception. exc is an exception object. The value of the exception is taken from the errno variable in the C library.
void PyErr_SetFromErrnoWithFilename(PyObject * exc, char *filename)	Like PyErr_SetFromErrno, but includes the filename in the exception value as well.
void PyErr_SetObject(PyObject *exc, PyObject *val)	Raises an exception. exc is an exception object and val is an object containing the value of the exception.
void PyErr_SetString(PyObject *exc, char *msg)	Raises an exception. exc is an exception object and msg is a message describing what went wrong.

The exc argument in these functions can be set to one of the following:

C Name	Python Exception
PyExc_ArithmeticError	ArithmeticError
PyExc_AssertionError	AssertionError
PyExc_AttributeError	AttributeError
PyExc_EnvironmentError	EnvironmentError
PyExc_EOFError	EOFError
PyExc_Exception	Exception
PyExc_FloatingPointError	FloatingPointError
PyExc_ImportError	ImportError
PyExc_IndexError	IndexError
PyExc_IOError	IOError
PyExc_KeyError	KeyError
PyExc_KeyboardInterrupt	KeyboardInterrupt
PyExc_LookupError	LookupError
PyExc_MemoryError	MemoryError
PyExc_NameError	NameError
PyExc_NotImplementedError	NotImplementedError
PyExc_OSError	OSError
PyExc_OverflowError	OverflowError
PyExc_RuntimeError	RuntimeError
PyExc_StandardError	StandardError
PyExc_SyntaxError	SyntaxError
PyExc_SystemError	SystemError
PyExc_SystemExit	SystemExit
PyExc_TypeError	TypeError
PyExc_ValueError	ValueError
PyExc_ZeroDivisionError	ZeroDivisionError

An extension module can create a new exception by using the following function:

```
PyObject *PyErr_NewException(char *excname, PyObject *base, PyObject *dict)
```

Creates a new exception object. *excname* is the name of the exception of the form *modulename.excname*, *base* is an optional base class for the exception, and *dict* is an optional dictionary used as the __dict__ attribute of the resulting exception class. Both of these arguments are normally set to NULL. The returned object is a class object.

The following example shows how a new exception is created in an extension module:

```
static PyObject *SpamError;
...

/* Module initialization function */
void initspam() {
    PyObject *m, *d;
    m= Py_InitModule("spam",SpamMethods);
    d= PyModule_GetDict(m);
    SpamError = PyErr_NewException("spam.error", NULL, NULL);
    PyDict_SetItemString(d,"error",SpamError);
    ...
}
```

Reference Counting

Unlike programs written in Python, C extensions occasionally have to manipulate the reference count of Python objects. This is done using the following macros:

Macro	Description
`Py_INCREF(obj)`	Increments the reference count of *obj*, which must be non-null.
`Py_DECREF(obj)`	Decrements the reference count of *obj*, which must be non-null.
`Py_XINCREF(obj)`	Increments the reference count of *obj*, which may be `NULL`.
`Py_XDECREF(obj)`	Decrements the reference count of *obj*, which may be `NULL`.

Manipulating the reference count of Python objects in C is a delicate topic, and readers are strongly advised to consult the "Extending and Embedding the Python Interpreter" document available at `http://www.python.org/doc/ext` before proceeding any further. With this in mind, all Python objects are manipulated in C through the use of pointers of type `PyObject *`. Furthermore, these pointers are classified into two categories: owned references and borrowed references. An *owned reference* is a pointer to a Python object in which the reference count of that object has been updated to reflect the fact that some piece of C code or a C data structure is holding a pointer to it. A *borrowed reference*, on the other hand, is simply a bare pointer to a Python object in which the reference count of the object has not been updated.

Owned references are most commonly created by functions that create new Python objects, such as `Py_BuildValue()`, `PyInt_FromLong()`, and `PyList_New()`. When called, a new Python object is created and the object is said to be owned by the calling function. Borrowed references often appear when a function obtains a pointer to a Python object from elsewhere or when the contents of Python objects such as lists and dictionaries are extracted. For example, the `self` and `args` parameters of a wrapper function are borrowed references, as is the pointer returned by functions such as `PyList_GetItem()`.

The owner of a reference must either give up ownership using the `Py_DECREF()` macro or transfer ownership elsewhere. For example, temporary objects created inside a wrapper function should be destroyed using `Py_DECREF()`, whereas the return value of a wrapper is an owned reference that's given back to the interpreter. Likewise, the holder of a borrowed reference can obtain ownership using the `Py_INCREF()` macro. However, special care is in order. For example, decrementing the reference count of a borrowed reference may cause the interpreter to crash with a segmentation fault at a later time during execution. Likewise, failure to release an owned reference or inadvertently increasing the reference count of an object will lead to memory leaks.

Figuring out Python's reference counting scheme is tricky because there are several inconsistencies in its treatment of references. However, here are a few general rules:

- Functions that create new Python objects always return owned references.
- If you want to save a reference to a Python object, use `Py_INCREF()` to increase the reference count.
- To dispose of an owned reference, use `Py_DECREF()`.

- Many (but not all) functions that return pointers to objects contained in sequences and mapping objects return owned references.

- Many (but not all) functions that store objects in containers such as sequences and mappings increase the reference count of objects they contain.

- All C wrapper functions must return an owned reference.

Exceptions to these rules are noted in later sections of this appendix.

Abstract Object Layer

The functions in Tables B.3 through B.6 are used to manipulate objects from C, much in the same manner as from the interpreter. All the functions in this section that return an int return -1 if an error occurs. Likewise, functions that return a PyObject * return NULL on failure. Note that an "error" in this context is not the same as the false result of a test. For instance, the PyNumber_Check(PyObject *obj) function returns 0 if obj is not a number, but this isn't the same as an error. Finally, unless otherwise noted, all functions in this section that return a PyObject * return ownership with the object. It's up to the caller to decrement the reference count of the returned object if necessary.

Table B.3   Objects

Type	Function
int	PyCallable_Check(PyObject *o)
PyObject *	PyObject_CallFunction(PyObject *callable_object, char *format, ...)
PyObject *	PyObject_CallMethod(PyObject *o, char *methodname, char *format, ...)
PyObject *	PyObject_CallObject(PyObject *callable_object, PyObject *args)
int	PyObject_Cmp(PyObject *o1, PyObject *o2, int *result)
int	PyObject_Compare(PyObject *o1, PyObject *o2)
int	PyObject_DelAttr(PyObject *o, PyObject *attr_name)
int	PyObject_DelAttrString(PyObject *o, char *attr_name)
int	PyObject_DelItem(PyObject *o, PyObject *key)
PyObject *	PyObject_GetAttr(PyObject *o, PyObject *attr_name)
PyObject *	PyObject_GetAttrString(PyObject *o, char *attr_name)
PyObject *	PyObject_GetItem(PyObject *o, PyObject *key)
int	PyObject_HasAttr(PyObject *o, PyObject *attr_name)
int	PyObject_HasAttrString(PyObject *o, char *attr_name)
int	PyObject_Hash(PyObject *o)
int	PyObject_IsTrue(PyObject *o)
int	PyObject_Length(PyObject *o)
int	PyObject_Print(PyObject *o, FILE *fp, int flags)
PyObject *	PyObject_Repr(PyObject *o)

continues >>

Table B.3   continued

Type	Function
int	PyObject_SetAttr(PyObject *o, PyObject *attr_name, PyObject *v)
int	PyObject_SetAttrString(PyObject *o, char *attr_name, PyObject *v)
int	PyObject_SetItem(PyObject *o, PyObject *key, PyObject *v)
PyObject *	PyObject_Str(PyObject *o)
PyObject *	PyObject_Type(PyObject *o)

The *flags* argument of PyObject_Print() is used to select printing options. Currently, the only option is Py_PRINT_RAW, which forces PyObject_Print() to produce output using PyObject_Str() as opposed to PyObject_Repr() (the default).

PyObject_Hash() and PyObject_Length() return a positive integer result on success and -1 on error.

Table B.4   Numbers

Type	Function
PyObject *	PyNumber_Absolute(PyObject *o)
PyObject *	PyNumber_Add(PyObject *o1, PyObject *o2)
PyObject *	PyNumber_And(PyObject *o1, PyObject *o2)
int	PyNumber_Check(PyObject *o)
PyObject *	PyNumber_Coerce(PyObject **p1, PyObject **p2)
PyObject *	PyNumber_Divide(PyObject *o1, PyObject *o2)
PyObject *	PyNumber_Divmod(PyObject *o1, PyObject *o2)
PyObject *	PyNumber_Float(PyObject *o)
PyObject *	PyNumber_Int(PyObject *o)
PyObject *	PyNumber_Invert(PyObject *o)
PyObject *	PyNumber_Long(PyObject *o)
PyObject *	PyNumber_Lshift(PyObject *o1, PyObject *o2)
PyObject *	PyNumber_Multiply(PyObject *o1, PyObject *o2)
PyObject *	PyNumber_Negative(PyObject *o)
PyObject *	PyNumber_Or(PyObject *o1, PyObject *o2)
PyObject *	PyNumber_Positive(PyObject *o)
PyObject *	PyNumber_Power(PyObject *o1, PyObject *o2, PyObject *o3)
PyObject *	PyNumber_Remainder(PyObject *o1, PyObject *o2)
PyObject *	PyNumber_Rshift(PyObject *o1, PyObject *o2)
PyObject *	PyNumber_Subtract(PyObject *o1, PyObject *o2)
PyObject *	PyNumber_Xor(PyObject *o1, PyObject *o2)

Table B.5   Sequences

Type	Function
int	PySequence_Check(PyObject *o)
PyObject *	PySequence_Concat(PyObject *o1, PyObject *o2)
int	PySequence_Count(PyObject *o, PyObject *value)
int	PySequence_DelItem(PyObject *o, int i)
int	PySequence_DelSlice(PyObject *o, int i1, int i2)
PyObject *	PySequence_GetItem(PyObject *o, int i)
PyObject *	PySequence_GetSlice(PyObject *o, int i1, int i2)
int	PySequence_In(PyObject *o, PyObject *value)
int	PySequence_Index(PyObject *o, PyObject *value)
PyObject *	PySequence_Repeat(PyObject *o, int count)
int	PySequence_SetItem(PyObject *o, int i, PyObject *v)
int	PySequence_SetSlice(PyObject *o, int i1, int i2, PyObject *v)
PyObject *	PySequence_Tuple(PyObject *o)

Table B.6   Mappings

Type	Function
int	PyMapping_Check(PyObject *o)
int	PyMapping_Clear(PyObject *o)
int	PyMapping_DelItem(PyObject *o, PyObject *key)
int	PyMapping_DelItemString(PyObject *o, char *key)
PyObject *	PyMapping_GetItemString(PyObject *o, char *key)
int	PyMapping_HasKey(PyObject *o, PyObject *key)
int	PyMapping_HasKeyString(PyObject *o, char *key)
PyObject *	PyMapping_Items(PyObject *o)
PyObject *	PyMapping_Keys(PyObject *o)
int	PyMapping_Length(PyObject *o)
int	PyMapping_SetItemString(PyObject *o, char *key, PyObject *v)
PyObject *	PyMapping_Values(PyObject *o)

Low-Level Functions on Built-in Types

The functions in Tables B.7 through B.16 can be used to manipulate various built-in types. Functions of the form Py<*type*>_Check() are used to check the type of an object. Functions of the form Py<*type*>_From<*type*> are used to create a Python object from a C datatype. Functions of the form Py<*type*>_As<*type*> are used to convert from Python to C. These functions are presented without further description.

Table B.7   Integers

Type	Function
long	PyInt_AsLong(PyObject *iobj);
int	PyInt_Check(PyObject *obj)
PyObject*	PyInt_FromLong(long);
long	PyInt_GetMax();

Table B.8   Long Integers

Type	Function
double	PyLong_AsDouble(PyObject *lobj);
long	PyLong_AsLong(PyObject *lobj);
long long	PyLong_AsLongLong(PyObject *lobj);
unsigned long	PyLong_AsUnsignedLong(PyObject *lobj);
unsigned long long	PyLong_AsUnsignedLongLong(PyObject *lobj);
void *	PyLong_AsVoidPtr(PyObject *lobj);
int	PyLong_Check(PyObject *obj);
PyObject *	PyLong_FromDouble(double);
PyObject *	PyLong_FromLong(long);
PyObject *	PyLong_FromLongLong(long long);
PyObject *	PyLong_FromUnsignedLong(unsigned long);
PyObject *	PyLong_FromUnsignedLongLong(unsigned long long);
PyObject *	PyLong_FromVoidPtr(void *);

Table B.9   Floats

Type	Function
int	PyFloat_Check(PyObject *obj);
double	PyFloat_AsDouble(PyObject *fobj);
PyObject *	PyFloat_FromDouble(double);

Table B.10   Complex

Type	Function
Py_complex	PyComplex_AsCComplex(PyObject *cobj);
int	PyComplex_Check(PyObject *obj);
PyObject *	PyComplex_FromCComplex(Py_complex *cobj);
PyObject *	PyComplex_FromDoubles(double real, double imag);
double	PyComplex_ImagAsDouble(PyObject *cobj);
double	PyComplex_RealAsDouble(PyObject *cobj);

Table B.11   Strings

Type	Function
char *	PyString_AsString(PyObject *str);
int	PyString_Check(PyObject *obj);
PyObject *	PyString_FromString(char *str);
PyObject *	PyString_FromStringAndSize(char *str, int len);
int	PyString_Size(PyObject *str);

Table B.12   Lists

Type	Function
int	PyList_Append(PyObject *list, PyObject *obj);
PyObject *	PyList_AsTuple(PyObject *list);
int	PyList_Check(PyObject *obj);
PyObject *	PyList_GetItem(PyObject *list, int index);
PyObject *	PyList_GetSlice(PyObject *list, int i, int j);
int	PyList_Insert(PyObject *list, int index, PyObject *obj);
PyObject *	PyList_New(int size);
int	PyList_Reverse(PyObject *list);
int	PyList_SetItem(PyObject *list, int index, PyObject *obj);
int	PyList_SetSlice(PyObject *list, int i, int j, PyObject *slc);
int	PyList_Size(PyObject *list);
int	PyList_Sort(PyObject *list);

Note: PyList_GetItem() returns a borrowed reference.

Table B.13   Tuples

Type	Function
int	PyTuple_Check(PyObject *obj);
PyObject *	PyTuple_GetItem(PyObject *tup, int index);
PyObject *	PyTuple_GetSlice(PyObject *tup, int i, int j);
PyObject *	PyTuple_New(int size);
int	PyTuple_SetItem(PyObject *tup, int index, PyObject *obj);
int	PyTuple_Size(PyObject *tup);

Note: PyTuple_SetItem() increments the reference count of *obj* even if it fails, and PyTuple_GetItem() returns a borrowed reference.

Table B.14   Dictionaries

Type	Function
int	PyDict_Check(PyObject *obj);
void	PyDict_Clear(PyObject *dict);

continues >>

Table B.14   continued

Type	Function
int	PyDict_DelItem(PyObject *dict, PyObject *key);
int	PyDict_DelItemString(PyObject *dict, char *key);
PyObject *	PyDict_GetItem(PyObject *dict, PyObject *key);
PyObject *	PyDict_GetItemString(PyObject *dict, char *key);
PyObject *	PyDict_Items(PyObject *dict);
PyObject *	PyDict_Keys(PyObject *dict);
PyObject *	PyDict_New();
int	PyDict_SetItem(PyObject *dict, PyObject *key, PyObject *val);
int	PyDict_SetItemString(PyObject *dict, char *key, PyObject *val);
int	PyDict_Size(PyObject *dict);
PyObject *	PyDict_Values(PyObject *dict);

Note: PyDict_GetItem() and PyDict_GetItemString() return borrowed references.

Table B.15   Files

Type	Function
FILE *	PyFile_AsFile(PyObject *file);
int	PyFile_Check(PyObject *obj);
PyObject *	PyFile_FromFile(FILE *, char *, char *, int (*)(FILE *));
PyObject *	PyFile_FromString(char *name, char *mode);
PyObject *	PyFile_GetLine(PyObject *file, int);
PyObject *	PyFile_Name(PyObject *file);
void	PyFile_SetBufSize(PyObject *file, int size);
int	PyFile_SoftSpace(PyObject *file, int);
int	PyFile_WriteObject(PyObject *file, PyObject *obj, int);
int	PyFile_WriteString(char *str, PyObject *file);

Table B.16   Modules

Type	Function
int	PyModule_Check(PyObject *obj);
PyObject *	PyModule_GetDict(PyObject *mod);
char *	PyModule_GetFilename(PyObject *mod);
char *	PyModule_GetName(PyObject *mod);
PyObject *	PyModule_New(char *name);

Defining New Types

New types of objects can also be defined in extension modules. However, this process is considerably more advanced than simply accessing a few C functions. Because of this complexity, you should consider implementing a new type only in the following situations:

- The type is not easily constructed from existing Python types.

- The application requires high performance—for example, if you want to have an efficient matrix type.

- The type requires interaction with the operating system or another special feature not provided by the interpreter or the standard library.

- The type hasn't already been implemented elsewhere. For example, efficient matrix types have already been implemented so it would make little sense to reinvent them. It's always a good idea to check the Python libraries and newsgroup before implementing a new type.

The process of creating a new Python type involves the following steps:

1. Define a data structure that contains the actual data stored in the type—for example, the List type has an array of elements containing the list items.

2. Define the functions that are going to serve as methods of the type—for example, the append() method of a List object.

3. Define a pair of functions for creating and destroying the type.

4. Define a set of functions that implement the special methods such as __add__() and __getitem__() that are supported by the type, as described in Chapter 3, "Types and Objects."

5. Fill in a data structure containing pointers to the numeric operations of a type.

6. Fill in a data structure containing pointers to the sequence operations of the type.

7. Fill in a data structure containing pointers to the mapping operators of the type.

8. Define a type object that contains all the properties of the object and its associated methods.

9. Register methods and any additional functions with the interpreter in the module initialization function.

The following example illustrates the process of creating a new Python type by implementing a SharedBuffer object. A *shared buffer* is a special data structure that contains data shared by multiple Python interpreters running as different processes. Whenever a change is made by one interpreter, it's automatically reflected in shared buffers of the other interpreters. This implementation of a shared buffer utilizes an operating system feature known as *memory mapped files* in which the contents of a "file" are mapped into the address space of a process and can be accessed as ordinary memory. Memory mapped files are supported on both Unix and Windows, although the following example shows only the Unix implementation.

```
/**********************************************************
 * sbuffer.c
 *
 * A shared buffer object implemented using mmap().
 **********************************************************/
#include "Python.h"
#include <unistd.h>
#include <fcntl.h>
#include <sys/mman.h>
#include <sys/stat.h>
```

```
/***************************************************************
 * sbufferobject information
 ***************************************************************/
typedef struct {
    PyObject_HEAD
    char     *buffer;    /* Memory buffer */
    int       size;      /* Size of the structure */
    int       fd;        /* File descriptor */
    int       prot;      /* Protection bits */
    int       offset;    /* File offset */
} sbufferobject;

/* Exception object used by this module */
static PyObject *AccessError;

/* Forward declaration of type descriptor */
staticforward PyTypeObject SharedBufferType;

/***************************************************************
 * Instance methods
 *     sbuffer.lock()    - Lock the shared buffer
 *     sbuffer.unlock()  - Unlock the shared buffer
 *     sbuffer.get()     - Get data as a NULL-terminated string
 *     sbuffer.store()   - Store data as a NULL-terminated string
 ***************************************************************/
static PyObject *
sbuffer_lock(sbufferobject *self, PyObject *args) {
    if (!PyArg_ParseTuple(args,"")) return NULL;
    lockf(self->fd,F_LOCK,0);
    return Py_BuildValue("");
}

static PyObject *
sbuffer_unlock(sbufferobject *self, PyObject *args) {
    if (!PyArg_ParseTuple(args,"")) return NULL;
    lockf(self->fd,F_ULOCK,0);
    return Py_BuildValue("");
}

static PyObject *
sbuffer_get(sbufferobject *self, PyObject *args) {
    int i;
    if (!PyArg_ParseTuple(args,"")) return NULL;
    if (self->prot & PROT_READ) {
        for (i = 0; i < self->size; i++) {
            if (!self->buffer[i]) break;
        }
        return PyString_FromStringAndSize(self->buffer,i);
    } else {
        return PyString_FromString("");
    }
}

static PyObject *
sbuffer_store(sbufferobject *self, PyObject *args) {
    char *str;
    int len;
    if (!PyArg_ParseTuple(args,"s",&str)) return NULL;
    if (self->prot & PROT_WRITE) {
        len = strlen(str)+1;
        if (len > self->size) len = self->size;
        memcpy(self->buffer,str,len);
    } else {
        PyErr_SetString(AccessError,"SharedBuffer is read-only");
```

```
    return NULL;
  }
  return Py_BuildValue("");
}

/* Instance methods table.  Used by sbuffer_getattr() */
static struct PyMethodDef sbuffer_methods[] = {
  {"lock",    sbuffer_lock,    METH_VARARGS},
  {"unlock",  sbuffer_unlock,  METH_VARARGS},
  {"get",     sbuffer_get,     METH_VARARGS},
  {"store",   sbuffer_store,   METH_VARARGS},
  { NULL,     NULL }
};

/***************************************************************
 * Basic Operations
 ***************************************************************/

/* Create a new shared buffer object */
static sbufferobject *
new_sbuffer(int fd, int size, int offset, int prot)
{
  sbufferobject *self;
  void *buffer;
  buffer = mmap(0,size,prot,MAP_SHARED,fd,offset);
  if (buffer <= 0) {
    PyErr_SetFromErrno(PyExc_OSError);
    return NULL;
  }
  self = PyObject_NEW(sbufferobject, &SharedBufferType);
  if (self == NULL) return NULL;
  self->buffer = (char *) buffer;
  self->size = size;
  self->offset = offset;
  self->prot = prot;
  self->fd = fd;
  return self;
}

/* Release a shared buffer */
static void
sbuffer_dealloc(sbufferobject *self) {
  munmap(self->buffer, self->size);
  close(self->fd);
  PyMem_DEL(self);
}

/* Get an attribute */
static PyObject *
sbuffer_getattr(sbufferobject *self, char *name) {
  if (strcmp(name,"prot") == 0) {
    return Py_BuildValue("i", self->prot);    /* self.prot */
  } else if (strcmp(name,"fd") == 0) {
    return Py_BuildValue("i", self->fd);      /* self.fd   */
  }
  /* Look for a method instead */
  return Py_FindMethod(sbuffer_methods, (PyObject *)self, name);
}

/* repr() function */
static PyObject *
sbuffer_repr(sbufferobject *self) {
  char rbuffer[256];
```

```
    sprintf(rbuffer,"<SharedBuffer, fd = %d, length = %d, prot = %d at %x>",
        self->fd, self->size, self->prot, self);
    return PyString_FromString(rbuffer);
}

/**************************************************************
 * Sequence operations
 **************************************************************/

/* len() */
static int
sbuffer_length(sbufferobject *self) {
    return self->size;
}

/* getitem - Get a single character */
static PyObject *
sbuffer_getitem(sbufferobject *self, int index) {
    if (index < 0 || index >= self->size) {
        PyErr_SetString(PyExc_IndexError, "index out-of-bounds");
        return NULL;
    }
    if (!(self->prot & PROT_READ)) {
        PyErr_SetString(AccessError,"SharedBuffer is not readable");
        return NULL;
    }
    return Py_BuildValue("c",self->buffer[index]);
}

/* setitem - Store a single character */
static int
sbuffer_setitem(sbufferobject *self, int index, PyObject *obj)
{
    char *str;
    int    strsize;
    if (!PyString_Check(obj)) {
        PyErr_SetString(PyExc_TypeError, "Expected a string.");
        return 1;
    }
    if (PyString_Size(obj) != 1) {
        PyErr_SetString(PyExc_ValueError,"Expected a one character string.");
        return 1;
    }
    if (index < 0 || index >= self->size) {
        PyErr_SetString(PyExc_IndexError, "index out-of-bounds");
        return 1;
    }
    if (!(self->prot & PROT_WRITE)) {
        PyErr_SetString(AccessError,"SharedBuffer is read-only");
        return 1;
    }
    self->buffer[index] = *(PyString_AsString(obj));
    return 0;
}

/* getslice - Get a slice out of the buffer */
static PyObject *sbuffer_getslice(sbufferobject *self, int start, int end) {
    if (start < 0) start = 0;
    if (end > self->size) end = self->size;
    if (end < start) end = start;
    if (!(self->prot & PROT_READ)) {
        PyErr_SetString(AccessError,"SharedBuffer is not readable");
        return NULL;
```

```
    }
    return PyString_FromStringAndSize(self->buffer+start, (end-start));
}

/* setslice - Set a slice in the buffer */
static int
sbuffer_setslice(sbufferobject *self, int start, int end, PyObject *obj)
{
  int size;
  if (start < 0) start = 0;
  if (end > self->size) end = self->size;
  if (end < start) end = start;
  if (!PyString_Check(obj)) {
    PyErr_SetString(PyExc_TypeError, "Expected a string.");
    return 1;
  }
  if (!(self->prot & PROT_WRITE)) {
    PyErr_SetString(AccessError,"SharedBuffer is read-only");
    return 1;
  }
  size = PyString_Size(obj);
  if (size < (end-start)) end = start+size;
  memcpy(self->buffer+start,PyString_AsString(obj),(end-start));
  return 0;
}

/* Sequence methods table */
static PySequenceMethods sbuffer_as_sequence = {
  (inquiry)          sbuffer_length,    /* sq_length   : len(x)      */
  (binaryfunc)       0,                 /* sq_concat   : x + y       */
  (intargfunc)       0,                 /* sq_repeat   : x * n       */
  (intargfunc)       sbuffer_getitem,   /* sq_item     : x[i]        */
  (intintargfunc)    sbuffer_getslice,  /* sq_slice    : x[i:j]      */
  (intobjargproc)    sbuffer_setitem,   /* sq_ass_item : x[i] = v    */
  (intintobjargproc) sbuffer_setslice,  /* sq_ass_slice : x[i:j] = v */
};

/* Type object for shared buffer objects */
static PyTypeObject SharedBufferType = {
  PyObject_HEAD_INIT(&PyType_Type) /* Required initialization */
  0,                                /* ob_size      : Usually 0  */
  "SharedBuffer",                   /* tp_name      : Type name  */
  sizeof(sbufferobject),            /* tp_basicsize : Object size */
  0,                                /* tp_itemsize  : Usually 0  */

  /* Standard methods */
  (destructor) sbuffer_dealloc,    /* tp_dealloc,  : refcount = 0 */
  (printfunc)  0,                  /* tp_print     : print x    */
  (getattrfunc) sbuffer_getattr,   /* tp_getattr   : x.attr     */
  (setattrfunc) 0,                 /* tp_setattr   : x.attr = v */
  (cmpfunc)    0,                  /* tp_compare   : x > y      */
  (reprfunc)   sbuffer_repr,       /* tp_repr      : repr(x)    */

  /* Type categories */
  0,                               /* tp_as_number  : Number methods   */
  &sbuffer_as_sequence,            /* tp_as_sequence: Sequence methods */
  0,                               /* tp_as_mapping : Mapping methods  */
  (hashfunc)   0,                  /* tp_hash      : dict[x]    */
  (binaryfunc) 0,                  /* tp_call      : x()        */
  (reprfunc)   0,                  /* tp_str       : str(x)     */
};
```

```
/**************************************************************
 * Module level functions
 **************************************************************/

/* Create a new shared buffer object as
   SharedBuffer(filename,size,offset,prot) */
static PyObject *
sbufferobject_new(PyObject *self, PyObject *args) {
  char *filename;
  int size;
  int fd, flags;
  int prot = PROT_READ | PROT_WRITE;
  int offset = 0;
  struct stat finfo;

  if (!PyArg_ParseTuple(args,"si|ii",&filename,&size,&offset,&prot)) {
    return NULL;
  }
  if (stat(filename,&finfo) < 0) {
    PyErr_SetFromErrno(PyExc_OSError);
    return NULL;
  }
  if (size + offset > finfo.st_size) {
    PyErr_SetString(PyExc_IndexError,"Requested size and offset is too large.");
    return NULL;
  }
  if ((fd = open(filename,O_RDWR, 0666)) < 0) {
    PyErr_SetFromErrno(PyExc_OSError);
    return NULL;
  }
  return (PyObject *) new_sbuffer(fd,size,offset,prot);
}

/* Module Methods Table */
static struct PyMethodDef sbuffertype_methods[] = {
  { "SharedBuffer", sbufferobject_new, METH_VARARGS },
  { NULL, NULL }
};

/* Module initialization function */
void initsbuffer() {
  PyObject *m, *d;
  m = Py_InitModule("sbuffer",sbuffertype_methods);
  d = PyModule_GetDict(m);

  /* Add a few useful constants for the prot parameter */
  PyDict_SetItemString(d,"PROT_READ",PyInt_FromLong(PROT_READ));
  PyDict_SetItemString(d,"PROT_WRITE",PyInt_FromLong(PROT_WRITE));

  /* Define the exception */
  AccessError = PyErr_NewException("sbuffer.AccessError",NULL,NULL);
  PyDict_SetItemString(d,"AccessError",AccessError);
}
```

Finally, following is an example that uses the new SharedBuffer type. In this case, a shared buffer is used to exchange data between a parent and child process created with os.fork(). The example (motivated by a problem posted to the Python mailing list) performs a hostname-to-IP address translation with a timeout.

```
# Hostname lookup with a timeout.
# (with apologies to Andy D.)

import sbuffer, socket, os, sys, signal
```

```
# Create the memory mapped region
buffer = open("address","w")
buffer.write(" "*2048)
buffer.close()

# Open the file as a shared buffer object
buffer = sbuffer.SharedBuffer("address",2048)

# Return hostname or "" if it can't be resolved
# in less than 1 second.
def gethostbyname(hostname):
    buffer.store("")         # Clear the address buffer
    pid = os.fork()          # Create a subprocess
    if pid == 0:
        # Child process
        signal.alarm(1)      # Start the clock
        try:
            name = socket.gethostbyname(hostname)
        except:
            sys.exit()
        buffer.store(name)   # Save the name in the buffer
        sys.exit()           # Done
    else:
        os.wait()            # Wait for completion
        return buffer.get()  # Get the address
# Try it out
ip = gethostbyname("www.python.org")
```

Special Methods for Types

Most of the special methods for a type are encapsulated in three data structures:
PySequenceMethods, PyMappingMethods, and PyNumberMethods. Tables B.17 through B.20
show the contents of these structures.

Table B.17   **PySequenceMethods** Structure

C Datatype	Name	Python Method
(inquiry)	sq_length	__len__(x)
(binaryfunc)	sq_concat	__add__(x,y)
(intargfunc)	sq_repeat	__mul__(x,n)
(intargfunc)	sq_item	__getitem__(x,n)
(intintargfunc)	sq_slice	__getslice__(x,i,j)
(intobjargproc)	sq_ass_item	__setitem__(x,n,v)
(intintobjargproc)	sq_ass_slice	__setslice__(x,i,j,v)

Table B.18   **PyMappingMethods** Structure

C Datatype	Name	Python Method
(inquiry)	mp_length	__len__(x)
(binaryfunc)	mp_subscript	__getitem__(x,key)
(objobjargproc)	mp_ass_subscript	__setitem__(x,key,value)

Table B.19   **PyNumberMethods** Structure

C Datatype	Name	Python Method
(binaryfunc)	nb_add	__add__(x,y)
(binaryfunc)	nb_subtract	__sub__(x,y)
(binaryfunc)	nb_multiply	__mul__(x,y)
(binaryfunc)	nb_divide	__div__(x,y)
(binaryfunc)	nb_remainder	__mod__(x,y)
(binaryfunc)	nb_divmod	__divmod__(x,y)
(ternaryfunc)	nb_power	__pow__(x,y,n)
(unaryfunc)	nb_negative	__neg__(x)
(unaryfunc)	nb_positive	__pos__(x)
(unaryfunc)	nb_absolute	__abs__(x)
(inquiry)	nb_nonzero	__zero__(x)
(unaryfunc)	nb_invert	__invert__(x)
(binaryfunc)	nb_lshift	__lshift__(x,y)
(binaryfunc)	nb_rshift	__rshift__(x,y)
(binaryfunc)	nb_and	__and__(x,y)
(binaryfunc)	nb_xor	__xor__(x,y)
(binaryfunc)	nb_or	__or__(x,y)
(coercion)	nb_coerce	__coerce__(x,y)
(unaryfunc)	nb_int	__int__(x)
(unaryfunc)	nb_long	__long__(x)
(unaryfunc)	nb_float	__float__(x)
(unaryfunc)	nb_oct	__oct__(x)
(unaryfunc)	nb_hex	__hex__(x)

Table B.20   C Prototypes for Methods Defined in This Section

C Datatype	Prototype
(inquiry)	int (*)(PyObject *)
(unaryfunc)	PyObject (*)(PyObject *)
(binaryfunc)	PyObject (*)(PyObject *, PyObject *)
(ternaryfunc)	PyObject (*)(PyObject *, PyObject *, PyObject *)
(coercion)	int (*)(PyObject **, PyObject **)
(intargfunc)	PyObject (*)(PyObject *, int)
(intintargfunc)	PyObject (*)(PyObject *, int, int)
(intobjargproc)	int (*)(PyObject *, int, PyObject *)
(intintobjargproc)	int (*)(PyObject *, int, int, PyObject *)
(destructor)	void (*)(PyObject *)
(printfunc)	int (*)(PyObject *, FILE *, int)
(getattrfunc)	PyObject (*)(PyObject *, char *)
(getattrofunc)	PyObject (*)(PyObject *, PyObject *)

C Datatype	Prototype
(setattrfunc)	int (*)(PyObject *, char *, PyObject *)
(setattrofunc)	int (*)(PyObject *, PyObject *, PyObject *)
(cmpfunc)	int (*)(PyObject *, PyObject *)
(reprfunc)	PyObject (*)(PyObject *)
(hashfunc)	long (*)(PyObject *)

Threads

When using threads, a global interpreter lock is used to prevent more than one thread from executing in the interpreter at once. If a function written in an extension module executes for a long time, it will block the execution of other threads until it completes. To fix this, the following macros can be used in a wrapper function:

Macro	Description
Py_BEGIN_ALLOW_THREADS	Releases the global interpreter lock and allows other threads to run in the interpreter. The C extension must not invoke any functions in the Python C API while the lock is released.
Py_END_ALLOW_THREADS	Reacquires the global interpreter lock. The extension will block until the lock can be successfully acquired in this case.

The following example illustrates the use of these macros:

```
PyObject *spamfunction(PyObject *self, PyObject *self) {
        ...
        PyArg_ParseTuple(args, ...)
        Py_BEGIN_ALLOW_THREADS
        result = run_long_calculation(args);
        Py_END_ALLOW_THREADS
        ...
        return Py_BuildValue(fmt,result);
}
```

Many more subtle aspects of threads are not covered here. Readers are strongly advised to consult the C API Reference Manual. In addition, you may need to take steps to make sure that your C extension is thread-safe, as it could be invoked by other Python threads shortly after the interpreter lock is released.

Embedding

The Python interpreter can also be embedded into other applications. When embedding the interpreter on Unix, you must include the file config.c (usually found in a place such as /usr/local/lib/python1.5/config/config.c) and link against the library libpython1.5.a. (A comparable but more complex process is required on Windows and the Macintosh.) The functions in Table B.21 are used to call the interpreter to execute code and control its operation:

Table B.21   Embedding API

Function	Description
`int PyRun_AnyFile(FILE *fp, char *filename)`	If `fp` is an interactive device, calls `PyRun_InteractiveLoop()`. Otherwise, `PyRun_SimpleFile()` is called. If `filename` is NULL, `"???"` is used as the filename.
`int PyRun_SimpleString(char * command)`	Executes *command* in the `__main__` module of the interpreter. Returns 0 on success, -1 if an exception occurred.
`int PyRun_SimpleFile(FILE *fp, char *filename)`	Similar to `PyRun_SimpleString()`, except that the program is read from a file *fp*.
`int PyRun_InteractiveOne(FILE * fp, char *filename)`	Executes a single interactive command.
`int PyRun_InteractiveLoop(FILE * fp, char *filename)`	Runs the interpreter in interactive mode.
`PyObject* PyRun_String(char * str, int start, PyObject * globals, PyObject *locals)`	Executes the code in *str* in the global and local namespaces defined by *globals* and *locals*. *start* is a start token to use when parsing the source code. Returns the result of the execution or NULL if an error occurred.
`PyObject* PyRun_File(FILE *fp, char *filename, int start, PyObject *globals, PyObject * locals)`	Same as `PyRun_String()`, except that code is read from the file *fp*.
`PyObject* Py_CompileString(char * str, char *filename, int start)`	Compiles code in *str* into a code object. *start* is the starting token and *filename* is the filename that will be set in the code object and used in tracebacks. Returns a code object on success, NULL on error.
`void Py_Initialize()`	Initializes the Python interpreter. This function should be called before using any other functions in the C API, with the exception of `Py_SetProgramName()`, `PyEval_InitThreads()`, `PyEval_ReleaseLock()`, and `PyEval_AcquireLock()`.
`int Py_IsInitialized()`	Returns 1 if the interpreter has been initialized or 0 if not.
`void Py_Finalize()`	Cleans up the interpreter by destroying all the sub-interpreters and objects that were created since calling `Py_Initialize()`. Normally, this function frees all the memory allocated by the interpreter. However, circular references and extension modules may introduce memory leaks that can't be recovered by this function.
`void Py_SetProgramName(char *name)`	Sets the program name that's normally found in the `argv[0]` argument of the main program. This function should only be called before `Py_Initialize()`.
`char* Py_GetProgramName()`	Returns the program name as set by `Py_SetProgramName()`.
`char* Py_GetPrefix()`	Returns the prefix for installed platform-independent files.

Function	Description
char* Py_GetExecPrefix()	Returns the exec-prefix for installed platform-dependent files.
char* Py_GetProgramFullPath()	Returns the full program name of the Python executable.
char* Py_GetPath()	Returns the default module search path. The path is returned as a string consisting of directory names separated by a platform-dependent delimiter (: on Unix, ; on DOS/Windows, and \n on the Macintosh).
const char* Py_GetVersion()	Returns the version of this Python interpreter.
const char* Py_GetPlatform()	Returns the platform identifier for the current platform.
const char* Py_GetCopyright()	Returns the official copyright string.
const char* Py_GetCompiler()	Returns the compiler string.
const char* Py_GetBuildInfo()	Returns build information about the interpreter.
int PySys_SetArgv(int *argc*, char **argv*)	Sets command-line options used to populate the value of sys.argv. This should only be called before Py_Initialize().

Extension Building Tools

A number of tools are available to simplify the construction of Python extensions.

Extension Classes

Extension classes, written by Jim Fulton and available at
http://www.digicool.com/releases/ExtensionClass/, provide a mechanism for
defining extension types that are more class-like. In particular, they can be subclassed
in C or Python, and provide better interaction with documentation strings and other
aspects of the interpreter.

CXX

The CXX extension, developed by Paul Dubois and available at ftp://ftp-
icf.llnl.gov/pub/python, simplifies the process of creating C++ extensions and
provides a high degree of integration between built-in Python types and the standard
C++ library.

SWIG

SWIG (Simplified Wrapper and Interface Generator), developed by the author
and available at http://www.swig.org, can be used to create Python extensions automatically from annotated C/C++ header files. It hides most of the underlying details
and works well for development, debugging, and rapid prototyping.

While a full discussion of SWIG is beyond the scope of this book, it largely eliminates the need to know anything discussed in this appendix. In particular, you can use SWIG to create a Python extension module simply by writing a simple description like this:

```
// file : spam.i
%module spam
%{
#include "spam.h"
%}

int gcd(int x, int y);
void print_data(char *name, char *email, char *phone);
```

Now, running SWIG:

```
% swig -python spam.i
Generating wrappers for Python...
%
```

And that's about it. The output of SWIG is a wrapper file called `spam_wrap.c` that's compiled and linked and used in exactly the same manner as described in the earlier section "Compilation of Extensions." Of course, many more aspects of SWIG are worthy of discussion, but that's a topic for a different day—and the author needs rest.

Index

H

Q

R

T

X

Z

Open Source Resources

In MySQL, Paul DuBois provides you with a comprehensive guide to one of the most popular relational database systems, MySQL. As an important contributor to the online documentation for MySQL, Paul uses his day-to-day experience answering questions users post on the MySQL mailing list to pinpoint the problems most users and administrators encounter. Through two sample databases that run throughout the book, he gives you solutions to problems you'll likely face, including integratin MySQL efficiently with third-party tools like PHP and Perl, enabling you to generate dynamic Web pages through database queries.

ISBN: 0-7357-0921-1

This title is all about getting things done by providing structured organization to the plethora of available Linux information. Providing clear and concise instructions on how to perform important administration and management tasks, as well as how to use some of the more powerful commands, deal with shell scripting, administer your own system, and utilize effective security.

ISBN: 0-7357-08525

This book details the security steps that a small, non-enterprise business user might take to protect his system. These steps include packet-level firewall filtering, IP masquerading, proxies, tcp wrappers, system integrity checking, and system security monitoring with an overall emphasis on filtering and protection. The goal of the book is to help people get their Internet security measures in place quickly, without the need to become experts in security of firewalls.

ISBN: 0-7357-0900-9

Advanced Information on Networking Technologies

New Riders Books Offer Advice and Experience

LANDMARK

Rethinking Computer Books

We know how important it is to have access to detailed, solution-oriented information on core technologies. *Landmark* books contain the essential information you need to solve technical problems. Written by experts and subjected to rigorous peer and technical reviews, our *Landmark* books are hard-core resources for practitioners like you.

ESSENTIAL REFERENCE

Smart, Like You

The *Essential Reference* series from New Riders provides answers when you know what you want to do but need to know how to do it. Each title skips extraneous material and assumes a strong base of knowledge. These are indispensable books for the practitioner who wants to find specific features of a technology quickly and efficiently. Avoiding fluff and basic material, these books present solutions in an innovative, clean format— and at a great value.

CIRCLE SERIES

The *Circle Series* is a set of reference guides that meet the needs of the growing community of advanced, technical-level networkers who must architect, develope, and administer operating systems like UNIX, Linux, Windows NT, and Windows 2000. These books provide network designers and programmers with detailed, proven solutions to their problems.

DCE/RPC over SMB: Samba and Windows NT Domain Internals
By Luke Leighton
1st Edition
300 pages, $45.00
ISBN: 1-57870-150-3

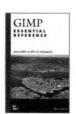

GIMP Essential Reference
By Alex Harford
1st Edition
400 pages, $24.95
ISBN: 0-7357-0911-4

Security people, system and network administrators, and the folks writing tools for them all need to be familiar with the packets flowing across their networks. Authored by a key member of the SAMBA team, this book describes how Microsoft has taken DCE/RPC and implemented it over SMB and TCP/IP.

As the use of the Linux OS gains steam, so does the use of the GIMP. Many Photoshop users are starting to use the GIMP, recognized for its power and versatility. Taking this into consideration, GIMP Essential Reference has shortcuts exclusively for Photoshop users and puts the power of this program into the palm of the reader's hand.

Grokking the GIMP
By Carey Bunks
1st Edition
350 pages, $39.99
ISBN: 0-7357-0924-6

Grokking the GIMP is a technical reference that covers the intricacies of the GIMP's functionality. The material gives the reader the ability to get up to speed quickly and start creating great graphics using the GIMP. Included as a bonus are step-by-step cookbook features used entirely for advanced effects.

UNIX/Linux Titles

Solaris Essential Reference

By John P. Mulligan
1st Edition
300 pages, $24.95
ISBN: 0-7357-0023-0

Looking for the fastest and easiest way to find the Solaris command you need? Need a few pointers on shell scripting? How about advanced administration tips and sound, practical expertise on security issues? Are you looking for trustworthy information about available third-party software packages that will enhance your operating system? Author John Mulligan—creator of the popular "Unofficial Guide to The Solaris™ Operating Environment" Web site (sun.icsnet.com)—delivers all that and more in one attractive, easy-to-use reference book. With clear and concise instructions on how to perform important administration and management tasks, and key information on powerful commands and advanced topics, *Solaris Essential Reference* is the book you need when you know what you want to do and only need to know how.

Linux System Administration

By M. Carling,
Stephen Degler,
and James Dennis
1st Edition
450 pages, $29.99
ISBN: 1-56205-934-3

As an administrator, you probably feel that most of your time and energy is spent in endless firefighting. If your network has become a fragile quilt of temporary patches and work-arounds, this book is for you. Have you had trouble sending or receiving email lately? Are you looking for a way to keep your network running smoothly with enhanced performance? Are your users always hankering for more storage, services, and speed? *Linux System Administration* advises you on the many intricacies of maintaining a secure, stable system. In this definitive work, the authors address all the issues related to system administration, from adding users and managing file permissions, to Internet services and Web hosting, to recovery planning and security. This book fulfills the need for expert advice that will ensure a trouble-free Linux environment.

GTK+/Gnome Application Development

By Havoc Pennington
1st Edition
492 pages, $39.99
ISBN: 0-7357-0078-8

This title is for the reader who is conversant with the C programming language and UNIX/Linux development. It provides detailed and solution-oriented information designed to meet the needs of programmers and application developers using the GTK+/Gnome libraries. Coverage complements existing GTK+/Gnome documentation, going into more depth on pivotal issues such as uncovering the GTK+ object system, working with the event loop, managing the Gdk substrate, writing custom widgets, and mastering GnomeCanvas.

Developing Linux Applications with GTK+ and GDK
By Eric Harlow
1st Edition
490 pages, $34.99
ISBN: 0-7357-0021-4

We all know that Linux is one of the most powerful and solid operating systems in existence. And as the success of Linux grows, there is an increasing interest in developing applications with graphical user interfaces that take advantage of the power of Linux. In this book, software developer Eric Harlow gives you an indispensable development handbook focusing on the GTK+ toolkit. More than an overview of the elements of application or GUI design, this is a hands-on book that delves into the technology. With in-depth material on the various GUI programming tools and loads of examples, this book's unique focus will give you the information you need to design and launch professional-quality applications.

Linux Essential Reference
By Ed Petron
1st Edition
350 pages, $24.95
ISBN: 0-7357-0852-5

This book is all about getting things done as quickly and efficiently as possible by providing a structured organization for the plethora of available Linux information. We can sum it up in one word—value. This book has it all: concise instructions on how to perform key administration tasks, advanced information on configuration, shell scripting, hardware management, systems management, data tasks, automation, and tons of other useful information. This book truly provides groundbreaking information for the growing community of advanced Linux professionals.

Lotus Notes and Domino Titles

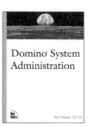

Domino System Administration
By Rob Kirkland, CLP, CLI
1st Edition
850 pages, $49.99
ISBN: 1-56205-948-3

Your boss has just announced that you will be upgrading to the newest version of Notes and Domino when it ships. How are you supposed to get this new system installed, configured, and rolled out to all of your end users? You understand how Lotus Notes works—you've been administering it for years. What you need is a concise, practical explanation of the new features and how to make some of the advanced stuff work smoothly by someone like you, who has worked with the product for years and understands what you need to know. *Domino System Administration* is the answer—the first book on Domino that attacks the technology at the professional level with practical, hands-on assistance to get Domino running in your organization.

Lotus Notes & Domino Essential Reference

By Tim Bankes, CLP and Dave Hatter, CLP, MCP
1st Edition
650 pages, $45.00
ISBN: 0-7357-0007-9

You're in a bind because you've been asked to design and program a new database in Notes for an important client who will keep track of and itemize a myriad of inventory and shipping data. The client wants a user-friendly interface that won't sacrifice speed or functionality. You are experienced (and could develop this application in your sleep), but feel you need something to facilitate your creative and technical abilities— something to perfect your programming skills. The answer is waiting for you: *Lotus Notes & Domino Essential Reference.* It's compact and simply designed. It's loaded with information. All of the objects, classes, functions, and methods are listed. It shows you the object hierarchy and the relationship between each one. It's perfect for you. Problem solved.

Networking Titles

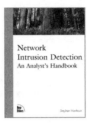

Network Intrusion Detection: An Analyst's Handbook, 2E

By Stephen Northcutt and Judy Novak
2nd Edition
450 pages, $45.00
ISBN: 0-7357-1008-2

Get answers and solutions from someone who has been in the trenches. The author, Stephen Northcutt, original developer of the Shadow intrusion detection system and former director of the United States Navy's Information System Security Office at the Naval Security Warfare Center, gives his expertise to intrusion detection specialists, security analysts, and consultants responsible for setting up and maintaining an effective defense against network security attacks.

Understanding Data Communications, Sixth Edition

By Gilbert Held
6th Edition
600 pages, $39.99
ISBN: 0-7357-0036-2

Updated from the highly successful fifth edition, this book explains how data communications systems and their various hardware and software components work. More than an entry-level book, it approaches the material in textbook format, addressing the complex issues involved in internetworking today. A great reference book for the experienced networking professional that is written by the noted networking authority, Gilbert Held.

Other Books By New Riders

Open Source

MySQL
0-7357-0921-1 • $49.99 US/$74.95
CAN
Web Application Development with PHP
4.0
0-7357-0997-1 • $39.99
PHP Functions Essential Reference
0-7357-0970-X • $35.00 US/$52.95
CAN
Available December 2000
Python Essential Reference
0-7357-0901-7 • $34.95 US/$52.95
CAN
Autoconf, Automake, and Libtool
1-57870-190-2 • $35.00 US/$52.95
CAN
Available October 2000

Linux/Unix

ADMINISTRATION

Linux System Administration
1-56205-934-3 • $29.99 US/$44.95
CAN
Linux Firewalls
0-7357-0900-9 • $39.99 US/$59.95
CAN
Linux Essential Reference
0-7357-0852-5 • $24.95 US/$37.95
CAN
UnixWare 7 System Administration
1-57870-080-9 • $40.00 US/$59.99
CAN

DEVELOPMENT

Developing Linux Applications with
GTK+ and GDK
0-7357-0021-4 • $34.99 US/$52.95
CAN
GTK+/Gnome Application Development
0-7357-0078-8 • $39.99 US/$59.95
CAN
KDE Application Development
1-57870-201-1 • $39.99 US/$59.95
CAN

GIMP

Grokking the GIMP
0-7357-0924-6 • $39.99 US/$59.95
CAN
GIMP Essential Reference
0-7357-0911-4 • $24.95 US/$37.95
CAN

SOLARIS

Solaris Advanced System Administrator's
Guide, Second Edition
1-57870-039-6 • $39.99 US/$59.95
CAN
Solaris System Administrator's Guide,
Second Edition
1-57870-040-X • $34.99 US/$52.95

CAN
Solaris Essential Reference
0-7357-0023-0 • $24.95 US/$37.95
CAN

Networking

STANDARDS & PROTOCOLS

Cisco Router Configuration &
Troubleshooting, Second Edition
0-7357-0999-8 • $34.99 US/$52.95
CAN
Understanding Directory Services
0-7357-0910-2 • $39.99 US/$59.95
CAN
Understanding the Network: A Practical
Guide to Internetworking
0-7357-0977-7 • $39.99 US/$59.95
CAN
Understanding Data Communications,
Sixth Edition
0-7357-0036-2 • $39.99 US/$59.95
CAN
LDAP: Programming Directory Enabled
Applications
1-57870-000-0 • $44.99 US/$67.95
CAN
Gigabit Ethernet Networking
1-57870-062-0 • $50.00 US/$74.95
CAN
Supporting Service Level Agreements
on IP Networks
1-57870-146-5 • $50.00 US/$74.95
CAN
Directory Enabled Networks
1-57870-140-6 • $50.00 US/$74.95
CAN
Differentiated Services for the Internet
1-57870-132-5 • $50.00 US/$74.95
CAN
Quality of Service on IP Networks
1-57870-189-9 • $50.00 US/$74.95
CAN
Designing Addressing Architectures for
Routing and Switching
1-57870-059-0 • $45.00 US/$69.95
CAN
Understanding & Deploying LDAP
Directory Services
1-57870-070-1 • $50.00 US/$74.95
CAN
Switched, Fast and Gigabit Ethernet,
Third Edition
1-57870-073-6 • $50.00 US/$74.95
CAN
Wireless LANs: Implementing
Interoperable Networks
1-57870-081-7 • $40.00 US/$59.95
CAN
Wide Area High Speed Networks
1-57870-114-7 • $50.00 US/$74.95
CAN
The DHCP Handbook

1-57870-137-6 • $55.00 US/$81.95
CAN
Designing Routing and Switching
Architectures for Enterprise Networks
1-57870-060-4 • $55.00 US/$81.95
CAN
Local Area High Speed Networks
1-57870-113-9 • $50.00 US/$74.95
CAN
Network Performance Baselining
1-57870-240-2 • $50.00 US/$74.95
CAN
Economics of Electronic Commerce
1-57870-014-0 • $49.99 US/$74.95
CAN

SECURITY

Intrusion Detection
1-57870-185-6 • $50.00 US/$74.95
CAN
Understanding Public-Key Infrastructure
1-57870-166-X • $50.00 US/$74.95
CAN
Network Intrusion Detection: An
Analyst's Handbook, 2E
0-7357-1008-2 • $45.00 US/$59.95
CAN
Linux Firewalls
0-7357-0900-9 • $39.99 US/$59.95
CAN

LOTUS NOTES/DOMINO

Domino System Administration
1-56205-948-3 • $49.99 US/$74.95
CAN
Lotus Notes & Domino Essential
Reference
0-7357-0007-9 • $45.00 US/$67.95
CAN

Software Architecture & Engineering

Designing for the User with OVID
1-57870-101-5 • $40.00 US/$59.95
CAN
Designing Flexible Object-Oriented
Systems with UML
1-57870-098-1 • $40.00 US/$59.95
CAN
Constructing Superior Software
1-57870-147-3 • $40.00 US/$59.95
CAN
A UML Pattern Language
1-57870-118-X • $45.00 US/$67.95
CAN

New Riders

We Want to Know What You Think

To better serve you, we would like your opinion on the content and quality of this book. Please complete this card and mail it to us or fax it to 317-581-4663.

Name_____

Address _____

City _____State _____Zip _____

Phone _____

Email Address _____

Occupation _____

Operating System(s) that you use _____

What influenced your purchase of this book?
- ❏ Recommendation
- ❏ Cover Design
- ❏ Table of Contents
- ❏ Index
- ❏ Magazine Review
- ❏ Advertisement
- ❏ New Riders' Reputation
- ❏ Author Name

How would you rate the contents of this book?
- ❏ Excellent
- ❏ Very Good
- ❏ Good
- ❏ Fair
- ❏ Below Average
- ❏ Poor

How do you plan to use this book?
- ❏ Quick reference
- ❏ Self-training
- ❏ Classroom
- ❏ Other

What do you like most about this book?
Check all that apply.
- ❏ Content
- ❏ Writing Style
- ❏ Accuracy
- ❏ Examples
- ❏ Listings
- ❏ Design
- ❏ Index
- ❏ Page Count
- ❏ Price
- ❏ Illustrations

What do you like least about this book?
Check all that apply.
- ❏ Content
- ❏ Writing Style
- ❏ Accuracy
- ❏ Examples
- ❏ Listings
- ❏ Design
- ❏ Index
- ❏ Page Count
- ❏ Price
- ❏ Illustrations

What would be a useful follow-up book to this one for you? _____

Where did you purchase this book? _____

Can you name a similar book that you like better than this one, or one that is as good? Why?
_____
_____

How many New Riders books do you own? _____

What are your favorite computer books? _____
_____

What other titles would you like to see us develop? _____
_____

Any comments for us? _____
_____
_____
_____

Python Essential Reference, 0-7357-0901-7

Fold here and tape to mail

- -

New Riders Publishing
201 W. 103rd St.
Indianapolis, IN 46290

New Riders | How to Contact Us

Visit Our Web Site

www.newriders.com

On our Web site, you'll find information about our other books, authors, tables of contents, indexes, and book errata. You can also place orders for books through our Web site.

Email Us

Contact us at this address:
nrfeedback@newriders.com

- If you have comments or questions about this book
- To report errors that you have found in this book
- If you have a book proposal to submit or are interested in writing for New Riders
- If you would like to have an author kit sent to you
- If you are an expert in a computer topic or technology and are interested in being a technical editor who reviews manuscripts for technical accuracy

nrfeedback@newriders.com

- To find a distributor in your area, please contact our international department at the address above.

nrmedia@newriders.com

- For instructors from educational institutions who wish to preview New Riders books for classroom use. Email should include your name, title, school, department, address, phone number, office days/hours, text in use, and enrollment in the body of your text along with your request for desk/examination copies and/or additional information.

Write to Us

New Riders Publishing
201 W. 103rd St.
Indianapolis, IN 46290-1097

Call Us

Toll-free (800) 571-5840 + 9 + 7494
If outside U.S. (317) 581-3500. Ask for New Riders.

Fax Us

(317) 581-4663

Colophon

Each year, thousands of people travel to the Northern Yucatan, to brave the heat and the bugs and to wait for the arrival of the Summer Solstice at the Pyramid named El Castillo, in what was once central downtown Chichén Itzá. At noon on the day of the solstice, if you stand in just the right place, you can see a particular pattern of light crawling down the sides of one of the stairways leading to the top of the pyramid. If your imagination is reasonably well-lubricated, you can see the body of a gigantic snake there, culminating in a grotesque head, ringed with feathers, at the base of the stairs.

This is the image of the feathered serpent. The one you can see at the solstice connects the top of the pyramid with the base. In April of 1999, tourists were forbidden to ascend to the platform at the top. At the peak of Mayan civilization, over a thousand years ago, commoners were also banned from that platform. The rulers of the polity that was Chichén performed religious rituals there, in the purview of those below, but they, too, were connected to a higher place by the body of a snake, yet another feathered snake. As above, so below.

As tourists, we can see this image of the feathered snake one day a year. If we choose, we too, like the Mayan rulers, may also see the living body of the celestial snake at some point in every night sky. The Milky Way is not a symbol of the snake, it is the snake; it is the sky, as is attested by the homophony of the two words in most Mayan languages.

A thousand years ago, the Mayan civilization was the greatest on this side of the planet. The Mayans listened to the sky, and left the words that were given to them in a book now called *Popol Vuh*. The Mayan rulers spoke to the governed, and left the words they wrote carved in stone, incised in stucco and in wood, relating how only the elite could intercede between and connect the commoners and the gods of the underworld, who lived in the sky. Scribes, of royal blood themselves, wrote down the paths of the planets and the moon, the locations of the killer snakes that ate the Sun during eclipses, and the many ways to calculate these things in exquisite calligraphy on fig bark paper, and they bound the paper into books. Nearly five hundred years ago, one of the first Europeans to meet the descendants of those who built Chichén Itzá burned most of their sacred books.

We have only four of those books left. In one of them, we see numbers written between the coils of great serpents. The meaning of those numbers remains a mystery, but we believe that, if we could but understand them, they should somehow connect above and below.

Pythons are denizens of the Old World, while the feathered serpent is a creature of the New, as is its natural model, the Anaconda.

Not all meetings between different worlds need end in book burnings.

Ivan Van Laningham